The Terrible but Unfinished Story
of Norodom Sihanouk,
King of Cambodia

The Terrible
but Unfinished Story
of
NORODOM
SIHANOUK,
King of Cambodia

Hélène Cixous

Translated by Juliet Flower MacCannell,
Judith Pike, and Lollie Groth

UNIVERSITY OF NEBRASKA PRESS
Lincoln and London

© 1994 by the University of Nebraska Press
All rights reserved
Manufactured in the United States of America
Originally published as *L'Histoire Terrible mais inachevée de Norodom Sihanouk roi du Cambodge*, © Théâtre du Soleil 1985, Tours.

The paper in this book meets the minimum requirements of American National Standard for Information Sciences—Permanence of Paper for Printed Library Materials, ANSI Z39.48–1984.

Library of Congress Cataloging-in-Publication Data
Cixous, Hélène, 1937–
      [Histoire terrible mais inachevée de Norodom Sihanouk, roi du Cambodge. English]
      The terrible but unfinished story of Norodom Sihanouk, King of Cambodia / by Hélène Cixous ; translated by Juliet Flower MacCannell, Judith Pike, and Lollie Groth.
          p.   c.m — (European women writers series)
      ISBN 0-8032-1455-3. — ISBN 0-8032-6361-9 (pbk.)
      1. Norodom Sihanouk, Prince, 1922–   —Drama.   2. Cambodia—History—Civil War, 1970–1975—Drama.   3. Cambodia—History—1975–   —Drama.
I. Title.   II. Series.
PQ2663.I9H4513   1994
842'.914—dc20   93-1916
                                                                         CIP

Contents

Introduction

CIXOUS AND MODERN CONSCIOUSNESS
Juliet Flower MacCannell

At times our collective consciousness can no longer find a way of conceiving itself: times when clinging to the past or moving reflexively with the current can no longer work.[1] Perhaps the old ways suddenly lose effectiveness as comfort or as resource for modeling what is yet to come; or the present becomes so unfathomable, or so deplorable, that to "experience" it is to be unable, properly, to bear full consciousness of it. At moments of great social and cultural change *history*, our own history, can become the subject of our experience only if it is marked as something else—as a merely "artistic" or "ritual" form. More and more often it appears as a story, even someone else's story. . . .

A story that has no ending, a history that is nevertheless not a "past": Hélène Cixous's terrible but not yet finished his/story (for the play is *histoire*—both history and story) of Norodom Sihanouk is a step in the formulation—the formation, really—of a collective *mod-*

---

[1]Portions of this essay appear in Juliet Flower MacCannell, *The Regime of the Brother: After the Patriarchy* (London: Routledge, 1991). I have revised and expanded them here. Verena Conley, *Hélène Cixous* (New York: Harvester Wheatsheaf, 1992) has done a valuable, brief, critical review of Cixous's multiform work. Conley is cited in the text hereafter.

ern consciousness. The world has turned on its axis, so that its orienting polarities are no longer East and West—spatially and politically. Instead Traditional and Modern are the poles of our fundamental opposition. A reorientation of our minds is called forth. And yet none comes. Except, perhaps, from writing. ("Northern" and "Southern" could provisionally and hemispherically offer a figure for it: since the end of World War II, most combat deaths have occurred below the equator.) We can argue that this reversal has been in effect since the invention of modernity sometime in the eighteenth century, and that, further, modern artists and writers who have articulated it are not only been rare, but highly resisted as well: think of Rousseau.

In their place, scientists, economists, political scientists, and some philosophers—often of doubtful political acumen—have been granted the last word on the attitude we are to take toward traditional forms. Here is a highly praised quote from the nuclear physicist, architect of the uncertainty principle, Werner Heisenberg from his book *Physics and Philosophy*:

> Modern science . . . penetrates in our time into other parts of the world where the cultural tradition has been entirely different from the European civilization. There the impact of this new activity in natural and technical science must make itself felt even more strongly than in Europe. . . . This new activity must appear as a decline of the older culture, as a ruthless and barbarian attitude that upsets the sensitive balance on which all human happiness rests. Such consequences cannot be avoided; they must be taken as one aspect of our time.

Claude Lévi-Strauss has already proffered one alternative, a *symbolic* modeling and remodeling he calls a "science of the concrete," to the imposition of modern rationality upon traditional societies, and he has been seconded by Michel de Certeau's work.[2] Yet the weight has been on the side of those—both pro- and antimodernists, from Heisenberg to Heidegger—who have assumed the inevitability of the march of Western rationalism and its technological arm, which somehow develop without the intervention of a desiring subject, and outside the context of the interpersonal relation.

---

[2] Werner Heisenberg, *Physics and Philosophy: The Revolution in Modern Science* (New York: Harper Torchbooks, 1958), p. 202. Michel de Certeau, *The Practice of Everyday Life* (Los Angeles and Berkeley: University of California Press, 1984).

The priority of modernity over traditional forms is one of our most cherished assumptions—it almost goes without saying. Its counterweight is an equally cherished nostalgia for the "old forms" as superior, in their simplicity and closeness to nature and/or innocence, to the modern. Unthought "modernity" exhibits, it appears, the contradictions and silent imperatives that Barthes named "mythic speech."[3] To accuse Lévi-Strauss (or Hélène Cixous for that matter) of nostalgia is to miss the essential: that it is modernity as an unconscious structure that has licensed the worst in its unmentioned name.

Thus, those human groups and epistemological forms that the Heisenberg paradigm both explicitly and implicitly (but absolutely) disenfranchises—family, tribe, clan, but also the woman—are also those about which we moderns have the most clearly guilty and reparational consciences. Liberal modern efforts to accommodate these forms are almost always rooted in the assumption that they are simpler, a more primitive stage, closer to innocence, or paradise or something that we know we have given up, lost willingly or not. To "bring them back in" has a false air, a bad conscience, it sentimentalizes: woman becomes "The Eternal" or "The Maternal" just as we have gotten rid of matriarchy; indigenous peoples who have been done away with are commemorated in monuments where they will remain, dead but idealized, ennobled by their troubles. Cixous brings the full range of sympathy into play without a trace of sentimentality. She does not simply put *herself* "in the other's place" but instead writes *as* each character. Like Hazlitt's and Borges's Shakespeare, she aims at the absolute dispossession of the self. Not ego-centered by definition, then, this self is free to explore the intersubjective relation as such—between sexes, races, and classes, even between the living and the dead.

Cixous's play deals directly and with great forthrightness with the clash between traditional and modern. We love the old women, so down to earth and so charmingly flighty at the same time, aristocrat and petty bourgeois, Cambodian royalty and Vietnamese immigrant shopkeeper, Queen Kossomak and the fishmonger Madame Lamné—we love them for each other—because they love each other. We grow passionate for and with Sihanouk because he is the King, and to be a king means for him precisely not to be a despot, arrogant, and ego-

[3]Roland Barthes, "Myth Today" in *Mythologies*, trans. Annette Lavers (New York: Hill and Wang, 1974).

centric. Interestingly, it is when he has been "elected" Prince that he becomes most egotistical—and most blind. As a "Papa" monarch, this means embodying—by marking himself as "lack"—the "people." Slavoj Zizek characterizes the idea of the people as a substance as "the sublime body of ideology."[4] Cixous's definition, via *Sihanouk*, attempts something else: her "people" is what it says, dreams, thinks, feels, creates, and nothing more. Thus, there is no "body" of Cambodians, and Sihanouk cannot be king of a land made up only of "real" Cambodians. He must embrace everyone, all the immigrants, and even the elephants and trees that are objects for the Cambodian subject. Embrace, and not expel. . . . But this version of monarchy, the classical patriarchy, comes to grief when Sihanouk is forced to situate it in a "democracy," a new order wherein he will become not the King-Father, but the Leader, the head of government as "simple citizen" and whose Cambodian people is renamed the "Community of the People" (Part 1, Act 1, scene 3). The "fatality" of this decision—a forced choice for him—constitutes the tragic essence of the play, the insistence of what I call "the regime of the brother" in the mutated forms of colonialism and imperialism today. Conley calls Sihanouk a "maternal father," but this is true only if the definition of the mother as a sublime body is radically revised (p. 97). No, Sihanouk as monarch is the oedipal and not totemic father/brother. Of course, at times, he is the latter as well.

This is why Cixous makes Lon Nol stand for the aberrant side of postmonarchical life. His vacillating, superstitious personality is dependent on the past in its worst aspects, and on the present for its most abusive forms. Weak yet authoritarian, it is Lon Nol's anti-Vietnamese campaign that launched—for "political" reasons—a racial pogrom against foreigners that ended in the Khmer Rouge's genocidal reign over the Cambodians themselves. The version of communism installed by the Pol Pot regime, less a great leap forward than a step back into a feudal structure, was nonetheless perfectly modern in this sense: it took advantage of the license to commit genocide that our post-Kantian ethics, an ethics of "nonfoundation," unfortunately licenses, a genocide we democracies have yet to proscribe adequately and from the point of view of the Law.[5]

---

[4]Slavoj Zizek, *The Sublime Object of Ideology* (London: Verso, 1989), p. 84.

[5]See discussions of the neo-feudal nature of Pol Pot's views in David P. Chandler, *A History of Cambodia* (Boulder, Colo.: Westview Press, 1983), p. 191. In my view, gen-

Cixous, in a surprise move—considering his historical identification with peace—therefore must have us hate the character of Henry Kissinger, admirer of Metternich and practitioner of "Realpolitik." The character grows mad with a lust to "sanitize" Cambodia for which he orders the 1969–70 secret Menu bombings along the Cambodian-Vietnamese border (Part 1, Act 2, sc. 3). We also hate Saloth Sâr/Pol Pot. The play depicts these two avatars of fanatical and unreflected "democracy" as working to enforce the health codes of our time. Pol Pot is determined to "purify"—to purge Cambodia of its noncommunist, traditional past; Kissinger wants to cleanse Cambodia of Communist/Chinese/Russian and Vietnamese "parasites" that are "infesting" it [Part 1, Act 2, sc. 4]. But Cixous shows them both as responding less to rational political ideals than to the unconscious demands of an Ideal Ego, a malevolent Superego, commanding them to rid themselves of a persistent, nagging "stain." That this is what the Lacanians call the stain of *enjoyment* is suggested by what it is that Cixous sees the war as attacking most directly: the "enjoyment" of Cambodian life both by Cambodians and those they took in. How often Samnol complains that the Khmer Rouge do not know how to *goûter*; Suramarit grows rightly fearful of Khieu Samphan when Sihanouk tells him how clean-cut and quasi-puritanical his choice for minister is. The unconscious complicity of these two ascetic forces working for modern political hygiene in only apparently opposed ways resulted, as we know, in the slaughter of millions. In the Cambodian-Kampuchean revolution, people were killed because they did not fit "the norm": they were too old, too short, they wore eyeglasses. With brilliant artistic economy, Cixous sums up this psycho-political profile by having the simple and yet perceptive Mme Khieu Samnol describe Saloth Sâr as a crocodile-like man "with a mouth full of teeth" and looking like he "eats men." Cannibalism indeed occurred during the Khmer revolution (Lon Nol's brother had his liver torn out and consumed by an angry crowd [Part 2, Act 1, sc. 4], making literal what Khmer Rouge rhetoric used as metaphor). But if Pol Pot eats his brothers and sisters it is only to purge them, spit them out.

To clean out, to evacuate the self, emptying it of all others—those

---

ocide is the only real ethical question for our time. See my "Facing Fascism: The Politics of Feminine Jouissance," forthcoming in a special issue of *Topoi* (September 1993) on ethics.

from its ghostly past as well as all those present before it—it is precisely this that Sihanouk, Sihanouk *as* King, Sihanouk *as* Papa, refuses to do. He is Cambodia, and he is all of it. He permits all to dwell within. Precisely because he is, at least for a while, nothing in himself.

From the viewpoint of the Western rational mind—politically,[6] psychoanalytically, economically—the forms Cixous's play seems in effect to celebrate (maternity, the feminine, the ethnic, even the homeland) are pathological *in the modern setting.* We have been enlightened about the darker sides of these forms of humanity when they atavistically surface in "our" world. Who could wish to see them operative or even dominant in modern life? And why does Cixous choose so risky a gesture?

I think it is because, from the viewpoint not of the *mind* but of contemporary, ongoing history, the question of traditional social forms is not merely hypothetical. We cannot permit our apprehension of traditional forms of human association to rest upon the unexamined assumption of the superiority of modernity. Great big modern countries—and Cixous's Sihanouk makes much out of America's continuing and unconscious reference to Cambodia as "tiny"[7]—the United States in Vietnam, the USSR in Afghanistan, and both in countless, secret little "wars," have seemed compulsively driven to bring their might to bear on these traditional societies, for reasons that remain largely unfathomable. Yet these nations clearly participate in the Imaginary, in phantasms of the traditional, phantasms of their own Self, their own collective being, that seem to have ever more tenuous links to rationality—scientific, economic or *Realpolitik.* The cultural unconscious, not collective, not racial or historic, but contemporary, is at work, shaping and shaped by an ego-ideal, the Ideal of the Modern Self.

---

[6]Sihanouk is aware of some of the problems of his position in Western eyes: in *Souvenirs doux et amers* (Paris: Librairie Hachette, 1981), p. 23, and p. 34, he examines his role as "neither Cesar Borgia nor the Marquis de Sade," but a melange of Sukharno and Nasser, and distinguishes the "authoritarian character" of his role from that of the dictators Idi Amin of Uganda, Macias N'Guema of Equatorial Guinea and, especially, from that of Pol Pot of "democratic" Kampuchea. In his later text, *Prisonnier des Khmers rouges* (Paris: Librairie Hachette, 1986), p. 425, Sihanouk calls himself an "actor-prince."

[7]See William Shawcross, *Sideshow: Kissinger, Nixon, and the Destruction of Cambodia* (London: Hogarth Press, 1986 [orig. ed. 1979]), p. 61.

What is the modern form of the collective? And against what in the traditional form has it so opposed itself that it feels it must fight it to the death? It is a question that, for the moment, has been asked best, perhaps, only by our artists. We call upon them and all their fierce forms to figure this life-and-death struggle for us. This is what Hélène Cixous's "history" play begins to do.

Modernity: Or When Will We Ever Get Over the Ancien Régime?

It is increasingly apparent that the *forms* of collective consciousness that have been developed under the conditions of modernity are failures. We have insufficiently attended to their construction and development, preferring to assume that the *ideals* of "liberté, égalité, fraternité" would somehow be born of themselves—which is to say, without parents—and with no further formalization than that produced in fact by the letter of the law. We seem blandly to have assumed that the overthrow of monarchism in the revolutions of the seventeenth and eighteenth centuries would yield the general form of the collective: through universal equality before the law, the substitutability of each for everyone else, through both imaginary (chiefly literary) and concrete political (chiefly through the vote) identification of our will with that of others. In short, through the installation of democracy, or the dream of collective freedom, equality and universal relation (brotherhood, fraternity).

In democracy, after all, anyone can grow up to be president, and anyone can see oneself in the role, in the place of the Leader. Ever since Kant (mis)read Rousseau as rooting the collective in an imaginary, ideal, and infinite projection of the "I"—the general self—we have had only one way of forming collective identifications: we can exchange places with another, equal, "I." There is, however, a paradox, and it is the paradox of Narcissus, of the mirror and its stage. For what is licensed by the mechanism of identification and exchange as the exclusive collective form in democracy also fosters the greatest of inequalities. It is in the interests of an ego that identifies itself with its own ego-ideal for there to exist an objective, ideal ego: a greater Other, a Leader, a focal point. As a relay of the self the greater He is the greater one's own self-esteem: if one could also at any moment fill the Leader's shoes, perform the same role, all the better that the Leader be all-powerful, the greatest of ideal egos.

We have been insufficiently vigilant: in the guise of the ego modernity has permitted the return of what Stendhal once called the "monarchical principle" in its implicit modeling of the *collective* as a generalized "I"—an I the later Freud could not distinguish from the Unconscious (in *Ego and Id*). The modern *individual* imagines himself the sovereign subject, a minor or major despot, a sum of his wills.

The advantage that the ancien régime, the actual rather than the phantasmatic monarchy, has over ours is purely one of *consciousness*. The peasant, structurally, is incapable of switching places with the King.[8] If there is identification—and if Freud is to be believed about group psychology there must be—it has to be a two-way street: we accept the Father/King's rule (and in this play it is always a question of "Monseigneur Papa") not only when and if he deigns to love us, but rather to the degree that he is conscious of the fact that, apart from us, he simply does not, cannot exist. Cixous presents "the King" not *as* Norodom Sihanouk, the living being, but the continuous stewardship of a people by itself through his figure. When she has Sihanouk say "I am three thousand years old," it reads both as his self-centered sulking ("I have nothing more to lose") *and* as his insertion into and submission before "the immense tranquil field of legend" (Part 2, Act 5, sc. 4). When she has Sihanouk at his most egotistical-seeming, his most improbable, most exasperating (as in Part 1, Act 1, sc. 2, when his rhetoric is exaggerated by means of a self-abasing aggrandizement—he says he will "represent" both the gods and the people), he is always redeemed by this identification in reverse ("And here we are, you and I, you who are I and I who am you, my prince-people, we are going to win [the elections], yes, and in an orderly and democratic fashion" [Part 1, Act 1, sc. 3]). He is characterized not by "l'état c'est moi" but by his strict awareness of the *multiplicity* of selves—his people, Cambodians, Vietnamese, men, women, children, trees, rivers, plants, cities, even and especially *the dead*—that go into making up his "identity" as monarch. And she traces this correspondence through and beyond the critical "demo-

---

[8] In contrast to Cixous's interpretation, in his *Souvenirs*, Sihanouk himself stressed his modern attitude (he cultivated rice alongside the peasants), p. 34. Still, for him the peasants—he calls them "le petit peuple"—remain the single human link that ties him to Cambodia: thousands of peasant men and women, the humble provincial Buddhist monks set themselves, according to Sihanouk, against the intellectual and bureaucratic hierarchies of the clergy and the party of Lon Nol who proclaimed Sihanouk the agent of atheist communism.

cratic" event—the time when one can no longer be "at one and the same time, god and King" (Part 1, Act 1, sc. 2). The failure of Sihanouk's effort—to be, as he says, "both classical and modern, guardian of inherited values and inventor of new strategies" (Part 1, Act 1, sc. 3)—is the strong impasse of modernity and its failure at political creativity.

Psychoanalysis and social science have uncovered the degree to which the individual self is blind to the fact that *in itself* it is also a collective form. Hélène Cixous would seem to teach us our history: that this condition of blindness is a structural feature of a democracy that is lived mythically, unconsciously, and unaware of itself. It is democracy, not "traditional" society, that will be—unless it realizes itself in the almost old-fashioned Hegelian sense of the term—in consciousness. And that consciousness is, currently to be found only in art like Cixous's.

Modernity and its failure of consciousness, failure of nerve, is both cause and effect, then. Our story, our *modern history* is replete with events so shocking to consciousness that they cannot be faced: even to enumerate them is in a way to be complicitous with them. The principal forms of artistic representation fail specifically to render the horror of horror, and they also fail, collectively, to form our consciousness. When they are reproduced or represented their horror is dulled, made into something different, even something attractive, something that secretly supports the conditions that made the horrible event possible: imaginary exchange with and phantasmatic replacement of self for other. When Marguerite Duras wrote *Hiroshima, mon amour* in 1960 she made the radical claim that she was going "to be done with the depiction of horror by horror": the film graphically depicts the pleasure her film's heroine (whose body and mind remain occupied by her dead German-soldier lover) takes in fixing the images of nuclear victims in her mind while she is making love. Cixous's epic effort has worked to transform at least some of the ways and means of artistic representation.

Cixous's play was published in 1985. Little has changed historically in the political conditions that persist in Cambodia. Sihanouk lives, and so do the Khmer Rouge. Vietnam and the United States continue to be players in the destiny of that people. The singularity of the assault on the totality of Cambodia as a people can be eloquently stated in the notes that explain why and how the Cambodian

Royal Ballet came to be invited to perform at the 1990 Los Angeles City Festival, curated by Peter Sellars. The Khmer Rouge exterminated more than 90 percent of the dancers and artists of the country. Apparently only one octogenarian puppet master-ballet teacher remained alive to pass on the traditions of the dance, which uses shadow puppets. The Khmer Rouge offensive against "traditional" art can, hopefully, be read now, in the light of Cixous's masterfully analytic as well as beautifully crafted play, for what it is— "modernity" and its "regime of the brother" at the worst. "Le père ou le pire," Lacan taught us; and Cixous agrees to that extent with his reading of the Freudian discovery.

What follows now is a brief sketch of the "epic" nature of the play and its relation to Cixous's work with the Théâtre du Soleil.

SIHANOUK AND CONTEMPORARY "EPIC" THEATER
Judith Pike

In recent years a number of contemporary playwrights, and Cixous is among them, have taken theater in a new direction. Whereas Beckett marked the culmination of minimalist theater with his short pieces such as *Come and Go* (1966) or *Breath* (1969) lasting only thirty-five seconds, Cixous and others such as Robert Wilson and Peter Brook have headed in the opposite direction with a new epic theater.[9] They are "epic" not only in the sense of their subject matter but also in terms of the actual duration of these pieces. The performances in Paris of both Cixous's *Sihanouk* and Brook's *Mahabharata* could be seen in performances that were each eight to

---

[9]Samuel Beckett, *Come and Go: Dramaticule* (London: Calder and Boyars, 1967) and *Breath and Other Shorts* (London: Faber and Faber, 1971); on Robert Wilson's *The Forest,* see Laurence Shyer, "*The Forest:* A Preview of the Next Wilson-Byrne Collaboration," *Theater* 19 (Summer–Fall 1988): 6–11. The reader might wish to consult Wilson and David Byrne's *CIVIL WarS,* in collaboration with East German playwright Heiner Müller, in *The Knee Plays: The American Section from the CIVIL WarS: A Tree Is Best Measured When It Is Down* (Minneapolis: Walker Art Center, 1984). *Mahabharata* is a collaborative piece by Peter Brook and Jean-Claude Carrière. See Jean-Claude Carrière, *Le Mahabharata* (Paris: P. Belfont, 1989) and *The Mahabharata: A Play Based upon the Indian Classic Epic,* trans. Peter Brook (New York: Harper & Row, 1987). For information on *Einstein on the Beach* see Samuel Lipman, "Einstein's Long March to Brooklyn," *New Criterion* 3 (February 1985): 15–24.

ten and one-half hours long, or one could attend two consecutive evening performances. Such large-scale works have placed Cixous and Brook in league with Wilson and his master production *Einstein on the Beach* (1977) and his later *CIVIL WarS* (1985), a twelve-hour work yet to be performed in its entirety. As with Cixous, an involvement with history characterizes Wilson's early works as well as his most recent one, *Forest* (1988), a collaborative piece with David Byrne. India's history has been taken as the dramatic subject for Brook's *Mahabharata* and Cixous's *L'Indiade* (1987), the latter depicting India's critical years, from 1937 to 1948. *Sihanouk* falls into this line.[10] In the shadow of the Geneva Peace Conference, Cixous's play begins with Sihanouk's abdication in 1955 and traces the political upheaval of the next twenty years, ending with Sihanouk's house arrest by the Khmer Rouge in the late 1970s.

One critic has called this new theater "Super-Wagnerian" (Rockwell, the *New York Times*), but the works seem less "total art works" than radical re-visionings, politically alert, of turbulent and critical historical moments. For Cixous at least, the epic quality of her work is less Wagnerian than Shakespearean: "I don't want to compare myself with Shakespeare, I just want to follow his path," she told the audience at Irvine in 1988.[11] Both she and the creator and director of the Théâtre du Soleil (founded in 1964), Ariane Mnouchkine, have a great affinity for Shakespeare (witness Part 1, Act 2, sc. 1, where John of Gaunt's "scepter'd isle" from *Richard II* is a model—"this other Eden, this demi-paradise . . . this little world, this blessed plot,") and over the years the Théâtre du Soleil has performed a number of Shakespeare's plays including *Richard II* (1982), *Henry IV* (1984), and *Twelfth Night* (1982–83). It is to the historical plays that Cixous tells us she is drawn:

---

[10] *The Forest*, Wilson's rewriting of the Gilgamesh epic, it is reset in Germany during the Industrial Revolution. See Judith G. Miller, review of Théâtre du Soleil productions of *Richard II* and *Twelfth Night*, *Theater Journal* 35 (March 1983): 87. *Sihanouk* has been viewed by more than 108,000 spectators in Paris and on tour in Amsterdam, Brussels, Madrid, and Barcelona. *L'Indiade, ou L'Inde de leurs rêves* toured Israel in 1988 and has been made into a film version by Bernard Sobel. Hélène Cixous, *L'Indiade, ou, L'Inde de leurs rêves: Et quelques écrits sur le théâtre* (Paris: Théâtre du Soleil, 1987).

[11] John Rockwell, "If Length Were All, or Why a 10½ Hour Play," *New York Times*, June 7, 1986, 12N. Hélène Cixous, "The Two Countries of Writing: Theatre and Poetical Fiction," paper presented to the Focused Research Program in Gender and Women's Studies, University of California, Irvine, May 11, 1988.

My type of writing for the theater one might situate in the line of Shakespearean historical plays. I've always loved them, I've always read them, but I've never considered these plays as giving me a political message. . . . History is the daylight or stagelight in which human beings are steeped.[12]

The imposing presence of this playwright in Cixous's work resurfaces in Sihanouk's words when he calls Shakespeare a "gigantic giant," unable to be contained, for he is "like an empire" (Part 1, Act 2, sc. 2). No doubt, Cixous is also speaking about here the immensity of her own project of dramatizing Cambodian history. What made this project even more difficult than her later piece L'Indiade was that the major political figure in this work was still alive. Although she was captivated by Sihanouk, there were ethical issues of misrepresentation to be considered:

> I was completely taken by the story of Cambodia, but all the time I wrote the play which became L'Histoire Terrible Mais Inachevée de Norodom Sihanouk, Roi du Cambodge, I thought I was doing something forbidden, so I decided that when I finished it I would change all the names. . . . But I didn't.[13]

Not only did Cixous retain the real names of all the political figures but before writing her final scenes she met with Sihanouk who later went to see the play.

While she disclaims being "political," Cixous is known best in the United States, through her career as theorist, as having been responsible for a certain kind of politicization of poetics for feminism, notably in her "Laugh of the Medusa." The one theatrical piece of hers with which most are familiar also has a theoretical air: Portrait of Dora (1976) is a rewriting of Freud's famous case. The dramatic force of Cixous's work bears witness to critical historical epochs, however, in such a way that each work becomes what she has called "the epic of the heart." In other words, the easy slogans of politics are reframed with the understanding of the intersubjective relation

---

[12]Hélène Cixous, "The Two Countries of Writing: Theater and Poetical Fiction," in The Other Perspective in Gender and Culture: Rewriting Women and the Symbolic, ed. Juliet Flower MacCannell (New York: Columbia University Press, 1990), p. 201.

[13]"Interview with Hélène Cixous," conducted by Catharine Franke and Roger Chazal, Qui Parle? 3 (Spring 1989): 154.

that they all too often fail to acknowledge as their motivation. In short, her political disclaimer is correct only if "political" is taken in the traditional sense of the term. Cixous says that she began writing "the epic of the heart" on a modest level with *Portrait of Dora*, but as she adds: "Already it was something that had to do with modern fate. I am interested in writing about fate . . . Destiny . . . it belongs to the vocabulary of tragedy or epic."[14]

In *Sihanouk* Cixous has moved further in the direction of the "vocabulary of tragedy [and] epic," although, as in Shakespeare's dramas, to achieve "the epic of the heart," realism is not the sole route; elements of comedy and even the supernatural come into play. The ghost of Sihanouk's father Suramarit, a echo perhaps from Hamlet but also of Cixous's own father, plays a central role in the play. One critic has very nicely described his role: "Suramarit's ghost also provides humorous moments, as well as serving as a link between the past and the present. His stylized, ancient costume and head piece contrast sharply with the dark, formal suits worn by those in power."[15]

The force of Cixous's vision lies with the destiny of an entire people. She calls this destiny into question; the result can only be tragedy. In theatrical terms this has meant more than play with costuming: it means mobilizing many. Cixous is no longer working with only three of four people on stage: in *Sihanouk* there are more than fifty characters to give voice to destiny—from the troubled maternal voice of the Cambodian vegetable vendor Samnol to the cold and designing voices of the Americans Abrams and Kissinger. The recent turn of events in Kampuchea, makes Cixous's play prophetic about this destiny: it was first published in Paris in 1985.[16]

---

[14]Hélène Cixous, "The Laugh of the Medusa," in Elaine Marks and Elizabeth de Courtivron, eds., *New French Feminisms* (New York: Schocken Books, 1981), pp. 245–64. Cixous, "Two Countries," p. 14. Hélène Cixous, *Portrait de Dora* (Paris: des femmes, 1976).

[15]Celita Lamar, "Norodom Sihanouk, a Hero of Our Times: Character Development in Hélène Cixous' Cambodian Epic," in *From the Bard to Broadway*, ed. Karalisa V. Hartigan (Lanham, Md.: University Presses of America, 1987), pp. 163, 164.

[16]Hélène Cixous, *L'Histoire terrible mais inachevée de Norodom Sihanouk, roi du Cambodge* (Tours: Théâtre du Soleil, 1985, rev. ed. 1987). At the time of this writing, negotiations for the withdrawal from Kampuchea of the Vietnamese and their appointed president, and for the return of the Khmer Rouge and—possibly—of Sihanouk, are under way.

CIXOUS, MNOUCHKINE, AND THE
THÉÂTRE DU SOLEIL
Lollie Groth

Call it "Journalistic Theater" with a touch of magic. Call it "Theater for the Exiled." But whatever you call it, Cixous's writing is riveting, a weave of the historical and the primordial, sustained by what Cixous refers to as her "unknown autobiography." Her ability to enhance the political with the wealth of the unconscious is repeatedly demonstrated in *Sihanouk*. At one point Cixous recalls that during the writing of *Sihanouk*, she was haunted by an image, a "metaphor," that she could not quite grasp. When it finally came to her, "it was a very old bike that had been used throughout the ages," and in the play it is used by a dead king, the dead king of Cambodia, who, Cixous contends, might actually be her father.[17]

This propensity to interweave the personal with the political, and so willingly to lay trust in the unconscious, is characteristic of Cixous's writing. And perhaps it is these very qualities that led Ariane Mnouchkine to ask Cixous to collaborate with her on a play about Cambodia, a request whose result is *Sihanouk*. The match seems inevitable. For Mnouchkine, theater and history have a dynamic relationship: as Celita Lamar notes, Mnouchkine "considers it not only possible but necessary to depict the living present on the stage."[18] Furthermore, what Cixous outlines as a poetics of theater Mnouchkine's Théâtre du Soleil puts into practice: "If the stage is a woman, it will mean ridding this space of theatricality. . . . it will therefore be necessary to work at exploding the confines of the stage, lessening our dependency on the visual and stressing the auditory."[19]

Anyone who has seen the Théâtre du Soleil perform knows that "staginess" is strictly not part of its vocabulary; rather it is a theater that celebrates the fullness of an actor's emotional and physical range. Mnouchkine's research into the theater of other cultures, into "forms of theater which speak to the primordial in human life, and her concern with recounting the world in simple signs and gestures

---

[17]Cixous, "Two Countries," pp. 200–201.
[18]Lamar, "Norodom Sihanouk," p. 157.
[19]Hélène Cixous, "Aller à la mer," trans. Barbara Kerslake, in *Modern Drama* 27 (December 1984): 547.

has led her again and again to cultivate in her actors extreme stylization in movement and emotional expression."[20] On a bare proscenium stage, Mnouchkine's actors and actresses continue to blur the line between the spectator and the actor, between reality and theater. It is even difficult to determine when the play actually begins, for when one arrives, the actors and actresses are in the process of making up, in full view of the public, beneath the bleachers where the audience will eventually sit. When I arrived at the Cartoucherie in Vincennes to see a performance of *L'Indiade*, I was overcome by a smell of burning incense and an incomparable quiet—Georges Bigot, who portrayed Nehru, was seated in a half-lotus position upon a thatched cot, and many of the actresses in purdah bowed *namaste* to acknowledge our presence.

Mnouchkine's actors and actresses are able to embrace and inhabit the "other" in a way that one rarely witnesses in American theater; they truly become Cambodians, Hindus, Muslims. This hyperidentification with the characters heightens the spectator's sense of being party to history in the making. Convinced that theater and history belong together, Mnouchkine, with her twenty-five-member cast, brought the plight of the Cambodian people center stage in Cixous's *Sihanouk*. In a play that runs eight and one-half hours and can be viewed over a period of two evenings, the effect is such that a historical moment is not only remembered but relived. We witness the exile of Sihanouk, the fall of Phnom Penh, the mercenary tactics of Kissinger, the rise of Pol Pot. The intrinsic nature of a play, its ability to be performed and repeated, is itself a grim and ironic comment on world affairs and the never-ceasing plays for power. How can we not be cynical when we realize along with Sihanouk the motives of the American government, that Cambodia served foremost as "the little silk footstool" they climbed up on "to look over the wall into our neighbor's [Vietnam's] garden" (Part 1, Act 1, sc. 2)?

From the vantage of her own country of writing, Hélène Cixous gives what has been exiled a voice. Whether it is the literal exile of Norodom Sihanouk, or the exile of an entire people, Cixous has made a habit of bringing the marginal, the almost forgotten into focus. Exile, for Cixous, is at once literal and metaphoric: it can

---

[20] Miller, review, p. 116.

mean losing the earth under one's feet, it can mean losing the nostalgic vision of one's country—India before partition, Cambodia before the killing fields. But for Cixous exile is a given, "a kind of earthly condition," not to be considered as "unhappy." She writes, "I consider it as having to be lived through and corrected. . . . Losing and re-winning, regaining and reconquering—for me these things go together."[21]

This unwavering determination to re-create what is lost seems almost innate in Cixous's work; in fact, it may very well, as Cixous suggests, grow out of her own personal experience of exile, of growing up in the French colony of Algeria:

> My writing was born in Algeria. No. I should say out of Algeria; out of a lost country, out of a lost father and of a foreign mother. All of these little traits which might appear as unsatisfactory were very fertile for me. I've had that luck to know first foreignness, exile, war, the phantom memory of peace, mourning. . . . I knew that uprooting existed and that human moods know no borders, no nationality.[22]

Somehow this early education in mourning and loss places Cixous in the exile's range, giving her the ability and authority to write about those who have experienced the loss of their country. Regarding the story of *Sihanouk* as a "contemporary legend," Cixous evokes "a story that becomes pure tragedy: a people driven from Paradise . . . the experience of infinite regret and infernal exile."[23] And yet the play also affirms that state in which there are no boundaries, where magic, and dignity, and a sense of otherness abide. To reduce these many others simply to being a resource for new formalizations may be to miss the essential: these cultures are, on stage, the theater, in another country, peoples and cultures *in exile*. Their exile has already transformed them, and it is to this event that Cixous's work, together with Mnouchkine, bears witness.

---

[21] Cixous, "Two Countries," p. 193.

[22] Ibid., p. 196.

[23] Hélène Cixous, "The Two Countries of Writing" (From personal notes on the address delivered to the Focused Research Program in Gender and Women's Studies at the University of California, Irvine, May 1988). In Cixous's view, this paradise was by no means one of free enjoyment. We moderns tend to imagine a savage, unrestrained jouissance as a feature of paradise; Sihanouk's pre–Khmer Rouge Cambodia, in Cixous's treatment, is clearly one of ethical limitations and responsibility. TR

Note on the Translation

WHY WE TRANSLATED *SIHANOUK*

This play was translated originally as part of the activities sur-
rounding the visit by Hélène Cixous to lecture at the University of
California, Irvine, in May 1988. We undertook this translation pri-
marily for pedagogical reasons, having to do with the shaping of
Women's Studies in the academic institution in which we work. We
had invited Professor Cixous to present a major address to our three-
year-old Focused Research Program in Gender and Women's Studies.
She was to be featured prominently in the context of a conference on
"Women and Creativity," organized to highlight women as cultural
producers. We included traditional craftswomen, artists of the avant-
garde, theorists of feminism, writers, and film makers, in ways that
we hoped would be unusual in its mix of old and new, theory and
practice, art and life. We were, furthermore, anxious to hear from
those who were accomplished in more than one field, and in settings
and institutions not often seen on college campuses, not for anti-
institutional reasons, but rather because we wanted to see them in relation to the academic, not excluded from or relegated to extramural
status. For example, we invited "Voices from the Pen," members of
the California Women's Prison Writing Project; a family of Puebla Indian women (several generations—Roxanne Swentzell, Rina
Swentzell, and Tessie Naranjo), who were accomplished in both traditional and modern arts (one had a doctorate); Judith Baca, coordi-

nator of the Great Wall of Los Angeles project, which commemorates the local history of that city; Suzanne Lacy, a performance artist committed to depicting with generosity the aging female; and Lynne Tillman, aka "Madame Realism," a writer and critic who collaborated on the film biography of Frances Farmer. The list suffices to elaborate our hoped-for vision of how creative "women" could relate to the academic study of women.

In such a context, we intended for Cixous to be first among peers—not different in approach from these others. She combines intellect and art, criticism and tradition. She has also eloquently articulates the limits and possibilities of gender, class, and cultural identification. Who can read her "Laugh of the Medusa" and not understand how these have been overdetermined in relation to each other?

The trouble was that except for a few in our community, and for fewer still in the United States, her recent creative work—as a playwright—remains largely unknown. While she is renowned for her feminist theory and her insistence on an *écriture féminine*, and though many had heard of her poetry and novels, except for *Portrait of Dora* her theater work has not received sufficient attention. Since her lecture was to concern her reflections on the differences between poetic and theatrical writing, we felt a certain consternation at having none of her plays at hand, in English. So we announced that my students and I would translate *Sihanouk*. We did not at that moment realize of what epic proportions the play was. . . .

PROBLEMS OF THE TRANSLATION

The basis for our translation is the 1985 edition, published at Tours by the Théâtre du Soleil. The play also appeared in a slightly abridged version in 1987, but we wanted to use the 1985 edition because it was the one mounted first by Mnouchkine at the Cartoucherie in Vincennes on September 11, 1985, and reflected the practical intervention by women in the arts that was the subject of the conference. (It was also the version Sihanouk himself attended.)[1] We have taken the liberty of reconverting some of the names of the

---

[1] Cixous, *L'Histoire terrible.* See Sihanouk, *Prisonnier des Khmers rouges*, p. 425, "Envoi: J'ai trois mille ans," whose title is a quote from the play ("I am three thousand years old").

historical characters familiar to citizens of the United States to their usual English spelling ("Melvyn Laird" becomes again "Melvin Laird," "MacClintock" becomes "McClintock," and "MacCloskey" becomes "McCloskey." "Zhou Enlai" has been converted to our practice of calling him "Chou En-lai"). We have also tried to offer some insight into certain phrases used by the Cambodian characters which refer to wordplay in Cambodian: for example, *sihan* means "lion" in Cambodian, and its presence in the Prince's name accounts in part for Sirik Matak's reference in Part 1, Act 1, sc. 3, to the monkey wearing "the lion's skin," and Lon Nol's reference to the "white lion" that threatens him (Part 1, Act 3, sc. 2).[2] Cixous's text often omits exits and entrances for characters, and we have not inserted those that are missing, delegating responsibility for these to the future director's discretion. Finally, the question of "Monseigneur" and "Monseigneur Papa": at times, especially when Sihanouk retains his association with the deified ancestors, we have chosen to translate "My Lord" or "Your Grace." Later, when he is elected Prince, we use "Your Grace." At first we considered "Royal Highness" for the opening parts of the play, but the intimate terms on which Sihanouk-as-King is deemed to consort with the dead and the gods in his first appearances on stage demanded, we felt, the broader and less Eurocentric determination of royalty.

Similarly, in the Shakespeare-like soliloquies that close many of the first scenes, we have opted for the formal, often declamatory style, modified, as in Shakespeare, to suit the particular psychic conflicts Cixous has evidently read in each of their hearts—Saloth Sâr's anal obsession with purgation and evacuation (Act 1, sc. 1) is wrapped in the rhetoric of moral fervor to clean up the state; Sirik Matak's egocentric "melancholia" (Act 1, sc. 3) reminds us of some of Hamlet's more vivid maledictions in the name of his rightful ascendance to the throne; Khieu Samphan's utopianism (Act 1, sc. 5) has a romantic ring. We have tried to render these less colloquially than the greater part of their dialogue in the rest of the play because we feel that Cixous intended to set them apart in this way, showing how political rhetoric is too often rooted in pathologies of the subject.

---

[2]Sihanouk makes reference to the lion in his name in his autobiography, *Souvenirs doux et amers,* p. 25. *Siha* (*singha* or *singa*) means lion in *pâli;* Singapour, for example, means "city of the lion" (*poura* = city). Sihanouk's grandfather, Prince Norodom Sutharot, gave him the name so he could become a "Khmer Richard the Lionhearted."

In the long run, we have not made the effort to create a seamless, smooth American English text. This is what all language teachers strive for in their conversation classes, and it may certainly be one legitimate aim of literary translation, particularly for the stage. But another equally valid aim is the one Goethe and Walter Benjamin knew about: they knew that hearing one's own "native" language in the syntactical forms of another tongue permits insights unavailable to someone perfectly at ease and at home with his or her own language. Neither Cixous nor Sihanouk count French as their pure and single native tongue; and since Cixous's epic theater recalls Brecht's, and like his, also tries to make the familiar uncanny, we did not think that striving to make the reader/listener perfectly at ease (out of fear of literalism, stylistic awkwardness, or a desire to lighten up) was a primary or even a desirable goal. (And after having met the Chilean actor who played Khieu Samphan [he cofounded El Grán Teatro del popolo in Chile] and hearing him discuss how strongly he and his fellow actors of the Théâtre du Soleil felt that they were inhabitants of no nation, but citizens of the "country of theater" it seems all the more appropriate that the translation ought to aim at this sort of *dépaysement* on the model of Mnouchkine/Cixous.)

Finally, along more practical lines, the French use of the present tense for a quasi future seemed to us to demand occasional use of the English future tense, especially when the characters discuss their machinations, often in monologue, as when at the end of Act 2 Sirik Matak imagines Sihanouk's downfall as a tree hanging by a sliver of bark: "Encore une poussée et je le renverse," which we translate as "One more shove and I'll overturn it."

THE PLAY'S TREATMENT OF HISTORICAL CHRONOLOGY

Norodom Sihanouk was called by the royal family to succeed his grandfather, King Sisowath Monivong, on April 23, 1941. Vichy France, which ruled Cambodia, had just signed a treaty with Japan, ceding the province of Battambang and several other important provinces to Thailand. Son Ngoc Thanh was named Prime Minister of Cambodia six days before Japan's surrender to MacArthur. Ngoc Thanh, arrested by Allied French forces, became the founder of the *issarak Khmer* movement, which later split into pro-Thai and pro-

Viet Minh (communist) factions. Limited internal independence from France came in 1949, after the construction of a constitutional monarchy in 1947, with guarantees of press and other freedoms. In 1952, Norodom Sihanouk campaigned to be appointed the crown and won under a "Royal Crusade for Independence" borne on a wave of popular feeling for him. In 1953 Sihanouk attempted to oust the Viet Minh from Cambodia. He received a critical letter from several Cambodian students in Paris, among them Ieng Sary, Saloth Sar, and Hou Youn (but not Khieu Samphan). The formation of the South East Asia Treaty Organization (SEATO) in 1954 prompted Sihanouk to declare Cambodia nonaligned. In 1955, Sihanouk held a popular referendum on his action and won 925,812 to 1,834. He then abdicated in favor of his father, Suramarit, and not, as in the play, his mother. He did this in order to draw closer to his people, to disempower the clique of antidemocratic elites who opposed him, and to create the *Sangkum Reastr Nium* (the Popular Socialist Community). He was elected Head of State. At the Bandung conference of April, 1955, he subscribed to the doctrine of peaceful coexistence. With the *Khmers sereis*, a CIA-run party of the right, installed in Thailand under Ngoc Thanh in 1956, the United States began an economic blockade of Cambodia, in part for its recognition of Communist China and for maintaining strict military neutrality. From 1957 to 1959 several assassination attempts on Sihanouk and others were made by the *Khmer sereis*, who were eventually installed in power after the fall of Sirik Matak in October, 1971. King Norodom Suramarit died in 1960, and was succeeded by Sisowath Kossomak Nearath, though Sihanouk was the real power. The country continued to support Sihanouk's policy of strict neutrality in a referendum. These details are supplied in Norodom Sihanouk *Chroniques de guerre . . . et d'espoir*. Paris: Librairie Hachette/Stock, 1979, pp. 231–39.

The translators wish to thank Robert Oventile for his help with a portion of the early version, Doug White for his research on aspects of contemporary Cambodian history, Tracy McNulty for further help with the diction of the manuscript, and Daniel MacCannell for his assistance in reading the final draft. We are grateful to the Organized Research Initiative (ORI) in Women and the Image for funding in support of this project, and to the series editor, Alice Jardine, for her continuing encouragement. We also thank Hélène Cixous.

The Terrible but Unfinished Story
of Norodom Sihanouk,
King of Cambodia

CAST OF CHARACTERS

Cambodia

The Royal Palace:
Norodom Sihanouk, first King, then Prince of Cambodia
Norodom Suramarit, deceased King, Sihanouk's father
Queen Kossomak, Sihanouk's mother
The Princess, Sihanouk's wife
Madame Mom Savay, Queen's friend

Loyal Friends of the King:
Lord Penn Nouth
Captain Ong Meang, aide to the Prince
Chea San, Cambodian Ambassador to Moscow

The Enemies of the King:
Prince Sisowath Sirik Matak
General Lon Nol
The Cambodian Ambassador to Paris

The Royal Household:
Rama Mok, musician
Dith Boun Suo, Prince's servant
Dith Sophon, Queen's servant
Captain Nissai

Phnom Penh

Madame Khieu Samnol, vegetable merchant,
mother of Khieu Samphan
Madame Lamné, Vietnamese fish merchant
Yukanthor, their adopted son

Household of Lon Nol:
The Soothsayer
Captain Sim Narang
Captain In Sophat

The Republic of Lon Nol:
General Seksaket
Colonel Um Savuth
Cheng Heng, president of the National Assembly
Long Boret, Prime Minister

Saukham Khoy, president of the Republic

Members of the Khmer Rouge:
Saloth Sâr [Later: Pol Pot]
Khieu Samphan
Hou Youn
Ieng Sary
Ieng Thirit[1]

Other Characters:
Peasants
The Radio Technician
The Japanese Ambassador
The Chorus
The Chinese Merchant
The Kamaphibal, Khmer Rouge cadre
Chorn Hay, Khmer Rouge cadre
Loudspeaker voice

The United States of America

Henry Kissinger
Melvin Laird, Secretary of Defense
General Abrams, Commander in chief of the American Forces in
South Vietnam
Robert McClintock, U.S. Ambassador to Cambodia
General Taber
Hawkins, CIA agent
William Watts, head of the National Security Council
John Gunther Dean, U.S. Ambassador to Cambodia
Keeley, Dean's secretary
Pete McCloskey, Republican Senator
John Holridge, U.S. envoy to Peking

The USSR

Alexis Kosygin, Prime Minister
The Interpreter

China

Chou En-lai, Prime Minister

---

[1]Spelling "Thirith" used in the 1987 edition. TR

Liu Kiang, Special Envoy to Chou En-lai
Cambodian Ambassador to Peking
Etienne Manac'h, French Ambassador to Peking
Secretary to the envoy

Vietnam

Pham Van Dong, Prime Minister of the Republic of North Vietnam
General Giap, Minister of Defense and Commander in chief of the
North Vietnamese Army
General Van Tien Dung, his assistant

FIRST EPOCH, ACT 1, SCENE 1

[Phnom Penh. The Royal Palace. Enter Sihanouk, King of Cambodia, Penn Nouth, Prince Sirik Matak, U.S. Ambassador McClintock, ambassadors, servants, peasants, Khieu Samnol, Khieu Samphan.]

SIHANOUK:

What a lovely crowd today!

Behold my favorite landscape.

Come stand close by my side, Lord Penn Nouth.

I like to feel your fidelity on my right

During the ceremony, which is so ancient,

And yet always so new.

Mr. Ambassador of the United States of America, you will see me mete out my justice under my flame trees.[2]

This is one of those very rare moments when reality becomes sweet and miraculous forgiveness and when one can relish being king.

Let's go ahead, for this beautiful day of complaint[3] and reparation.

Let us wade into the river of the people, up to our ears.

My children, my venerable mothers,

And you, my fathers of rice and of fish,

I am here for this entire day, the friend of your needs,

And the interpreter of your rights

Right beside[4] the gods of whom I am the heir.

My Majesty is at your service.

Let them come forward, those who have a petition to be heard.

Come forward, my children, and complain freely.

Musician: O, heavenly scales, cheat not.

O, plumbline, slant not.

---

[2] *Flamboyant:* flame trees are generally found in Western Australia and the West Indies, not Cambodia. TR

[3] *Plainte* carries connotation of judicial complaint, but with overtones of serious injustice, injury, and pain. *Larousse classique,* 6th ed. (Paris: Librairie Larousse, 1957), p. 916. TR

[4] *Auprès des* means at close hand, right next to, as well as suggesting the power to influence. We have chosen the sequence ". . . right/Right . . ." as the best solution in English for carrying both connotations, and to show the "power" of the King—to preserve his people's "rights" by recourse to an effective fiction of his "authority," which he and they both know to be metaphoric. TR

O, Buddha's gaze, shift not.
O, Vessel of the Sun, sink not.

FIRST PEASANT: For me, this is the third time I've come with a grievance and both times before My Lord Papa said I was right.

SIHANOUK: What was your complaint, my uncle?

FIRST PEASANT: The first time, I complained because our governor makes us pay so many taxes on our own harvests, and then after that, without even thanking us, he steals our fattest pigs for his own kitchen, without even inviting us. Our beloved King gave us satisfaction, may his voice be blessed.

SIHANOUK: And the second time?

FIRST PEASANT: The second time it was for the same thing.

SIHANOUK: Why is this? Didn't I grant[5] your wish?

FIRST PEASANT: My Lord, you gave me satisfaction, but the governor would not hear of it.[6]

SIHANOUK: And it's for the same business again today?

FIRST PEASANT: No, Your Grace, today it is more serious. Drought!

SIHANOUK: Speak, my uncle.

FIRST PEASANT:
Drought, Your Grace. For two years it grips us between its teeth and won't let us go. You, Who embody the divine essence,
You, who order who comes and goes,
Couldn't you come and say a prayer over our fields?
The earth is hard as a rock and our granaries are empty to the bare ground.

SIHANOUK: Where are you from, you who are asking me to order the sky about?

FIRST PEASANT: From Ratanakiri, My Lord Papa.

---

[5] *Exaucé:* granting of a wish that is usually reserved to the power of a deity. TR
[6] Note the discrepancy between figurative and executive power. TR

SIHANOUK: And you have no more water up there? But you have a Rain King in your mountains. Have you, perchance, offended him?

FIRST PEASANT: Yes, Your Grace. We did not offer him the sacred buffalo two years ago. Since then he no longer speaks to us.

SIHANOUK: Chief, do not ask me to intercede with my gods under these conditions. We must respect all our kings equally as our greatest gods. Nevertheless, since you had the strength to admit your error, you will not leave without some consolation: the buffalo you owe the Rain King, I offer it to you.
Go and greet the King of the noble element on my behalf.

FIRST PEASANT: O, High-and-Mighty One,[7] you are husband for the widow, mango tree for the starving, mother hen for the chick!

MUSICIAN: Full breast for the infant, jug of rice wine for the drunkard, cucumber for the King. . . .

KHIEU SAMPHAN: [aside] How easy it is to seduce the hearts of the peasants with a little crumb of justice.

SIHANOUK: Let us continue our festivities. Whose turn is it?

SECOND PEASANT: Royal Father, I speak for the village of Pangrolim, northwest of Battambang. They're driving us off our land. To build a sugar factory.

SIHANOUK: Who's driving you off?

SECOND PEASANT: A company from the city, Blessed Power, the Amirac Company . . . American-Khmer . . . for the develop. . . . They say our land does not belong to us but to the governor. Your Grace, these are our lands! We have all sprung from this land[8] from the time our ancestors were born.

---

[7] *Puissance-et-Faveur:* lit. "Power-and-Favor." We have chosen "High and Mighty" here because the term is used again, sarcastically, by Khieu Samnol further on in response to Saloth Sâr (the future Pol Pot), and contrasts with its nonironic use here. TR

[8] *Poussé de cette terre:* we have chosen "sprung from" (in the sense of "grown up out of") rather than the more usual English "we have grown up on this land" because of Cixous's imagery of peasant "roots" later in the scene. TR

PENN NOUTH: This business, My Lord, once again bears the mark of Sankroun, your cousin's brother-in-law, Prince Sirik Matak. He is president of this company. But behind him already crowd five or six directors, attracted by the smell of sugar.

SIHANOUK: Your rice field belongs to you, it is the King who owns this Kingdom and it is he who gives it to you. There will be no sugar factory, I'll see to it. Lord Penn Nouth, you see to it. Tell Sankroun what I think of his greed and of his imbecile feudal behavior.

MCCLINTOCK: Your Majesty! It's one of our citizens who's financing the establishment of the refinery on your cousin's land; may I draw your attention—

SIHANOUK: Sankroun is not my cousin! And those are neither his lands nor yours, Mr. United States Ambassador!

MCCLINTOCK: Surely there's some misunderstanding. . . .

SIHANOUK: Of course, Mr. Ambassador. In that case I'm sure it will please you to please us. That's why I request that you inform the American-Khmer Company it's not welcome. Kindly have its director contact Lord Penn Nouth to settle this matter.

MCCLINTOCK: I shall, Your Majesty, but, there is a contract.

SIHANOUK: Please, settle this with Penn Nouth.

MCCLINTOCK: Your Majesty, Prince Sirik Matak is the one with a handle on this business . . . and on this region—

SIHANOUK: With Penn Nouth, I said. Make them understand my decision. Period.

KHIEU SAMNOL: [to the audience] He's quite a king, this one, he knows how to soothe the sufferer's heart. I find him even more regal than my neighbor told me he'd be.

SIRIK MATAK: Your Royal Highness, my cousin!

SIHANOUK: Prince Sirik Matak?

SIRIK MATAK: Your Royal Highness my cousin, do you realize the enormous harm you are doing to developing industry in Cambodia? You will put investment to flight. I won't even mention the moral injury you're doing my wife's family.

SIHANOUK: In that case, I won't mention it either.

SIRIK MATAK: My brother-in-law obtained a license from the royal ministry for that refinery, and paid a great deal for it in dollars. You'd promised to watch over the fortunes of that portfolio.

SIHANOUK: But in the meantime, and before all the people, I promised otherwise.

SIRIK MATAK: Certain people could also choose to forget their word, and make you false promises under other circumstances.

SIHANOUK: I foresaw all this, my cousin. I know your crowd. Your riches weigh upon you, and blind you. So, then: move. This peasant cannot uproot himself. He is a millennial tree. But your brother-in-law, behind the wheel of his Mercedes, he has only to go build his refinery farther away. How about over by Pursat?

PENN NOUTH: My Lord! I don't agree! For then next year we'll have the peasants from Pursat here!

SIHANOUK: Even farther off, then. Our Cambodia is vast. Any more complaints? My children, I am listening.

KHIEU SAMPHAN: Sire, I have a request.

SIHANOUK: Who are you, my son, and what is it you wish?

KHIEU SAMNOL: Your Grace! That's my son! My god! What's he going to say?

KHIEU SAMPHAN: I'm a graduate of the University of Paris.

SIHANOUK: That's what I thought.

KHIEU SAMPHAN: I hold a doctorate in Economics. Three years ago I returned to this country, I applied for a position in the University and the Lycées. They've sent my dossier back to me six times asking me to complete it. They told me that it's missing a letter of recommmendation.

SIHANOUK: Well? So?

KHIEU SAMPHAN: They ask if I know anyone at the Palace.

SIHANOUK: What? You want a recommendation?

KHIEU SAMPHAN: I want an explanation, your Royal Highness. I'd like to know if one is named to a post in our university for competence or for loyalty.

SIHANOUK: Ah! I also would like to know. But you will ask our Rector that yourself. Someone go get the Rector. This graduate wants explanations.

[Dith Boun Suo exits.]

KHIEU SAMNOL: Give thanks, my son, give thanks.

SIHANOUK: [to the U.S. Ambassador] Ah yes! Mr. Ambassador, our country still suffers from corruption. It's a tropical disease, stubborn and contagious. I wonder how we could cure it since, you see, unfortunately everyone wants to catch it. And we never know whom to treat first, the corrupted or the corrupter.

[Dith Boun Suo returns.]

DITH BOUN SUO: The Honorable Rector is in the countryside for a month for his daughter's marriage.

SIHANOUK: There you have it! The Rector is at his daughter's wedding. You, what is your name?

KHIEU SAMPHAN: Khieu Samphan, Your Royal Highness.

THE KING: Ah! you're the one who sent me that letter signed "Khieu Samphan and Hou Youn, Doctors of the University of the Sorbonne of Paris" in which you demand the Rector's dismissal.

KHIEU SAMPHAN: Your Royal Highness, I'm not the only one in this fix; there are four of us. My comrades would like to express their—

SIHANOUK: What! What?! Four graduates? What is it you want? Four solutions? You want something else? You were in France? You had scholarships? Did you know someone in the scholarship service? What is this? A plot? A revolt of the privileged? I am not here to discuss their careers with graduates! What! You go to Paris at our expense! Thanks to our scholarship fund! Then you join the Union of Communist Students. Then with our money you treat yourself to the complete works of Marx and Mr. Mao Zedong.

You pile them up, climb up on them, and from the top of this mountain of Marxism, you look down with contempt on the poor Cambodian people who continue to live, stupidly happy. That's right! The people and we, we bleed ourselves to pay for you young people's scientific studies! But you return to us graduates in ingratitude and protest. And to top it all off you ask for our royal recommendation! You are making me waste the people's time, but you are not the people. Go! Leave us alone! The people and I have serious business to deal with. You bore us and you exploit us. This is the Hall of Justice for those who can't write French. Go, go back to the Latin Quarter, to Hanoi, to Peking!

[Khieu Samphan exits.]

Write your articles, believe me I read them, because I read everything.

Lord Penn Nouth, next time, allow no one with a sad face in, no one who stares at us with those unblinking eyes. They made us sweat. Well, let's have a little music to cleanse the heart. And serve everyone a drink. We start our festivities again in one hour.

[The King and the Court exit. Enter Khieu Samphan and Saloth Sâr.]

SALOTH SÂR: Your declaration surprised me, my brother. And frankly, it disturbed and even pained me.

KHIEU SAMPHAN: Pained? But why?

KHIEU SAMNOL: Didn't I tell him to hold his tongue! Now the King is angry with us. You see? Saloth Sâr is more reasonable than you.

KHIEU SAMPHAN: Mother! Please don't.

SALOTH SÂR: If you don't mind, Madame Khieu Samnol. . . ?

KHIEU SAMNOL: Excuse me, Mr. High-and-Mighty. I'll shut up. The old lady holds her tongue. I'm leaving. The old lady is leaving. *[She exits.]*

SALOTH SÂR: As I was saying: I didn't like your speech very much. Besides, you will have noticed that none of the rest of us spoke out. You alone stepped forward.

KHIEU SAMPHAN: His farce exasperated me, I wanted . . .

SALOTH SÂR: But of course. We certainly agree. I understand you.

13

But look, objectively—as the enemy has already noted—you put yourself ahead of the people. Objectively.

KHIEU SAMPHAN: I'm completely crushed.

SALOTH SÂR: Do you understand? It seemed to me and to our brothers Hou Youn and Ieng Sary, therefore, that you had not yet found that humility we absolutely must observe in our relations with the people. Without realizing it, I'm sure, you have brought popular resentment down on us. Just when we have to do everything to earn the people's love. Do you see what I mean? We must never distinguish ourselves from the peasant.

KHIEU SAMPHAN: Oh! Yes. Now I see! Ah! I am ashamed! I was thoughtless. I beg your pardon.

SALOTH SÂR: We all thought you had made a little more progress since our Paris meetings. But that's how it is, right? The spirit of the revolution isn't found in front of the door like a ladder. You have to struggle to get it. Ah! Well, brother, I leave you. Good-bye.

KHIEU SAMPHAN: What? But . . .

SALOTH SÂR: Oh! No, no. I don't think you're in any shape to go to our meeting today. If you don't mind, let me give you some advice: take a few days to reflect. If the monks taught me anything, it's that you have to take some time to know yourself. It could be you'll discover after a few days you're not cut out for our cause!

KHIEU SAMPHAN: Brother! It's all I live for!

SALOTH SÂR: I'm sure. But one can be mistaken.
Think of the people, my brother! Don't use just your head, use your heart too. Go on, go home.

KHIEU SAMPHAN: I'm on my way. I would be grateful if you would convey my most humble apologies to Ieng Sary and to Hou Youn.

[Khieu Samnol returns.]

KHIEU SAMNOL: Well then, my son, are you coming? The fish is going to get cold.

KHIEU SAMPHAN: I don't want to eat fish, mother.

14

KHIEU SAMNOL: What! But see here, my son, you're the one who made me buy it this morning.

KHIEU SAMPHAN: I don't want to eat fish this week, mother.

KHIEU SAMNOL: What! Then is it pork week?

KHIEU SAMPHAN: I intend to fast for a few days.

KHIEU SAMNOL: Are you sick? It's that Saloth Sâr who killed your appetite, I bet.

KHIEU SAMPHAN: I'm not sick, mother, I'm very happy. Please don't ask me so many questions, revered mother.

KHIEU SAMNOL: Revered mother! I would rather you were sick than acting strange. Such a fish! I'll take your portion over to Madame Lamné then? You're sure. . . ?

KHIEU SAMPHAN: I'm sure, mother.

KHIEU SAMNOL: Come along, anyway. Go with me.

[Khieu Samphan and Khieu Samnol exit.]

SALOTH SÂR:
>I hate them all, those who haven't the noble courage to hate,
>And those who are mere dilettantes in hatred, paying it lip-
>	service on tiptoe.
>O hatred, I shall do you justice.
>Hatred, you are power, you are intelligence.
>And I dare proclaim you
>The true Sun of my destiny.
>In return, help me tear this country from the shameful spells of
>	this junk Buddha.
>Indecent monarchy, I hate your effeminate countenance,
>Your foolish moods, your whorish profusion.⁹
>I shall tear off your silken gowns
>And I shall unveil to the stunned world
>Our next Cambodia, virgin, virile, incorruptible.
>One fine day, beginning tomorrow,

---

⁹*Luxe* has the connotation of showy splendor, and, coupled with *putain*, overtones of *luxure*, or carnal pleasure. TR

at History's turning point,
Our insolent neighbors, those land-guzzlers,
And this horrendous plunderer, this blind ogre, this America,
Will see looming before them—
Invincible Cambodia descending from the mountains
To hound them all beyond our borders
In a magnificent slaughter.
Oh! I cannot wait, I cannot wait.
O, that my furious heart might pour out freely
Its torrent of bitterness.
I'll burn everything in my way.
Arrogant Vietnamese, you who for centuries
Have used our sacred land as a scullery,
I'll burn you to a cinder.
And you, Cambodians, my brothers, you who are made
Out of the my country's mud,
I'll be your potter, I'll smash you to bits,
I'll return you to primal matter
And then I'll mold from this clay a new Khmer people.
How far my thoughts go today!
My plan strides forward all by itself like a giant before
My amazed and admiring eyes.
Go forth, my hate, guide my imagination beyond all known
     bounds. I feel I'll do what no man has done before.
Oh! I'm capable of anything![10] You'll see!
The Universe will be dumbfounded by my deeds.

[He exits.]

PART 1, ACT 1, SCENE 2

[The sanctuary. King Suramarit's statue. Enter Sihanouk.]

SIHANOUK:

For three years I've been awaiting you,
My most holy, most missed, and most ardently loved Father.

---

[10] *Capable de tout:* we have chosen "anything" over "everything" partly out of the more ominous sense the former has in English, and which predicts his transformation into Pol Pot. TR

August and most eminent Majesty,
You still don't want to talk to me?
If I've taken so much time to perfect your statue,
It has been neither from laziness nor from negligence.
I wanted you to be the most handsome, my revered Father,
You, sacred fire, you Rhinoceros of the fire
I wanted your fathers to know how much
Your son honors you.
Forgive me if I've made you wait some time for the mask.
I was searching for a Bang bird to pluck its ritual feathers.
I roamed half our kingdom from forest to forest.
Would you believe me?
At last, near Preah Vihear, where the King of the
Buffaloes lives, I spot one!
I chase it, I capture it, I pluck the three feathers of
Rama, and I release it back into the air. The last Bang bird is
    alive and
Why, you're magnificent.
But tell me something!
Now that you are seated among your own,
You, henceforth forever awake,
You, blissful companion of our gods,
I would like very much to discuss things awhile with you.

[The statue comes to life.]

SURAMARIT: I've waited a long time for this packaging.
    You've made me a solid body again and a magnificent appearance.
    I am happy. I'm listening. Give me the news.

SIHANOUK: Things are not good for me and for our country.
    Never have I known a period so tense, so confused, never have the
    hostile forces which oppose my kingdom been so numerous and so
    brutal.

SURAMARIT: Are we still independent?

SIHANOUK: We're still independent. But . . .

SURAMARIT: We're no longer King!

SIHANOUK: We still are. Let me explain my problem to you. You remember that we accepted the principle of free elections? It was just before your death.[11]

SURAMARIT: ...!...!...!

SIHANOUK: There are going to be elections in the spring by universal suffrage. Already six parties have formed to take power.

SURAMARIT: Several parties? That's disastrous. Still such greed, still more divisions. And you?

SIHANOUK: I am alone. Tomorrow they're going to present themselves at the palace gates to demand a piece of my throne. If I am king, I shall lose all, I shall be nothing. I shall reign over my own chair, if I even am king.

SURAMARIT: Defend us, my son! Forbid these elections! Think of something!

SIHANOUK: I've found a way: I have a secret and very subtle plan which will surprise that greedy crowd. With one breath, I'm going to upset all the pawns on the chessboard. Are you listening to me?

SURAMARIT: I'm all ears.

SIHANOUK: With your permission, I'm stepping down. Wait, hear me out: I'm abdicating because I'm determined to rule. I'll explain: I cede the throne to my mother and I step down. So, I'm a prince. I stand for election and since it is me, I win. Then, I'm king of sorts once more, but freer and stronger. What do you think?

SURAMARIT: Quit your throne . . . what a shame . . .

SIHANOUK: The throne stays in our family. Believe me. I'm right. To-day, one can no longer be, at one and the same time, both god and King. I remain god, of course, but in addition I become party leader.
I already see my future, my face, my statue. A king who deposed himself in order to propose a great adventure to the people. I will be without precedent: the man who exchanged his throne for a seat in Parliament.

---

[11]Here Cixous plays with historical chronology: See The Play's Treatment of His-torical Chronology in the Note on the Translation. TR

He who trades the silence of majesty for the thunder of the speaker's platform is greater than a king. Can you see me next month making the entire country tremble with a few words?[12]

SURAMARIT: My son, it's getting so dark here. In principle we only see the past clearly. But I'll try.

SIHANOUK: Then, more prestigious and more powerful than a king, I shall represent both the gods and my people and I'll be able to struggle with redoubled force for sacred Independence.

SURAMARIT: I feel you're going to convince me.

SIHANOUK: You see! As soon as I speak out. . . .

SURAMARIT: You will be able to convince. Come on, my son, let's abdicate! But you will be hated for being a politician. Have you a few allies?

SIHANOUK: I have all the people. Inside the palace, it's the same old circus with all its wild animals. But once we're on the other side of the gates, it's love.

SURAMARIT: Certainly. You are loved but that doesn't help. To achieve a great destiny, it takes gold, factories, weapons. It isn't the peasants with their debts and their bare hands who will make your history.

SIHANOUK: That is debatable . . .

SURAMARIT: Consider the matter, though, and choose your partners well. But say, my son, how are we doing with the Bigfoot? Tell me, how are you getting on with the Americans?

SIHANOUK: They never let up on me, my father.

SURAMARIT: Why don't you get rid of them? When I picture them in our palace, the Bigfoot, with their coarse voices, I'm appalled. Come on, my son, make a clean sweep!

SIHANOUK: Sweep them out, my father? Why, I do nothing but! I

---

[12]Here Sihanouk yields, briefly to the demagogic potential in all self-empowering acts of self-denial. He is also asking for a prophetic seeing by his father, who does not grant it. TR

throw them out through one window, but your cousins let them back in through the other.

SURAMARIT: Oh, it's disheartening and humiliating! I've never understood why our Khmer race, so graceful, so rich, so well endowed by the gods still suffers from an insistent penchant for corruption. Tell me, you at least, my son, you . . . ?

SIHANOUK: Me?! Me?! My own father dares to wound me with such an insulting suspicion?

SURAMARIT: Hush! don't shout so. . . .

SIHANOUK: I, who paid so dearly for my glorious refusal to enter SEATO . . .

SURAMARIT: SEATO? What's that?

SIHANOUK: You'd been dead a year when this SEATO business started: South East Asia Treaty Organization. It's an enormous citadel America built up against China, full of disparate countries united by the same hostility: Pakistan, Australia, Thailand, New Zealand . . .

SURAMARIT: Thailand!

SIHANOUK: Thailand, England, France, . . . Me? Protect me? by force? in a cage? with the Thai foxes outside the cage? I refused.

SURAMARIT: You did the right thing.

SIHANOUK: Yes, but just afterward, as if by accident, bands of looters out of Thailand and South Vietnam attacked our border villages, falling upon our peasants and massacring them. And a conspiracy seeking to separate our northern provinces from the body of the state just happened to arise, sheerly by coincidence, of course. Might as well have torn off our arms! Only a slaughter got us out of it.
I receive these "messages"—and I answer them like this: I establish ties with the Russians.

SURAMARIT: With the Russians! Once, my blood would have frozen in my veins. Go on.

SIHANOUK: With the Russians, then. Meanwhile to be prudent and fair, I'm accepting aid from the Chinese.

SURAMARIT: My god! But you could do nothing else! Continue.

SIHANOUK: We have to deal with reality. So, I accepted Chinese aid. But aid equals debt equals a dangerous poison. I thus provided a counterpoison: United States aid. Are you following me?

SURAMARIT: The United States . . . I'm with you. . . . But . . . aren't we back where we started?

SIHANOUK: No! We're advancing, but in a circle. I come back, then, to the Americans.

SURAMARIT: There they are again! It's a trick! It's a trap!

SIHANOUK: Everything is a trap. It's a game of traps that's very difficult to play. Sometimes when I go up Independence Boulevard, I feel like Mickey Mouse lodging a Cat Convention in his hotel. Ultimately, this is all the fault of the Vietnamese.
My compatriots sometimes think the Americans are interested in them, in their culture, and in their destiny. But the Americans have eyes only for the Vietnamese. They're the ones the Americans come to see. They fear only the Vietnamese. They dream only of the Vietnamese. We're nothing but the little silk footstool they climb on with their big feet to look over the wall into our neighbor's garden.

SURAMARIT: For seven centuries everything that has befallen us has been Vietnam's fault. I spoke again yesterday with our Fathers. They all say that since the Origin only destruction and misery has come to us from them. They all say the thorny North, inflexible and somber, will never pardon our having received a heritage of joy, dancing, and smiles. Why do you allow them to move in on our home, these land-eaters? Does one let rats into the granary? How many are there?

SIHANOUK: Frankly, there are still the 500,000 who live and trade among us as during your lifetime, but from those we have nothing to fear. What has changed a little is their number at the borders. There, I don't know exactly. They come and go like nocturnal birds that are never seen but whose movements are divined in the night. Those are the communists.

SURAMARIT: Those you must chase out. They don't come to be added in like the others, but to divide and subtract.

SIHANOUK: How impatient and quick to anger you have become since your departure. If I listened to you, I would have already set the country on fire. The hatred smoldering between our races will rekindle instantaneously if I interfere with those who sneak in. Immediately all those who are already lying in wait for us will shout "Fire!" and fling themselves upon us, stamping us out, pell-mell.

SURAMARIT: How wise you have become!

SIHANOUK: My father, I must take my leave.

SURAMARIT: I haven't been much help to you.

SIHANOUK: It did me good to speak with you.
I understand myself much better when I explain myself to you. [They exit.]

PART 1, ACT 1, SCENE 3[13]

[The Royal Palace. Enter McClintock, United States Ambassador.]

MCCLINTOCK: What a country! You spend your time dressing, undressing, dressing and undressing! Who does he take us for! Summoning us at midnight! Making all of high society rush over here at this ridiculous hour in ceremonial dress: princes, ministers, venerable ones, and all the ambassadors!
All this, I was told, just to hear the King make one more speech on the radio. Talk about arrogance in these little two-bit kings! The less power they have, the more pretentious they are!

[Enter Prince Sirik Matak.]

SIRIK MATAK: Mr. Ambassador, you do us the honor of coming to hear our noble cousin deliver his precious thoughts? Ah! But I see this doesn't exactly charm you.

MCCLINTOCK: And do all these dramatics please you, Prince Sirik Matak?

SIRIK MATAK: It's all odious to me, as usual.

MCCLINTOCK: Really, your king has a strange way of exercising the

---

[13]For the performance, this scene was greatly modified. AU

abnormal power this magical and accidental accessory "the crown" confers on a completely ordinary man.

SIRIK MATAK: Stop saying "*your* king," Mr. Ambassador. I take those words as an insult. This king is not mine and if he is still on our throne, it's not as if you had nothing to do with it.
I hate him, I hate him.
I have seven reasons to hate him.
First of all, he stole from me my throne, which he dishonors with his capers and his silly formalities. Next, I hate him because he is popular, very basely popular, very vulgarly and easily popular. Judging from what he says, he has all the virtues. If impudence, perversity, megalomania, and demagoguery are virtues, then he has them all.
Next, I hate him because he is disgracefully anti-American. He is a backward despot, inimical to all progress and more concerned with schools and amusements than with industry and armaments. He is an adulterous king, an accomplice and slave of totalitarianism, who betrays his ancestors, his gods, and his family with Communists, all the Communists! Not only the Russians and the Chinese, but with those from Annam—rabid, raw-boned skinny Vietnamese wolves who have stalked us at the borders for centuries, without counting all the others. He would invent them if they were not coming out of woodwork everywhere. And my final reason for hating him is the scandalous blow of this week: his proclaiming an alleged neutrality without having asked anybody's advice or consent.

MCCLINTOCK: That makes six reasons. You said seven.

SIRIK MATAK: I could have said a hundred. Each contains ten. His neutrality! What a hollow word.

MCCLINTOCK: Didn't he say "passionate neutrality"?

SIRIK MATAK: The passionate neutrality of Cambodia! Why not call it "passionate ubiquity"? It's being both to the left and to the right at the same time. For socialism and for capitalism, for Buddhism and for atheism.
If he is a king, then he is the king of dreams. He wants to trick everyone, Mr. Ambassador. And do you know what all his tricks

and oddities conceal? In the first place he hates me. All he thinks of is harming me.

And next, he sold his soul to the Vietnamese. Yes, observe him and examine our innocent country. Go and look at our borders: you won't find them. The highlands are already Vietnam. We're being eaten alive.

MCCLINTOCK: We've been there, Prince.

SIRIK MATAK: And our cities? And our capital? More and more foreigners, I mean Chinese and Vietnamese, and fewer and fewer Khmers. The North is devouring us. And this is what he calls "neutrality." It's us he's neutralizing. Us, the direct descendants of the gigantic kings who built the greatest city on earth at the time when Vietnam was only a miserable uncultivated rabble. And he is also capable of conning you.

MCCLINTOCK: Prince, don't get yourself so worked up. We've already set in motion a few very secret and very nasty little conspiracies.

SIRIK MATAK: I'm getting upset! This is the fourth one I've seen fail. Why, if were plotting, I'd pull it off!

MCCLINTOCK: In that case why don't you?

SIRIK MATAK: A Sisowath doesn't conspire. To each his own. Ah! The King comes!

MUSICIAN:

Enter the greatest of the Greats,
Who is the greatest of all the Greats of this realm.

[Enter the King, Penn Nouth, the ministers, the ambassadors, etc.]

Here enter the four sacred bulls,
The handsomest, the noblest of the assembly.
Here enter the monkeys of this realm.
Next comes the elephant, light as a bird,
And finally the one who deceives not . . .

SIHANOUK: [to the radio technician] Shall I do a test? Testing, testing, testing, 1, 2, 3, . . . 1, 2 . . . Princes, Ministers, Mandarins, I'm not going to speak to you, but, over the tops of your honorable heads and your decorated chests, I'm speaking to my people, personally, and to you, the gods. . . .

24

[Enter the Japanese Ambassador, shaken.]

No, Mr. Japanese Ambassador, I haven't started, but hurry up and get settled. There, there's a place next to the French ambassador.

TECHNICIAN: Thirty seconds, Your Majesty . . . Twenty seconds, Your Majesty . . . Ten seconds, Your Majesty. . . . You're on, Your Majesty!

MUSICIAN:
Microphone, Microphone, Microphone, carry the voice of the Prince of Princes
Far into the heart the forests.

SIHANOUK: My most beloved people, my loyal friends! Greetings and Benedictions! You, my compatriots, my race, my millennial tribe, you inhabitants of my valleys and of my heart, you my cousins, my children, you who are all my family, my earthly mother, and even—permit me the expression—my fiancee, hear the news: Today, the third of March 1955, I step down from the throne and cease being King, to become, with the permission of the gods, one of my simple citizens.
In other words, Mr. Foreign Ambassadors, as I am honored to tell you, I abdicate. You didn't expect this? I thought not. Oh! faithful friends listening to me, would you were near me at this moment! Listen to this silence! I have just petrified, with a few words, this entire assembly. A bomb, my children, here in the hall of honor, my abdication is a veritable atomic bomb! But for us, for you and me, my people, it is the happiest of events. In truth, this abdication liberates me and gives me to you. What was I until now? One of these sacred elephants who's only taken out of its wooden palace to be led to water. Around his noble feet stick the leeches of the court. And he never can go freely into the forest to visit his peasants. In truth, I was a pampered and helpless invalid. And when you, my friends, more deprived but freer than I, when you come to me demanding justice, it's you who do me a favor. Therefore, today, if I take from you a king of good faith but with no power, it is to return to you a prince whose power is from now on inseparable from his word. That's what I have to say to you.
Now what am I going to do?
First of all, starting tomorrow, aboard my helicopter, I'll fly over our country and I'll swoop down from the sky among you, arms

full of gifts, and I'll warn no one: neither the police, nor the army, nor the governor. We will be able to talk heart to heart without being watched. Wait for me because you'll see I'm coming.

Ha! Ha! To look at the faces of certain governors in front of me I feel I've hit the mark. Oh! Well, now, my friends, it seems that my words have bitten their ears. I continue.

Second, what am I going to do with our throne? The monarchy is part of our body and of our nature, it is our eternal mother, who unites us, and gathers us all around her knees. Well, I entrust it to the one you love as much and more than your own mothers, Her Majesty the Queen Kossomak, my revered mother. If anyone or any party contests our choice, let them telephone our secretary before the end of this evening.

Because, as of tomorrow, Her Majesty our Queen, my mother and the Nation's, will incarnate before the gods and before the ambassadors our loyalty towards Buddhism and the monarchy. We, however, will incarnate the political spirit of the Cambodian people. We will show the world how you can be both classical and modern, a guardian of inherited values and the inventors of new strategies.

Because, third, and after this I'll stop, we will distinguish ourselves from the other Asian nations, so readily servile, by defending our Independence at any cost. Our country will be Neutral. As a citizen who comes down to the city to espouse our historical destiny, I solemnly swear it. Therefore today Sihanouk sows Neutrality. And now, who will bring the tender sprouts to maturity? Who will help me? One peasant can't plant a great rice field. But we have been reflecting here for many hours together planting the future. I propose then that we give our imaginations a moment of musical repose. Let's convene again in a half hour, because I have yet another happy surprise for you. It is a lucky find of which I am more than a little proud.

[music]

And you, too, my most honorable guests, I invite you to savor these few moments of rest. No? I gather that this noble audience does not care much for my song?

THE JAPANESE AMBASSADOR: Your Majesty, am I to understand that you're abdicating, or that you're not abdicating?

26

SIHANOUK: Mr. Japanese Ambassador, one moment ago King
Sihanouk left the throne room through here. Well, when this music stops, look over at that window there, that's where he'll come
back in.

My cousin, Sirik Matak, my abdication pleases you, yes?

SIRIK MATAK: No.

SIHANOUK: No! You see, Mr. Ambassador, my cousin never ap-
proves of me. If I put my crown on, he gets blue, and if I take it
off he goes white. He abhors me.

SIRIK MATAK: I detest you as much as you detest me.

SIHANOUK: That didn't stop me from granting you the most sump-
tuous embassies.

You're bilious. Fifteen years ago the French gave my family back
the throne they had mistakenly loaned to yours, and that still
sticks in your craw.

SIRIK MATAK: You were not so proud then, and you glued yourself to
the throne they'd stolen from us, yowling like an alley cat.

SIHANOUK: A cat! You lie, snake! I am a tiger and my mother is a
lioness! Go ahead, renounce the crown; it flies too high for you,
up there among the eagles.

TECHNICIAN: Ten seconds, Your Majesty.

SIHANOUK: Ah! The music is over.

MUSICIAN:
> The Prince who is less King, the
> Prince who is more King
> Than all the Kings, the Prince will raise his voice.
> Microphone, Microphone, carry the voice of the most Princely
>   of Princes
> further into the heart of hearts
> Than the voice of the King of Kings.

SIHANOUK: Cambodian men, Cambodian women. No, rather: Cambodian women, Cambodian men. Have you noticed how cool the
air is this morning, how it feels good, like a fountain on our temples? It is a bit stormy here, but it will clear up.

Well! a fourth surprise: elections.

So, these famous elections will soon take place. And here we are, you and I, you who are I and I who am you, my prince-people, we're going to win them, yes, and in an orderly and democratic fashion.

How? Pay close attention. I have no lack of ideas. I'm going to create a party for us that will be the strongest of all parties. . . .

MUSICIAN:
> The party of all parties,
> the biggest of the Biggest Parties? . . .

SIHANOUK: A party which will clasp to its bosom everything that makes up Cambodia. Everything, from left to right and from top to bottom, all religions and all doctrines: all our patriots as well as all our women. And this all-encompassing party, this great Socialist and Monarchist Community of the People, shall headed by me, as a simple citizen. I present myself at the elections, everyone will vote, I will vote too, and you will elect me. This very evening, at the first coolness of dusk, in all the schools and pagodas, the Social and Monarchist Community party will register voters.

Bring the children, too, because there will be cakes and Bengali fireworks.

Long live royal, Buddhist, socialist, neutral and independent Cambodia! Till then!

I think that, apart from you, Lord Penn Nouth, I was the only one to be pleased about my coup. Come on, let's leave these long faces. This evening at the river, there will be happier ones.

[Exit Sihanouk, Penn Nouth, the ambassadors.]

MUSICIAN:
> Here leaves the Maddest of Mad
> The Strongest of Strong in this realm.
> The most lion, the most hare, the most eagle.

MCCLINTOCK: Have you ever seen such a campaign? He has already proclaimed the winner. It's an illegality that's positively oriental.

[He exits.]

SIRIK MATAK: Ah! Eat out his liver and sleep on his skin! The Kingship is lost and descends toward its twilight. In ten years, maybe five, we shall be no more than a memory.

And we won't even have a tomb.
There will no longer be a place for the dead kings on this earth.
    And I, I am alone at the edge of the world,
The only one to see the sad sun of the monarchy
Dwindle afar as it sinks to its last sunset. O gods, give me a
    chance!
Allow me at least to be the last king of Cambodia.
Give me back the throne, if only for a single year, if only for a
    single month!
But if it is he who is to remain in the memory of humanity as
    the last reminder of what Kingship was, then I hope there's
    no life after death.
I've already suffered too much in this one seeing the monkey
    wear the lion's skin.
O you who make and unmake kings and regimes,
Grant me a single day
Not of power itself, but of royal destiny. *[He exits.]*

PART 1, ACT 1, SCENE 4

First Period

[The sanctuary. The Ghost of King Suramarit. Enter Sihanouk.]

SIHANOUK: My father, I come all in a flurry.

SURAMARIT: What happened?

SIHANOUK: A triumph.

SURAMARIT: Your fortune has always had found sympathy with the
gods.

SIHANOUK:
    So here I am, head of the government. Even though I am no
        longer King,
    My person is sacred and more secure on the throne than ever.

SURAMARIT: For your Prime Minister you ought to choose . . .

SIHANOUK: I've already made my choice, father. It is Lord Penn
Nouth.

29

SURAMARIT: That's the one I wanted. I'm completely reassured. Tell me about the malcontents.

SIHANOUK: Malcontents? No one.

SURAMARIT: Nobody?

SIHANOUK: Only the cousins, the mandarins, the usual obstructionists. I told you.

SURAMARIT: Don't tell me that the Communists are delighted!

SIHANOUK: They rejoice in the few seats they've been able to win.

SURAMARIT: Communist seats in the house? Now, you're casting a pall over my joy.

SIHANOUK: Those are very dear and very necessary to me. They are proof of my loyal and affectionate tolerance for all the inclinations of my people, for all their desires and all their dreams. I value my Communists. We have named three to ministerial posts. We'll overwhelm them with responsibilities and marks of confidence. There is one, Mr. Khieu Samphan, to whom I've entrusted the Ministry of the Finance, who would please you greatly. He thinks only of work. He rides a bicycle. He doesn't even have a wife.

SURAMARIT: No wife? Why do you think he'd please me?

SIHANOUK: He's very unobtrusive, strict, and indifferent to honors; I could have named him undersecretary of state. He would have done the work even if only through simple self-sacrifice.[14]

SURAMARIT: It's quite extraordinary. Beware, though, of a man who doesn't have a wife and has no taste for honors. . . . *[pause]* What about the press? Did you bring me the newspapers?

SIHANᴏUK: I forgot. Pardon me. Next time I'll think of it.

SURAMARIT: Next time . . .

SIHANOUK: Good-bye, Father.

---

[14]*Devouement:* although this can mean simply "devotion" since he is devoted to the Khmer Rouge and not to Sihanouk, and since he is suggesting a kind of personal asceticism and puritanism in Khieu Samphan, we have chosen "self-sacrifice." TR

SURAMARIT: Wait! Wait! Oh! What was it I was about to say? Ah!
Yes! And tell me, Madame Mom Savay . . .

SIHANOUK: Forgive me, my father, I should have remembered!
Madame Mom Savay, notwithstanding the sincere grief your
death has caused her, is well and is as ravishing as ever. She no
longer teaches dance. She's living now at the Royal Palace close to
Her Majesty Queen Kossomak. My mother is very kind to her
since you are dead. The two women console each other . . . but
they haven't forgotten you.

SURAMARIT: That's a consolation. Yes. What women . . . I suddenly
feel . . . more peaceful and . . . less peaceful.

SIHANOUK: Don't worry. They love you truly. My father, I must take
my leave. I shall come back to seek advice.

SURAMARIT: Come back soon! You will come back?

[They leave.]

PART 1, ACT 1, SCENE 5

[In front of Khieu Samnol's house. Enter Khieu Samnol.]

KHIEU SAMNOL: Oh, My Buddha! How nice it is outside under the
stars!
I feel like I've leapt out of the witches' cauldron! That's the last
time that I'll allow those devils in my house.
Tell me, my god, is there a single fault that they don't have, these
animals who cover my floor with spit! Ugh! How those crocodiles
shout! It's because their bowels must be consumed with rage today. Because of the great honor which came to my son, may
Buddha protect him from claws and teeth, or they'll cut my little
one to ribbons like a rabbit, those jealous fellows!
O Buddha! Who would have believed it? That even though he was
so small, so skinny, and so naughty,[15] the son of the vegetable
merchant, Madame Khieu Samnol, his Majesty the King would in-

---

[15] *Vilain:* can mean ugly, but we have chosen "naughty" because, applied to small
children, this is what the epithet means. TR

vite him to lunch yesterday? I mean our beloved Prince, but it's the same thing. As soon as the Prince called him, I said, "This is it, it's the prediction come true: If your son doesn't fall into the claws of a great wild beast, he will fly very high." And until today I thought he would be an airplane pilot! It did not please him: "If you believe that I owe my rise to a meteor you have nothing to be proud of." He has become quite dried up. Ever since he was in France and he fell in with those Communist savages, he has changed so much that at times I ask myself if it's really him, the same boy who left here five years ago.

Yes, I'll go look at him, at my son, sometimes when he is sleeping just to make sure.

To come back to the honor that our Prince has done us: at the end of the meal, Samphan was named Minister of Finance for the entire kingdom. And me, I'm waiting two hours for him, two whole hours in front of the gates of the Royal Palace, and under the boiling sun, but I had my gold-striped party umbrella. Finally, there he is, coming out looking hurried, like this, and not at all as if he were leaving the Palace of the King.

And, of course, Buddha, right away I ask: "Well, what did you eat? Was it good?" But he just dashes past me, rushing because he is afraid of being late to the meeting with these savages, him, who's just left—the Palace—as Minister—him, who's just gotten up from the table of Our Father the Prince. So finally, he must feel I'm going to make a scene, and he slows down.

"Well then, tell me what you ate?" I ask him. Well, Buddha, he didn't even remember!

"Chicken," he tells me. "Chicken!!?" I say. "Don't tell me that they cooked you chicken at the Royal Palace! For a Minister of the whole country! Chicken!!??!"

"Well, it might have been fish, I was distracted, and I didn't touch it. . . . "

That's my own son who said that, my god, the son I raised and nourished with my milk and then with my vegetables, and who was made Minister by your grace!

And as for those guys there inside, busy baring their teeth at each other for hours!? Well, I made them a crab *extraordinaire*, just to see, on purpose. Well, did you see? They never even touched it. What do you have to say about that, My Buddha?

I myself would say they're so strange and unnatural, these Com-

munists, that they no longer know how to live, laugh, or savor. And I swear to you that at times there's so . . . strange an aspect to their mouths that . . . I've thought . . . that they might be eating men! . . . In the old days there used to be tiger-men, they said so in my village, but I never believed it.
Careful, my children, here they come.

[Enter Saloth Sâr and Khieu Samphan.]

SALOTH SÂR: The time to go underground has arrived and you don't see it! After what happened this week can you hesitate, Khieu Samphan?

KHIEU SAMPHAN: I don't doubt your wisdom, Saloth Sâr. But this time I see things completely differently from you. I think that we must stay right in the center of the country precisely because of what happened this week.

SALOTH SÂR: Brother, please take a moment to reflect further. As for me, I'll try to understand you, really.

KHIEU SAMPHAN: I ask nothing more. But when I think of all we have done. . . .

SALOTH SÂR: Hush . . . permit me to meditate, please. This disagreement should be able to fade.

KHIEU SAMPHAN: By all means.

[They meditate. Enter Hou Youn.]

HOU YOUN: What is going on here?

KHIEU SAMNOL: Shhh! They're thinking. Tell me, Mr. Hou Youn, what happened this week?

HOU YOUN: This week? The elections.

KHIEU SAMNOL: And so, that's a catastrophe?

HOU YOUN: Not at all. Socialist brothers were elected everywhere in the country. Your son and me too.

KHIEU SAMNOL: This week there were the elections and I, Samnol, for the first time in my life as a woman, Sunday, I voted. If my husband could have seen me!
Monday my son was elected by almost everyone in his district.

33

And you never saw such parties in the street, with fireworks all night. Tuesday, my son received a telegram of congratulations from the Prince, may all-powerful Buddha bless him. I took it right away to be framed and I'll have it Friday. Wednesday he was made Minister of the Realm, and immediately afterward my house was as full as a stable but I don't mind. This week there were only blessings! So then what is that guy talking about?

SALOTH SÂR: Well, have you considered the matter?

KHIEU SAMPHAN: Yes.

SALOTH SÂR: Welcome, Hou Youn. We were having a disagreement, Khieu Samphan and myself. Well. I have also thought it over. And I can't in all honesty change my opinion. Thirty-four seats for the left is too much, it's a unpleasant surprise.

HOU YOUN: What do you mean, an unpleasant surprise? We never expected more than six. Thirty-four seats! That means that the masses are beginning to listen to us. I am very excited. And honored.

SALOTH SÂR: Well, I'm telling you we have come to the decisive crossroads. Either we take the road of privileges, appointments, and sleaziness and collaborate with the dictator. Or in one leap we escape this pitfall, and clasping our young Revolution to our bosoms, we carry her far away from the city, to the noble and rugged retreat where we will rear her until she attains full bloom. Then we will gloriously descend once more upon the nation and we will make a pure, proud, impeccable conquest of it.
I beg you, flee this illusory, shabby victory which will drag us from corruption to degradation. Let's get out of here!

KHIEU SAMNOL: Get out of here! What about my shop? Who is going to help me pay for it?

KHIEU SAMPHAN: Brothers, only corruptible matter fears corruption. We asked for the trust of the people. We got it. We must fulfill it.

HOU YOUN: I agree. *[to Saloth Sâr]* Brother, I'm having trouble following you. You were hoping for a defeat?

SALOTH SÂR: Yes! Sometimes it's defeat that is the true victory.

KHIEU SAMNOL: !!!!

HOU YOUN: There has been a misunderstanding then?

SALOTH SÂR: Do I have to shout it? I trusted you. But I see that we aren't following the same paths. And I'm no longer certain that we have the same goals. You like to serve, I'm determined to make change. You are going to be manure for the Prince. I'm going to strike him like lightning and uproot him.

KHIEU SAMPHAN: I believe that we have the same exalted and noble goal, dear Saloth Sâr. But it is possible, indeed, that we don't get there by the same paths.

SALOTH SÂR: There is only one road to the truth.

HOU YOUN: And you believe that its yours?

SALOTH SÂR: I believe so. All right. Ieng Sary and I leave tomorrow. A splendid heroism awaits us in the forests. And don't tell me that it's love of the people which keeps you here.
Farewell, Mr. Ministers of his Majesty, I wish you all gorgeous Mercedes.

KHIEU SAMNOL: Mercedes?! Mercedes yourself, you jealous devil!

KHIEU SAMPHAN: You are mad. You bite without distinguishing friend from enemy.

HOU YOUN: Brothers, stop your quarrel.

KHIEU SAMNOL: Hold your tongue, nice guy! You, go on, go on!

KHIEU SAMPHAN: I shall go underground in my own sweet time! Don't imagine you can dictate a single decision to me. I'm one of those men who brook no tyranny.

SALOTH SÂR: I rejoice in going first and without you. Your presence by my side would have spoiled the purity of my gesture.

[Saloth Sâr exits.]

HOU YOUN: Wait! You could be mistaken. Listen! Anyone can make a mistake!

[Hou Youn exits on the heels of Saloth Sâr.]

KHIEU SAMNOL: May his venom sink back upon his own heart if he has one! Well, my son, you see? Who was right? He is a bamboo-monkey, I knew it!

KHIEU SAMPHAN: Listen mother! Leave me in peace!

KHIEU SAMNOL: That's how it is! Each time they argue, it all comes down on the old lady. I'm going to my next door neighbor's. If she only knew she elected a fool! *[She stays.]*

KHIEU SAMPHAN:

> I dream of a perfect society.
> We would erase everything. We would empty out the cities.
> We would start the world over again. We would know nothing.
> The earth would be virgin. Nothing, not even a house yet,
> Not a temple, not a trace.
> An innocent Cambodia would be born.
> It requires patience. The seasons are long
> In History.

KHIEU SAMNOL: I would have liked it better if he had become an airplane pilot. At least up above they ride along on real clouds!

[They both exit.]

PART 1, ACT 2, SCENE 1

[The Royal Palace. Enter Sihanouk, Penn Nouth, Lon Nol, Sirik Matak, Khieu Samphan, Hou Youn, Ambassador McClintock, General Taber, servants.]

SIHANOUK: Mr. Ambassador, General. Gentlemen, your government claims it has no hostile intentions toward me. Should I have faith in them?

MCCLINTOCK: Of course.

SIHANOUK: Nonetheless, I do not trust them. They want my death, they want the disappearance of Cambodia and I'm determined to let you know I'm absolutely opposed to that.

LON NOL: How's that, Your Eminence? What do you mean?

MCCLINTOCK: Who wants that, Your Eminence?

SIHANOUK: Why you, of course; you, our American friends, are what's giving me that impression—convincing me of it even—every day. Of course they are, they are, General Lon Nol.

MCCLINTOCK: Your Highness, I cannot listen to such unjust and gratuitous remarks calmly.

SIHANOUK: That's quite normal.

MCCLINTOCK: Doesn't our government give more and more aid to your tiny little country day by day?

SIHANOUK: Aha! Now I've caught you in the act, Mr. Ambassador! You heard it, Gentlemen! He said *tiny*! *Tiny*! You say it isn't a crime to say *tiny*? Then I'll answer you: it's a sign of malevolence, a mark of contempt, and evidence of a conspiracy, and I'm going to prove it!

LON NOL: My god! That does it, we're in for a crisis!

SIHANOUK: I know perfectly well the United States is immense, but I do not think an ambassador does honor to his country by characterizing the country that receives him as "rinky-dink"!

GENERAL TABER: We didn't say that!

SIHANOUK: Mr. McClintock doesn't stand on ceremony in front of servants, journalists, and even diplomats. Can't you accord us the same treatment as countries much smaller than ours yet which you respect? Do you say "Little Belgium"? "Tiny Israel"? You reserve contempt for Cambodia alone and foreordain its disappearance. You're systematically shrinking us. Why, just look at the newspapers. First Cambodia is small, then it's very small, the next day I read that it's extremely small, now it's minuscule, a pocket kingdom, a useless remnant, an eleventh toe, it's a speck of dust in your eye, a scab, it's nothing! Just where is it? It's going to disappear. It has disappeared! *[Lon Nol signals behind his back that Sihanouk is crazy and should not be paid attention to.]* That's what would happen if I let you have your way. Right, Gentlemen? But I'm here; Sihanouk is here, Cambodia exists! We are here, at the tip of great big Asia! You see? Here! The spearhead of neutrality, the white standard, neither *blue* nor *red*; the glorious haven of all manner of pride, this other Eden, this demi-paradise,

37

it's us, this happy breed of men, this little world, this blessed plot, this fortress Nature built against the contagion of the world and the arm of war, this ANGKOR, it is us! And speaking of fortresses . . .

MCCLINTOCK: Exactly, Your Highness, allow me to say a few words . . .

SIHANOUK: Go ahead, put in your word.

MCCLINTOCK: This fortress is protected by our diligent arms and is under our generals' supervision.

SIHANOUK: Protected! Indeed! I was getting to your way of protecting us! Yes! You're protecting us, Mr. American. You're protecting us from protecting ourselves.[16] One fine day, the troops of Mr. Diem, your employee from Saigon, enter our country, and steal a piece of land four kilometers wide from me. And when, indignant over this violation, this theft, I want to make a response, and send my soldiers to retake our property, "It is forbidden, he's off-limits!" Washington shouts at me, "Mr. Diem is our protégé. Don't touch a hair on his head!"

MCCLINTOCK: Your Eminence, you're talking about one very special case, where our government was, of course, obliged to limit the use of our arms.

SIHANOUK: He said *our* arms, did you hear it gentlemen? Well then, these famous weapons, are giving them to us or are you taking them back? Eh? Or would you rather I exhibited them in my museum?!

HOU YOUN: *[to Khieu Samphan]* You have to admit he has prodigious talent! I'm delighted!

KHIEU SAMPHAN: *[to Hou Youn]* The juggler and the idler, how cute!

PENN NOUTH: Besides, Your Eminence, why should we express re-

---

[16]The play on the word *défendre* is difficult to render in English, meaning both to forbid and to defend. An alternate use of "protect" ("You protect us from protecting ourselves") almost conveys the wordplay. TR

grets? We wouldn't have been able to use the American equipment. The last hundred trucks to arrive are, for some reason, all broken down; only the heaters seem to be working.

GENERAL TABER: You surprise me.

SIRIK MATAK: It's true, my general.

PENN NOUTH: As for the five thousand pairs of boots, Mr. Ambassador, undoubtedly this gift was sent to the wrong address. Our Khmer soldiers don't wear size eleven.

GENERAL TABER: It's clearly an error, indeed! Mr. Ambassador . . .

SIHANOUK: So what is Sihanouk to do? Should I allow your puppet to strip me to the bones because you like him and because you don't like me?

PENN NOUTH: The Americans are friends to our enemies so how could they be our friends as well?

SIHANOUK: Finally what is American aid doing for us? Making my beautiful city of Phnom Penh a dollar-addict.

HOU YOUN: [to Khieu Samphan] He has a way with words, doesn't he?

SIRIK MATAK: The corruption doesn't come from the Americans, cousin! Our industries, our banks, our economy are very grateful, Mr. Ambassador, for the generous aid from the United States. Let's give Washington its due . . .

SIHANOUK: That's just it, my cousin! Let's give it—back! Let's give it all back! That is indeed my intention. So, Gentlemen, have I any reason to accept this alleged American aid any longer? Comments?

KHIEU SAMPHAN: None, Your Eminence.

PENN NOUTH: Up till now I have only seen dishonorable reasons for such aid.

LON NOL: But wait! Gentlemen! We are taking a fatal step!

SIRIK MATAK: Don't worry, leave it be, let him lean to the left; he'll regret it.

GENERAL TABER: *[to McClintock]* How far does he want to push this?

MCCLINTOCK: How far? Severing relations, of course! And I wouldn't particularly oppose it. I've had enough of this parrot, and of this corrupt and pretentious country.

SIHANOUK: Mr. Ambassador, Ministers, Mesdames, Mesdemoiselles, Messieurs, our government, concerned for our national dignity and in the spirit of *extreme* neutrality, decides to renounce as of today all economic and military aid from the great big United States of America. We thank your mission's personnel. The Palace invites all American officials to a superb farewell party this evening.

HOU YOUN: He's expelling the Americans!

KHIEU SAMPHAN: He'll call them back tomorrow.

HOU YOUN: I barely recognize you! One could almost swear that Saloth Sâr in departing bequeathed his mistrust to you. At the very moment when the Prince is taking a step toward us!?

PENN NOUTH: The banks, Your Eminence.

SIHANOUK: His Excellency Penn Nouth is instructed to carry out the nationalization of all the banks and foreign enterprises.

SIRIK MATAK: This is an intolerable outrage! In-tol-er-a-ble!

LON NOL: Never mind, Prince, let him lean left. *[to the Americans]* Don't listen to him, you will be back.

SIHANOUK: And don't try to come back! Not if you haven't changed your attitude, it's pointless. As for you, Gentlemen of my left wing, I'll state publicly that I feel no more attracted to red wolves than to blue wolves.
Tomorrow I'll be beating my country's free air with my own two wings.

[He exits followed by Penn Nouth.]

MCCLINTOCK: Cambodia will pay us very dearly for this!

[McClintock exits followed by General Taber.]

MUSICIAN:

> Lightly, buffeted by four winds,
> The young man dances beneath his umbrella
> The rope of hemp sways from West to East.
> Down below, the crocodiles are wondering:
> How does that umbrella taste?
> Is it sweet, or is it salty?

LON NOL: Expel the Americans! But this amounts to disarming us! It delivers us over to Annam! To China! What will my general staff say?

SIRIK MATAK: But I'm surprised you're surprised! Don't you realize what a monkey you are serving? Ugh! Let go of me, General! There's still ground under your feet. If you stuck to our cause half as vigorously as to my arm, we would all be less disarmed.

LON NOL: My planes! My planes due to arrive this week! And training courses for my pilots!

SIRIK MATAK:

> Good-bye planes, guns, armored trucks
> And good-bye bank account, my poor general.
> Good-bye our hope and our liberty!
> What am I saying! Good-bye our survival
> If we don't respond without a moment's delay
> To the violent shameless blows
> This monster of pride, scorning his fatherland
> Seeks to rain upon us.
> I have some friends. Are you in? General! Are you with us?

LON NOL: What? What were you saying?

SIRIK MATAK: I said I have some friends . . .

LON NOL: Ah! My god! Merciful Buddha! I can't let General Taber leave like this! Prince, pardon me.

[Lon Nol exits, followed by Sirik Matak. Enter Queen Kossomak, followed by Sihanouk.]

QUEEN KOSSOMAK: My son, I don't understand you. Hanoi is winning its war. Tomorrow the skinny North will break upon our lakes and our rich rice fields. And this is the very moment you choose to break down our dikes? You bear pride so high you are going to pour it down over the clouds. Now who will defend our territories?

SIHANOUK: Ourselves, our pride, my foresight. And besides, leave it to me. I will retain Lon Nol in Defense.

QUEEN KOSSOMAK: You will retain Lon Nol! A man you have faith in for no more than one hour a day? You told me so yourself.

SIHANOUK: Lon Nol will not betray me. I know I hardly reign over a quarter of his heart; the rest belongs to his astrologer; but he has an interest in serving the strongest, and the strongest is me.

QUEEN KOSSOMAK: You are playing with a crocodile.

SIHANOUK: Reign, my mother, and let me rule.

[Kossomak exits. Enter Lon Nol and McClintock.]

SIHANOUK: Mr. McClintock, do you know what they said about me in *Newsweek*? Well, you must read this article. In it you learn my wife's family owns all the brothels in Phnom Penh. That explains my fortune and of my great relations with the American G.I.'s. This enlightening article was published with the help of the ambassador still here.

MCCLINTOCK: What?! But this is an outrage!

SIHANOUK: Why certainly, why certainly, a foul slander, look, it's written right here: copyright *Newsweek* and McClintock and Embassy, 1963, 1965 et cetera, et cetera.
Well, I royally trample this journal. Do as I do, General Lon Nol: when one has an untroubled conscience and the friendship of the gods, one forces vermin back underground! Mr. McClintock, I am giving you notice. You have just enough time to pack your bags.

MCCLINTOCK: Cambodia will pay us dearly for this.

[He exits, followed by Lon Nol.]

SIHANOUK: I'm finally going to be able to go for a walk in Phnom Penh without having to switch sidewalks.

[He exits singing. Lon Nol returns.]

LON NOL: Cambodia will soon be no more than a red fish in China's fishbowl. The Prince must come back to the Americans. But how can we persuade him? I have neither the eloquence of Penn Nouth nor the favor of the Princess to aid my timid speech. Since I can't hope to awaken in his impatient soul the sympathy and the respect the United States of America merits, I'll try to ignite an inextinguishable hatred between the Prince and the Communists. It is always easier to divide than to unify. But, I won't be creating hatred out of nothing. It's already there, but it is fragile and helpless like the eggs of serpents asleep everywhere in our country's caves. I will tend this fragile progeny until it hatches fearsome offspring I'll raise to monstrous size. I will make mountains with grains of salt. And I will be able to start giant fires from the least spark. Behold, I'll take Battambang and I'll work it in such a way . . . I can say no more on this before Buddha.
If suspicious Penn Nouth doesn't happen upon my tricks and spoil them. Merciful Buddha, this is a critical moment for your Cambodia. I won't ask you to put a little malaria in the way of His Excellency Penn Nouth to prevent him from fouling up my humble projects; but I will ask you to hasten the success of my tricky work in the Battambang region.

[He exits.]

PART 1, ACT 2, SCENE 2

[The Royal Gardens. The river. Enter Sihanouk and Penn Nouth.]

SIHANOUK: The year was happy overall, don't you think?

PENN NOUTH: Eventful, but in the long run, happy, Your Eminence.

SIHANOUK: Come, come Penn Nouth, let's go greet my stars. I want to have you visit to my celestial meadow.

PENN NOUTH: Your celestial meadow?

SIHANOUK: The stars, how I adore them! They're the divine faces of our desires.

PENN NOUTH: It's true there's nothing in the world more inspiring.

SIHANOUK: I want to tell you a secret: I gave the stars the names of those I love. Sometimes at night, when every one is dreaming in the palace, I hear the soft sweet call of the stars. I go outside, to speak to them. Look, there high overhead, that star burns like a Bengali firework candle. Do you see it?

PENN NOUTH: Yes, I see it.

SIHANOUK: That's Mozart. When he was little.
And this one which seems to be weeping is my young forebear King Leprous. Also a magnificent child. And that one, the next one over, somewhat gloomy, that's Pandit Nehru. And the one over there, to the west of the Great Bear, do you know who that is? I discovered it last year, one night in September of 1966. Can you guess?

PENN NOUTH: General de Gaulle! What an excellent idea!

SIHANOUK: Charles de Gaulle, my great friend.

PENN NOUTH: And which one is William Shakespeare, Your Grace?

SIHANOUK: William Shakespeare? Hmm . . . I don't know. Let's find it. Do you like William Shakespeare, Penn Nouth?

PENN NOUTH: As much as our own Royal Chronicles. Don't you admire William Shakespeare, Your Grace?

SIHANOUK: Of course, I admire William Shakespeare. But he is a little big. Whereas Mozart is so small I want to take him in my arms. William Shakespeare is immeasurable, like an empire. He's a gigantic giant. The one I like is the gigantic dwarf.

PENN NOUTH: It's true tonight seems blessed by all the gods, as if they'd wanted to mark your birthday with their high benevolence. I so want their divine will, rather than fearsome China's, to be right in History.
The sky is so clear it seems bigger than usual. It's like a heavenly sea. [*He sings alternately with the Musician.*]

"Divinity, garlands, affection, young maiden. The girl and the
    boy go nicely together. Do not tarry, Sir, go forward.
Enter my deep forest with joy.
Quickly, Sir, do not tarry.
Dear wife, dear love, have I come?
It seems to me, dear husband, you have indeed made it."

44

SIHANOUK: This has been a prehistoric day and I thank the gods for it.

[Enter Dith Boun Suo.]

DITH BOUN SUO: Royal Father! General Lon Nol has come from Battambang to offer you his best wishes.

SIHANOUK: I am expecting him. Go fetch him.

[Enter Lon Nol.]

LON NOL: May the gods grant Your Highness a hundred and twenty years of life and fill them with wealth, fidelity, and peace.

SIHANOUK: May your wishes be granted, dear friend, with the exception of the first. One hundred and twenty years is too much. What say you of my birthday sky, you who are such an expert?

LON NOL: It's an exceptional sky, Your Grace, like your destiny. Except for that cloud covering the constellation of Cassiopeia. . . . Do you see it? Ah! What a shame! Without this flaw, everything would be so beautiful today.

SIHANOUK: Ah! Yes! It wasn't there a minute ago. You're the one who brought it here, eh? Aha!

LON NOL: Ah! Yes! Your Grace! It could be me and I am sorry. I would have liked so much not to spoil this sublime night. But the heavens cannot lie.

PENN NOUTH: What do you mean, General?

LON NOL: The same above as below, Your Grace. That cloud has to be what took place in Battambang.

SIHANOUK: In Battambang? What happened?

LON NOL: There have been some incidents. . . . Your Grace, incidents. . . .

SIHANOUK: What? The Americans? A bombardment? The Chinese? The Vietcong?

LON NOL: The peasants, Your Grace, hundreds of peasants.

SIHANOUK: Massacred?

LON NOL: Massacred? No! Mad, Your Grace, agitated! An unbridled rebellion, Your Grace, for two days running. We didn't wish to crush them.

SIHANOUK: The peasants? Crush them?

LON NOL: A savage crowd armed with hoes and crossbows, and which even after two days, goes on crashing frightfully around in the center of the town, like a herd of buffaloes, smashing everything and shouting your name.

SIHANOUK: They called me? You should have received them.

LON NOL: They were calling you traitor.

SIHANOUK: Traitor?! Who called me traitor? Who?

LON NOL: A real pack of wild animals, Your Grace, who shouted: "Sihanouk sellout! Sihanouk thief! Sihanouk exploiter of the people!"

SIHANOUK: The peasants? Shouted? This? No! You've misunderstood.

LON NOL: Your Grace! Yes! The peasants! I was there, I wanted to speak to them as you would have. I opened the window of the governor's palace. Huge deadly stones rained down upon me. They slit the throats of ten of your Royal Guards and cut them to pieces!

SIHANOUK: My Royal Guards? Me?! Their father? My children? My peasants?! It's impossible! Impossible!

PENN NOUTH: The peasants against Your Grace? I'd really like to know who the wind was that stirred up this wave?

LON NOL: Your Grace, you know how the peasants love you. It must be they have been terribly misled.

SIHANOUK: Misled! Rather, you mean seduced, bewitched, and transformed into rabid dogs? It's the Khmer Rouge, right?

LON NOL: Your Grace, your wisdom sees correctly. It's the reds and they barely try to conceal it. I have proof right here, abominable terrorist tracts, whose origin is indisputable: it's Mr. Khieu Samphan's style.

PENN NOUTH: But it's unsigned, of course.

LON NOL: These are his inflated sentences.

SIHANOUK: To be at once minister and rebel is the height of treachery and hypocrisy! They're worse than the Bigfoot, these Khmer Rouge. They're wolves in sheep's clothing who cry "Wolf!" But how can they be so perverted? How can one be a Khmer Rouge and claim to be a Khmer? No! These rebels are aliens, Chinese Martians! Ah! Penn Nouth, I have told you for months I'm afraid of the plague coming from China.
It's a new race that's sprung up over there, since this revolution, called "cultural" but actually savage, barbarous, parricidal, and contagious. Those hateful robots are scribbling their slogans on my children's brains and driving them to hate Monseigneur Papa. But what do these demons want? To push me into the arms of Uncle Sam? I refuse to commit suicide!

LON NOL: Your Grace, after the expulsion of the Americans the left imagines. . . .

SIHANOUK: I am going to cut their imagination short. Oh! No, Mr. Chinese Khmers, it's not for your benefit that Sihanouk expelled the Americans, but for the sake of creating my own policy of purifying my country and restoring its pride and independence. My country will remain neutral, unstained, and monarchist. This is its nature and its calling. If the red dogs try to bite me, then sticks to their backbones.
Lon Nol, my faithful friend, return immediately to Battambang. And show these traitors my Royal Army knows what loyalty to my policy means. Go!

LON NOL: Your Grace, the Royal Army will prove its enthusiasm and its affection for Your Majestic Person, I promise you.

PENN NOUTH: Your Grace, give General Lon Nol precise orders.

SIHANOUK: Precise? Subdue the rebels, arrest the agitators, reestablish royal order. I have confidence in you, General.

LON NOL: I will be just and efficient in the name of Your Highness.

PENN NOUTH: General, while you're putting out these flare-ups take care not to stoke up a hotter and more dangerous fire.

47

LON NOL: I know what I have to do, Your Lordship. This won't be my first repression.

PENN NOUTH: Exactly. Pour water on the fire. My advice: water, not oil.

SIHANOUK: Go on! Go!! Go! Let law triumph and make the Great Helmsman's[17] red bastards realize once and for all what it costs if they don't steer clear of me! I will defend my neutrality against all subversions from the right and from the left, against moles, tigers, and snakes.

[Lon Nol exits.]

PENN NOUTH: You should not have said: "sticks to their backbones."

SIHANOUK: Why? It's only a metaphor.

PENN NOUTH: But General Lon Nol has an annoying tendency to take your expressions literally. I wouldn't be surprised if he makes use of the club in his own way.

SIHANOUK: So what! How would you want him to put down the rebellion? With sugar?

PENN NOUTH: Expect some deaths, Your Grace.

SIHANOUK: Lord Penn Nouth, keep your suspicions to yourself. It's a disease I don't want to catch. And don't annoy me with your croaking. I won't get caught in even one trap.
My sky has already lost all its stars. Nothing is sadder than a beautiful day which ends in sorrow. Eternity, *au revoir*! I feel History is going to begin again. *[They exit.]*

PART 1, ACT 2, SCENE 3

[Enter Hou Youn and Khieu Samphan.]

HOU YOUN: The Prince openly accuses us of being instigators of the rebellion and agents of China. And to think we had nothing to do with it!

---

[17]Presumably a reference to Mao, known as the Great Helmsman. TR

KHIEU SAMPHAN: That's not true. This rebellion is already a victory for us.

HOU YOUN: A victory? If we had been there, with them! But we were in the palace in our offices. So here we are stained with the people's blood.

KHIEU SAMPHAN: Stained? Why? Here we are, to the contrary, called upon by this blood. Justified. Even blessed. For me, this day is a festival, a promise. And then to have Sihanouk with bloody hands—it's more than we could have hoped for.
The fruits have ripened. There's nothing to regret. Except that Saloth Sâr will triumph. But that hardly matters.

HOU YOUN: Three hundred deaths!

KHIEU SAMPHAN: We'll have others. We must not count our dead. We must count only our victories. We are the sole masters of the meaning of these events. We can interpret them as we like. The massacre served our cause, so it is a good thing. Enough said. We leave right away this evening. The future begins in the forests.

HOU YOUN: I'll go to the north, into the Ratanakiri mountains. I have a brother and friends who have already won over the hearts of the villagers there.

KHIEU SAMPHAN: We'll go alone. Our families will follow us in one year.

HOU YOUN: Why alone?

KHIEU SAMPHAN: Your wives will bring complaint after complaint to the Parliament and to the Palace. They will spread the rumor that Sihanouk's police have assassinated us.
Presently I will go to the Chinese Embassy with Hou Nim. We'll confide our plan to our friends. We'll work out the bulletin announcing our executions with them for Radio Peking. And then we'll just vanish.

HOU YOUN: With all the gory details! It'll be a bloody execution, outdoing in horror and solemnity that of the martyred peasants. It would be really delicious, if Lon Nol believed it . . . he'll be afraid of Sihanouk . . .

KHIEU SAMPHAN: He'll be afraid of our ghosts!

HOU YOUN: And your mother, what will you tell her?

KHIEU SAMPHAN: My mother will know nothing. I'll vanish without a word.

HOU YOUN: She will weep a great deal.

KHIEU SAMPHAN: The joy of my reappearance one day will wipe out all trace of sorrow. And, besides, your wives' dignity in their grief will help to support her.

[They exit.]

PART 1, ACT 2, SCENE 4

[Saigon. Enter Kissinger, McClintock,[18] and General Abrams. Noise of airplanes.]

KISSINGER: What's that?

ABRAMS: Those are our old Dakotas we've armored. They're better adapted for the machine-gun missions than our helicopters. Thirty-six thousand bullets a minute.

KISSINGER: Well then, Mr. Ambassador, tell us how you managed to let our Cambodia slip away?

MCCLINTOCK: Mr. Advisor, Cambodia was never ours and it won't be as long as we continue to let Sihanouk to do just as he pleases. There's nothing to be done with this country. The people can't see past their pagodas. They adore their Prince, who hates us. These people still haven't learned other things exist on Earth besides their little bitty scrap of Asia. They're more afraid of ghosts than of us.
Any strategy that counts too much on diplomacy is going to fail. We can't seduce them. I had a list of 207 great ideas drawn up to persuade them to join the free world. I tried everything, from corruption all the way to the denunciation of corruption. Result: nothing. If they imagine in Washington . . .

---

[18] When this is staged McClintock doesn't appear in the scene. AU

50

KISSINGER: I haven't come to Saigon to imagine, but to observe, consider, and decide. President Nixon wants to finish off Vietnam this year. In that case, what do you advise us to do?

MCCLINTOCK: We don't need an embassy, we need an ultimatum.

KISSINGER: And you, General Abrams? What do you think about it?

ABRAMS: What do I think, Mr. Advisor?
I think if they stop me from mopping up the whole northern and eastern part of Cambodia completely and once and for all, I'll drop Vietnam and resign. Cambodia, Mr. Advisor, is where it's happening. There's where the Viets have their sanctuaries, hidden bases, headquarters.
I've had it with trying to drain the ocean teaspoonful by tiny teaspoonful! I want to bomb, here, here, and here. It's simple.

KISSINGER: But, how do you view these things in regard to neutrality, General?

MCCLINTOCK: We've got to force Sihanouk to choose between two neutralities: pro-communist neutrality and pro-American neutrality.

ABRAMS: Don't talk to me about their neutrality—there's not a soul left who believes in it. I've been saying this for years. Sihanouk has sold his soul to the red army. Mr. Advisor, Cambodia *is* Vietnam. Vietnam *is* Russia. So why wait? My planes have bellyaches. They're like pregnant cows wanting to drop their young. Well?

KISSINGER: We should get the Secretary of Defense's advice, right? He's just back from Phnom Penh.

ABRAMS: Melvin Laird is a civilian, Mr. Advisor.

KISSINGER: He saw Sihanouk last night.

MCCLINTOCK: But I've seen Sihanouk too—a hundred times and at all hours!

KISSINGER: President Nixon is anxious to get everyone's advice. Abrams, I'm a civilian, too, but believe me, I know how to read a map and I can assure you we take a deep interest in Cambodia. You'll see.
Have the Secretary of Defense come in.

ABRAMS: We'll see.

[Enter Melvin Laird.]

KISSINGER: Well then, Mr. Laird. You've been to see the unpredictable Prince. How are his little moods?

LAIRD: I found the Prince fairly reasonable. He understands that Asian communism will not permit him to remain neutral much longer. And he's ready to resume relations with Washington on the condition the United States recognizes the integrity of his borders.

MCCLINTOCK: Resume relations?! I'd like to see that. You can't believe any of his talk.

KISSINGER: What do you advise?

LAIRD: The reestablishment of relations with this little country which, after all, has no desire to go over either to Peking or the USSR. It would allow us a better sense of what is going on. I'm convinced the damage isn't extensive. I'm convinced there are no more than three or four thousand Communist Khmers.

KISSINGER: Three thousand? Communist Khmers?

LAIRD: Yes. Certainly.

KISSINGER: What? Khmer Rouge? They're not our concern! We're interested in the Vietnamese. How many Vietnamese Communists are there in Cambodia? Hundreds of thousands?

ABRAMS: At least a hundred thousand.

LAIRD: No, no. Ten thousand, maybe. Believe me, it would be best to support Sihanouk. He has his faults, he doesn't like us, but he's a Buddhist prince. He has every reason not to have faith in the Vietnamese. He demonstrated exceptional severity over the Battambang riots.

MCCLINTOCK: But he's denied publicly having ordered the massacre!

LAIRD: That doesn't alter the results. He's given up on the reds or else they've given up on him.
Besides, the masses are sincerely attached to him. He'd be our best internal defense against Vietnamese infiltration.

KISSINGER: I thank you for your good advice and for your convictions. But we have to deal with strategy not feeling. We must harass Sihanouk rather than let him believe we support him. We'll recognize his borders but we still won't rely on him. If he fails to block Vietnam's occupation of his own provinces, we will fly to his rescue. Let him close his little eyes while we strike.
The President wants to make the enemy feel, wherever he hides, the full weight of his determination. General, your little mopping-up operation of the borders completely failed?

ABRAMS: Not completely but . . .

KISSINGER: Completely, but that's not your fault, you hadn't the wherewithal.

ABRAMS: So give it to me!

KISSINGER: We will give it to you!

LAIRD: Which means? What do you intend to do?

KISSINGER: To sanitize. Abrams is going to bomb the border region parasites.

LAIRD: Bomb Cambodia!?

KISSINGER: Only the Vietnamese sanctuaries infesting Cambodia, correct, General?

LAIRD: But the sanctuaries are in populated areas!

ABRAMS: Mr. Advisor, we will only hit sanctuaries situated at least one kilometer from an inhabited zone.

KISSINGER: If we're going to go there, let's go. I won't haggle with you over our effort.

LAIRD: But civilian lives, Mr. Advisor, civilian lives!

KISSINGER: Our generals take all necessary measures to reduce risks incurred by the population. Do you doubt it, Mr. Laird?

LAIRD: Well . . . I don't doubt it . . . but these measures, will they be effective . . . ? And what sort of measures?

KISSINGER: The minimum necessary, since we can't jeopardize hopes for a rapid peace.

LAIRD: We don't understand one another, Mr. Advisor. I'm talking about civilian lives, innocent, humane . . . in a word . . . humans.

KISSINGER: We must be able to make sacrifices. Our era must accept being a tragic one. I bear in mind the victory of the free world.

LAIRD: But so do I, so do I.

KISSINGER: We aren't on the same wave length.[19]

LAIRD: But what if there are casualties and the Prince protests?

KISSINGER: We'll deal with his protests.

LAIRD: But our Congress will also protest.

KISSINGER: Protests? There will be none. We are not obligated to make such delicate and such decisive operations public. We owe the nation only a happy ending.

LAIRD: We *are* obligated, sir. There's law in our country. There's Congress. There's morality.

KISSINGER: Yes! And there is communism all around us. There are concentration camps. There's China, there are the Chinese. There are the Russians, there are the Soviets! There's the most menacing imperialism in the whole history of the world.

LAIRD: I'm opposed to concealing the bombing of Cambodia from Congress. Mark my words!

KISSINGER: I take note of your opposition!

LAIRD: I'm anxious for my protest to be on record and deposited in a safe place so it can be made public one day.

KISSINGER: It's already on record, and it will be made public.

LAIRD: Whenever I want it to be!

KISSINGER: Will you grant us one or two short months?!

LAIRD: I'm ashamed to be the same nationality as you.

KISSINGER: Then emigrate! Or rather, don't. Come General, come McClintock!

---

[19] *À la même vitesse:* lit. "at the same speed." TR

LAIRD:

>Sometimes I no longer know if I'm right or wrong.
>What I call vice others call virtue.
>Which one of us, he or I, is really defending the country?
>Me, so serious with my thousand scruples
>Or him, who, perching upon his audacity, dares to go above the law.[20]
>I am certain of nothing.
>Should I resign? Talk to me, God.
>Solitude weakens my courage and attacks my judgment. *[He exits.]*

PART 1, ACT 2, SCENE 5

[Enter Queen Kossomak and His Excellency Penn Nouth.]

QUEEN KOSSOMAK: You are abandoning us, Lord Penn Nouth. You mustn't get ill at the very moment our realm is itself suffering from so many evils. When the enemy overwhelms us, a real friend would stay on. But if the friend betrays us also, only despair abides.

PENN NOUTH: Majesty, the gods and your late husband himself are witnesses that, far from betraying my country which is to me my ward, my child dearer to me than my own children, when my own weakened hands betrayed me and refused to lift my bowl up to my lips, I continued carrying this country in my trembling arms; in your son's absence, twenty times I've told this illness "Wait a while longer, wait for My Prince to return; then crush me if you like." So, Your Majesty, have some indulgence for the extreme weakness which I am guilty of now, for it is a sign of the Prince's arrival. He should be here any time now.

QUEEN KOSSOMAK: What also upsets me so is that, according to my astrologer, you should be ill, but only next spring. Either my astrologer is mistaken and my entire existence and my son's since

---

[20] We thought it might be appropriate to use Fern Hall's terminology from the Iran-Contra congressional hearings to translate here. TR

birth—everything—have been only fatal errors. Or else the stars have abandoned us this year.

PENN NOUTH: I beg of you, Your Majesty, don't despair of your former counselors. I will also be sick next spring since they said so.

QUEEN KOSSOMAK: That doesn't suit me either.

PENN NOUTH: Majesty, I swear to you I'll do everything in my power to overcome this illness which has stricken me. I hate this malady which is causing me to resign and making Penn Nouth disloyal despite himself.

[Enter a servant.]

SERVANT: The Prince has come, Your Majesty.

QUEEN KOSSOMAK: Counsel him well, Lord. You know his fatal propensity: he is too fond of the Vietnamese.

PENN NOUTH: He likes them only as much as he has to, neither too much nor too little, Your Majesty. *[Enter Sihanouk.]*

SIHANOUK: So, Lord Penn Nouth, you are quite ill. It doesn't surprise me! I expected it. This year, 1969, holds only shoals and shipwrecks in store for me. The parties to my right have undermined my Parliament and my left sabotages me. Just before I came in, I was saying to myself: "Someone's going to be ill, and it won't be Sirik Matak!" And it's you! I'm burning with such rage it has made me clairvoyant. I see everything! And I'll tell you what I've just seen with my own eyes: I've seen Vietnam pass before me with my Cambodia under its arms.

QUEEN KOSSOMAK: Is that you speaking?!

SIHANOUK: Listen. Two weeks ago, I left on an inspection tour of our border zones with one of our valiant units. You saw me. Wearing field dress and these ankle boots I had made in Paris for just such rugged expeditions, I went into the forest and even into the thorny jungle with my men, drinking the muddy swamp waters like them, and I was unsuspecting. We get to Ratanakiri province. A desert.

QUEEN KOSSOMAK: A desert?

SIHANOUK: Silent villages. A few deaf old women nobody wanted. Not a hen. Not an exclamation. Nothing but mosquitoes.

PENN NOUTH: A massacre?

SIHANOUK: Not at all! A desertion! A crime against the country. I went into houses which, only even yesterday, would have been all fixed up for my visit. Tombs. Instead of finding the altar covered with flowers and my photo above it, my ever-so-confident smile, surrounded with wreaths, I was greeted by the old lizard head of Ho Chi Minh mocking me right to my face. Ho is everywhere! They had two or three per house. If I had not seen those old women, I would have thought I was lost somewhere in Vietnam. But no, I was ridiculed in my own house. These mountain dolts, they've been told they're not Sihanouk's children but of old Three-Hairs-for-a-Beard there—and they believed it. If I had been able to give them a walloping at least I'd have made them yowl in Khmer. My heart overflowing, I rushed to Bokeo, some thirty kilometers from there. The same desolation. And just so I'd know who robbed me, I'm confronted with piles of leaflets left behind by these Chinese Khmer dogs, accusing me of murder, of being a trai-tor, and enjoining my peasants to clear out ahead of me. Well, they did. They've taken my children from me, my smiles, my fes-tivals. They've emptied my fatherly arms and heart, but they have filled me with a rage nothing will be able to restrain. I shall never forget this desolation.

PENN NOUTH: Like the sickness in my body, the Chinese and the Vietnamese dig deep into our country's flesh.

SIHANOUK: To continue: I took a detour back to the sanctuary where our dead kings reside. I entered the dwelling of my ancestors, barely greeting them, and asked for advice, a sign. No response. Silence. I asked them a few questions:
"You don't want Buddhist socialism, do you?"
They said nothing.
"Then do you want pure, hard-line communism?"

QUEEN KOSSOMAK: You asked that? Of our ancestors?

SIHANOUK: No answer.
"Well, then, should I rent Cambodia out to the Bigfoot so they can make it their trash heap, their public dump . . . ?"

Silence. Silence. I wait. Finally, only my father sighs. And he says: "If you reflect carefully, everything is simple."

PENN NOUTH: That's all? He didn't say anything, even for me?

SIHANOUK: I left there as if I had just experienced a death. I no longer had anything. I no longer was anything. Coming back, my jeep broke down. I had to push it. I didn't care. And now, I thought to myself, what blow will land when I return? I arrive completely out of breath. It's you Destiny is taking from me.

PENN NOUTH: Your Grace, I am not dead yet.

SIHANOUK: True. Everything is simple. Let's not complicate things. You're not dead. I'm alive. Everything could have been worse. This evening our way is blocked by dark cliffs. I don't see where we're going. I let my legs follow the trail blindly. At dawn I'll see the world afresh and I'll know my way.

QUEEN KOSSOMAK: With whom will you replace your loyal minister, my son?

SIHANOUK: Well, let's see. I can see only Lon Nol in these parts. Do you see anyone else?

PENN NOUTH: No, Your Grace. For the time being I only see him.

SIHANOUK: And you, my mother?

QUEEN KOSSOMAK: Couldn't you name Lon Nol just Vice-Prime Minister?

SIHANOUK: What have you got against Lon Nol? He reveres you.

QUEEN KOSSOMAK: He'd rather take than get. And besides I have never heard anything but parroting you come out of him. Does he speak? Does he think? And besides are you even certain he exists? A reincarnated ghost is what he seems like.

PENN NOUTH: He's merely prudent, Your Majesty. He knows everyone but is at odds with no one.

SIHANOUK: Well, then, we'll name him Prime Minister.
While waiting for you, Your Excellency, I am going to be a very wise and cunning Prince. At least I'm going to try. What should I do?

PENN NOUTH: Do you ask my advice, Your Grace? You really want it?

SIHANOUK: Really. Yes, I'd like a little bit, for once.

PENN NOUTH: Here's some: You lead a herd of water buffaloes. Don't keep flying like a wild duck so far above their horns. Adjust your pace to that of your species. You go so fast you're often left alone. Whoever can't keep up with you wants you to fall. Slow down, turn around from time to time, make sure they haven't lost sight of you. You're already fully into the future while the bulk of the herd is still walking along in the dust from the past. Aren't you listening to me?

SIHANOUK: Yes, I was listening to you. You were saying my herd is raising the dust of the past as it goes forward. I agree. I'll try to speed them up.

[Enter Sirik Matak.]

Have you been brought by the news, cousin?

SIRIK MATAK: I've brought news myself, my cousin. Good news. Old Ho Chi Minh has just surprised us by dying.

SIHANOUK: Old Ho has retired. . . . What a pity! I would have liked to have met him. To be sure, he wasn't always very nice to the Kingdom of Cambodia, but what an extraordinary man, what an admirable patriot, what a respectable and magnificent enemy! So it was written that I would meet him dead.

QUEEN KOSSOMAK: How's that, meet him dead? You're not thinking of doing that!?

SIHANOUK: He had invited me to come see him, two years ago. I let the time pass when I could have seen him alive. But all is not lost. I'll not let the chance to go to his final convocation slip by.
First thing tomorrow I'm off to Hanoi. In my person Cambodia will bow down before the old demon.
Meanwhile, my mother, have them put up a large portrait of the dead President in front of the Khmer throne, and have an immense college of religious monks recite beautiful prayers for that great soul's bliss.

QUEEN KOSSOMAK: My son, I don't know if these very courteous decisions will please the Vietnamese but I am sure they will not please our Khmers. Wouldn't a small private ceremony be more suitable?

SIRIK MATAK: In the name of the Royal Family, I protest against your pretension to prostrate Cambodia in your person before our aggressor's remains.

SIHANOUK: I have no ear for those who are mere quarter-princes. Your opinion is worth only as much as your small portion of our monarchy. He was a hero, a genius, a man.
As for me, I am leaving for Hanoi with the Princess. Whatever our cousin's countenance, at least one King will mourn with Vietnam the man whose grandeur belongs to the whole of Asia. And that King is I. There's a time for rancor and a time for sorrow.

PENN NOUTH: Your Grace! Don't do this! This is a dangerous week. Tomorrow, I'll be in the hospital and will not be able to watch over anything.

QUEEN KOSSOMAK: Public opinion will be wrong about this trip. People will believe you are freely dropping the stability of neutrality. Don't go to Hanoi. Appoint a representative.

SIHANOUK: No one represents Sihanouk! I am irreplaceable. If I had to bow before public opinion, I wouldn't budge from my armchair. I'd remain seated equidistant from both its arms. So, in spite of everyone, but with my own complete approval, I'm going to Hanoi. My decision is set and I am happy with it.

SIRIK MATAK: *[to the audience]* In truth so am I. I would gladly turn myself into a helicopter to speed you even more quickly to your destruction. Come on, Sirik Matak, let's play our cards right. *[to Sihanouk]* I solemnly declare I disapprove of this trip and I consider it to be a national treason.

SIHANOUK: Actually, you are encouraging me. Because whatever displeases Sirik Matak is definitely a blessing for Sihanouk!

PENN NOUTH: But nevertheless, Your Grace, it also displeases your ailing friend Penn Nouth.

SIHANOUK: I would have preferred for Ho not to die this week!

I'd rather he'd waited for me! I'd rather you weren't sick! Nobody chose, neither you nor I, certainly not him. I want to see him. I must go to Hanoi. You must go into the hospital. Sometimes things really are simple.

[Sihanouk exits.]

QUEEN KOSSOMAK: Dearest Buddha, I would very much like to know, what's going on up above? Who is it assailing and whipping us? Is there a rebellion? Who rules: gods or demons?

[The Queen, Penn Nouth, and the servant exit.]

SIRIK MATAK:
The tree is hanging on by just a bit of bark.
Just one more shove and I'll overturn it.
Come, Prince of Monkeys, while you're traveling,
Your crown, weary of these distant adventures, will fly off
And will at last come to rest on the head of the true King.

[He exits.]

PART 1, ACT 3, SCENE 1

[Paris. The Cambodian Embassy. Enter Sihanouk.]

SIHANOUK: —Given that: the Chamber of Deputies of the extreme right emits a foul smell, more revolting than a dead elephant's, making Phnom Penh unbearable for me.
—Given that: the dignitaries putrefying it are drawn to my worst enemy Sirik Matak like iron to a magnet.
—Given that: the Vietnamese Communists, although they'd promised me over the sacred body of Uncle Ho to stop spreading Viet Minhs and Congs within my tender flanks, are continuing to infiltrate me in this month of March 1970, just like before.
—Given that: my Chinese friends are treacherously lenient toward the criminal Khmer Rouges.
—Given that: aside from my number one friend, Lord Penn Nouth, nobody understands that what Cambodia needs is not money and more money, but independence, ever independence.
—Given that: the wise Penn Nouth is in no position to support me.

—Given that: my number two friend, my Prime Minister General Lon Nol, administers his own strongbox better than he does my state and that his heart is in Switzerland.

—Given that: I must walk without leaning on either my right foot or on my left foot.

—Given that: everyone in the world but me wants war:

—I declare that: I'm exhausted, alone, and completely discouraged.

And so I travel, I wander, like Moses, I navigate, I cover ground: yesterday Hanoi. Today Paris which is no longer Paris. Tomorrow Moscow which will always be Moscow. The day after tomorrow . . .

[*Enter the Ambassador of Cambodia to Paris.*]

SIHANOUK: Ah! So, Mr. Cambodian Ambassador to Paris?

THE AMBASSADOR: Your Highness, Your Highness! It's Lord Penn Nouth!

SIHANOUK: Well, give it to me, Mr. Ambassador.

THE AMBASSADOR: But Your Highness, it's him in person. Lord Penn Nouth in person.

SIHANOUK: In person? But how? How?

THE AMBASSADOR: Standing, Your Grace. In the salon, the vestibule, in the hall.

SIHANOUK: Standing? Didn't you ask him to sit down? You made him wait?

THE AMBASSADOR: But of course, Your Grace. . . . But no, Your Grace. He's coming up, Your Grace.

[*Exit the Ambassador, enter Penn Nouth.*]

SIHANOUK: My Penn Nouth! But how! Why?

PENN NOUTH: I'll sit down, Your Grace, and then I can tell you everything.

SIHANOUK: Penn Nouth! What a joy! Or is it a sorrow? Tell me? You're no longer ill? To what do I owe this joy which nonetheless makes me anxious?

PENN NOUTH: To tell the truth, you owe it to my anxiety about your state, not about my own, Your Grace. Lon Nol, on the pretext of suffering from a broken shoulder, has transferred power to Sirik Matak and named him interim Prime Minister!
Lon Nol is bedridden, but this news put me right back on my feet: Sirik Matak is finally all powerful. The demon is going to undo all your political work in one moon. What do you intend to do? How can I serve you?

SIHANOUK: So, you are no longer sick? I have somehow cured you through anxiety?

PENN NOUTH: You evidently fail to recognize the imminence of the catastrophe. Prince, there's a fire, we have to do something. Two months of vacation is too much; I mean it's more than enough for a chief of state.

SIHANOUK: My pirate of a cousin dreams of hijacking my beautiful Khmer plane and of landing it at Washington airport. He will not succeed. My plane obeys only me.

PENN NOUTH: He'll go as far as a coup d'état.

SIHANOUK: He won't go that far. He'd need the army's support and therefore Lon Nol's. But Lon Nol is an unconditional supporter of Sihanouk. Sirik Matak is going to do all possible evil, but later the evil will turn against him.
No doubt it is good for a country to taste the bitter before the sweet. When we return, we will be appreciated all the more.

PENN NOUTH: You're wrong. Things will get worse. Disavow Sirik Matak. Recall Lon Nol. Don't leave the child with an evil nurse or he'll grow up irredeemably evil.

SIHANOUK: I'll do that when I get back from Moscow.

PENN NOUTH: From Moscow?!

SIHANOUK: From Moscow and Peking! Sirik Matak is not my only concern! The secret of his current strength is concealed beyond his person, in the horrible situation created by the heartless and unscrupulous Vietnamese. What are the people complaining of? Not of socialist Buddhism. But of the increasingly insupportable presence of the land-guzzlers on our soil. Not only do they eat us raw, bite after bite, they also draw American bombs down on us. Because of them, we've had more than five hundred deaths this month. Five hundred Khmer peasants who were moving along in their fields singing and who'll never know how beautiful their harvest would have been.

It's not Sirik Matak who upsets me, it's the American Ogre. The Bigfoot cretins aren't wiping out the men of Hanoi. No. Their bombs are murdering our children in our fields because we don't realize blind war is hunting us down, too! Meanwhile, the Vietnamese, who have learned to hear planes that can't be heard, run for cover. And where do they find refuge? Deeper and deeper in our arms, closer to our breast, in the very heart of our country. How many, how many are they now, to bring down upon our innocent land the horrible death intended for them?

PENN NOUTH: Your very respected Highness, they were thirty thousand before the escalation of the bombing. But they're dug in now; there must be forty thousand.

SIHANOUK: Well, I've had enough of dying on account of them. It's no longer Vietnam we need to demand some quarter from. It's to the higher gods headquartered in Moscow and in Peking we must address ourselves. They can make the Vietnamese bend like bamboo beneath the monsoon. I'll explain that Sihanouk is their best friend and that they have an interest in not shaking my regime. I'll be logical and impassioned. I'll cry out for mercy for my country to these distant ears. Would you come help Sihanouk not to shout too loudly and to choose brilliant words?

PENN NOUTH: I'll help, Your Grace. May you make these cold-hearted allies listen to reason.

SIHANOUK: So, we leave for the North of Norths in three days. I'll notify Her Majesty my venerable Mama right away of our trip. I ask one small favor of Lon Nol: that he keep an eye on Sirik Matak and organize, during our pilgrimage, a few small demonstrations of popular discontent in regard to Vietnamese excesses. In the provinces where they've infiltrated, for example. That way the voice of my people will accompany my petitions and they'll hear all Cambodia over there demanding the respect it deserves.

PENN NOUTH: Small anti-Vietnamese demonstrations . . . I don't entirely like this idea, Your Grace. Lon Nol interprets that type of order badly. Remember Battambang.

SIHANOUK: Hmm, right. I'll think it over. To Moscow, Penn Nouth! When we return to our capital, everything will be miraculously changed!

PENN NOUTH: What I would like more than anything would be for Sirik Matak to fall gravely ill. And for skies no longer to have anything but birds and clouds in them! *[They exit.]*

PART 1, ACT 3, SCENE 2

[Phnom Penh. Enter Lon Nol and his soothsayer.][21]

LON NOL: The reason I begged you to bring the oracle as quickly as possible is that yesterday I suffered an outburst of pain which damns me to hesitate. Up to now only my left thigh used to tremble. That was clear. Yesterday, lo, my right thigh was seized with painful tremors. I no longer know what to do. The same for my ears: ever since I conferred interim power on Sirik Matak, a little pernicious buzzing in the right, a little pernicious buzzing in the left. And what's more, for a whole week now my dreams are no longer telling me anything. My nighttime tape recorder is silent. All it records is a sssss . . . ssssss . . . sssssss. Sirik Matak's going too fast. Denationalizing the banks and the companies! De-Sihanoukizing the Ministries. In one week! Forbidding the officials to send memos to Sihanouk! He's going too far. The Prince is going to lash out. Total resumption of relations with the Americans. Should I inform Sihanouk? Should I keep quiet? My person is like an occupied country which doesn't know which master to obey. Should I choose this prince here? Should I choose that prince there?

THE SOOTHSAYER:
> The silver dragon will burn down the golden palace.
> The white lion will threaten the silvery chameleon.
> The chameleon will transform itself into a vulture.
> The vulture will take flight over the silver palace's roof.

---

[21] The character of the soothsayer is not present during the performance. AU

Having arrived above Peter's stony dome[22]
The vulture will alight in Buddha's position.
The white lion will go and grovel before it.
Then the vulture will put out his eyes.

LON NOL: Put out his eyes? Ah! Yes! Put out his eyes! Of course!
In other words and so that things are clear, do I have to take a
plane? To go meet Sihanouk? And once I've arrived, am I to blind
him?
Am I wrong?

THE SOOTHSAYER: The oracle has spoken. I have nothing to say.

LON NOL: Or else I should warn him? Whom should I be betraying?
Let's see. The vulture will take flight . . . lands above the Peter's
dome? Are you sure? Why Peter's dome? Sihanouk isn't in Rome,
he's in Paris. As for Sirik Matak, he's in Phnom Penh. I'm without
a compass. What are you saying?

THE SOOTHSAYER: The oracle has nothing more to say.

LON NOL: Yes! But you? Don't say anything. Just give me one little
sign. It'd be too foolish to go to Rome instead of Paris. Or is it the
Sacré Coeur then?

[Enter Captain In Sophat.]

THE CAPTAIN: General, Sirik Matak has arrived furious.

LON NOL: As usual!

THE CAPTAIN: Worse! Like a vulture who's had his carrion torn from
him!

LON NOL: A vulture? Oh, no!

THE CAPTAIN: Pardon, Your Excellency! I meant to say a lion. In
short a . . .

LON NOL: Say no more and have him come in! *[Enter Sirik Matak.]*

---

[22]*Dome de pierre* = dome made of stone. Lon Nol hears "pierre" as "Pierre," the
proper name, and thus can think only of St. Peter's dome in Rome, or analogous struc-
tures, like the Sacré Coeur in Paris. The ultimate referent becomes St. Petersburg
(Leningrad) in Russia. TR

SIRIK MATAK: My general, do you know what Sihanouk's next address will be?

LON NOL: He's not in Paris anymore?

SIRIK MATAK: He's leaving there. My cousin isn't a man of state, he is a grasshopper! So, can you guess his next stop?

LON NOL: Is he going to Rome?

SIRIK MATAK: To Rome? Why Rome? Why? Who told you that?

LON NOL: Gold . . . In fact . . .

SIRIK MATAK: Rome?! Why not London?

LON NOL: London?! Ah! Saint Paul's! But why?

SIRIK MATAK: You're haunted by churches! In two days Sihanouk will be in Moscow! In Moscow—Kremlin—Red Square!

LON NOL: In Moscow! I won't go to Moscow.

SIRIK MATAK: Why would you go to Moscow? You? With your crooked back. Besides you're not invited. Lord Penn Nouth is accompanying my cousin on his infamous expedition.

LON NOL: To Moscow! With Penn Nouth! He's going too far!

SIRIK MATAK: To Moscow! And then on to Peking!
As for you, while the fat Quixote and skinny Sancho are tilting with Moscow's windmills, Sihanouk beseeches you to organize a few cleverly spontaneous anti-Vietnamese demonstrations to accompany their little number. Does that please you?

LON NOL: Anti-Vietnamese demonstrations? He will have as many as he likes.

SIRIK MATAK: As many as he likes and then some. Do you follow me?

LON NOL: Perhaps I'm following. I don't know. Where is it all heading?

SIRIK MATAK: To the bitter end, step by step.
First anti-Vietnamese demonstrations. You'll organize them, but as if they were for me. With an extreme zeal. Let's be hardy, let's rid

the country of this damned race ourselves. Vietnamese out! And at long last we'll give Cambodia back her true face.

LON NOL: I've always dreamed of seeing that! A pure and natural Cambodia! But the Prince will never let us. He'll come back.

SIRIK MATAK: He will not return. We'll take Phnom Penh. We'll leave him Asia with all its Communists.

LON NOL: A coup d'état, Prince, are you sure?

SIRIK MATAK: Yes, I am. We'll win, step by step. A coup d'état to which I invite you wholeheartedly. You'll lend me your tanks in order to surround the National Assembly, and I'll leave you the honor and the reward of this great deed. Well? Are you with me this time or are you once again going to dash my hopes?

LON NOL: Me dash your hopes, Prince?

SIRIK MATAK: Yes, dash. You know what I mean. When you made me miss the superb opportunity of the outrageous trip to Hanoi.

LON NOL: But after all, my wife had died. I won't let you. . . .

SIRIK MATAK: Ah! Nor will I, precisely. I'll not let myself be blocked once again by your stars, your astrologer, or your dreams. This time, I'm pouncing on my prey and finishing it off. Your tanks, then? Agreed?

LON NOL: [aside] Oh! My Buddha! Must I betray Sihanouk?
[to Sirik Matak] What was I saying, Prince?

SIRIK MATAK: I was the one who was speaking, Your Excellency. I was saying: Ta-anks!

LON NOL: Tanks! Oh! my god! I had another lapse. Oh! Prince, if you knew how horrible it is. Right in the middle of a conversation, suddenly longer knowing where you are, nor why you're there.
The armored tanks . . . I'll give you a response before this evening.

SIRIK MATAK: The tanks, Your Excellency, and you're Head of State.

LON NOL: Me?

SIRIK MATAK: You'll be able to lead the kingdom as loyally and firmly as a prince.

68

LON NOL: Your Highness, you know I wouldn't do anything to make you regret your generous confidence in me. But first I must consult my star . . . my staff.

SIRIK MATAK: I'll let you consult. Think of the stars. *[He points to his sleeve.]*

LON NOL: I shall decide for whatever is in our country's best interest.

SIRIK MATAK: I'm convinced you will.

[Sirik Matak exits.]

LON NOL: Well, what am I going to do? Sirik Matak is audacious but Sihanouk is more solid than one might think. He won't permit himself to be done in. I can't bet on one prince or the other as long as the balance hasn't tipped.
One shouldn't trust anyone on this earth. Neither one's allies, nor one's own brother, nor, indeed, one's self. Whatever Lon Nol is about to do, it's best for him not to be consciously aware of it. Or rather for him not to tell himself about it. We'll see. You'll see. But as for the anti-Vietnamese demonstrations, that's practically already done.

[Lon Nol exits.]

PART 1, ACT 3, SCENE 3

[Phnom Penh. The Royal Palace. Enter the servant Dith Sophon, nephew of Dith Boun Suo, Khieu Samnol, and Madame Lamné.]

DITH SOPHON: You can stay on the terrace, my dear aunts, until the terrible storm blows over. I'll bring you your meals and your mats later. There. Don't be afraid any more. The rioters wouldn't risk coming all the way in here!

KHIEU SAMNOL: May all the gods of all the religions bless you, Dith Sophon. And may they annihilate this group of mad apes, murderers of poor Vietnamese!

[Dith Sophon exits.]

Do you see how beautiful it is here? Good heavens! This morning, we get up, a hellish riot is going on, I think that they're murdering my Madame Lamné, my neighbor, and all the Vietnamese living in my quarter, then I remember that I have the brother of the son-in-law of my sister-in-law who I never see, the poor soul, who's named Dith Sophon like his grandfather, who is the fifth assistant four-spoon cook in Papa Highness's kitchen, and so here we are: Samnol and Madame Lamné, installed for good and all in the Royal Palace. It's Heaven and no one's even dead.

MADAME LAMNÉ: Still, I would have preferred to arrive in Heaven without the deadly heart palpitations I am suffering from because of these bandits who pillaged me.

KHIEU SAMNOL: Let's not be extreme, all the same. You have the terrace, you have your life and me, you have me. What more do you want?

[Queen Kossomak, Mom Savay, Hawkins enter. The two old women hide.]

QUEEN KOSSOMAK: But the police? Hasn't anyone mobilized the police?

MOM SAVAY: The police, My Queen, were a part of this barbarian gang.

HAWKINS: Sacking the two Vietnamese embassies, hunting men in the streets, pillaging shops, this whole thing, Your Majesty, is contrived. The riot is coming straight from certain Ministers of His Highness the Prince.

QUEEN KOSSOMAK: My son's Ministers! I cannot bear that idea!

HAWKINS: Have you seen a single minister in the Palace this morning? Did anyone explain why to you?

QUEEN KOSSOMAK: No. No. Exactly. Madame Mom Savay alerted me. But why, why these villainies, these crimes, these deceits?!

MOM SAVAY: Why, why . . . ! When fire breaks out you must find firemen, not reasons why! Call His Highness back quickly, Your Majesty. He must return at the earliest possible moment. The city is sick with anxiety.

QUEEN KOSSOMAK: Yes. Yes. That's what must be done. I'll send him a telegram directing him to return immediately. His presence will

quickly reconcile our communities which are in such violent upheaval.

HAWKINS: Permit me, Your Majesty; this fire isn't an accident. It has
been set voluntarily. Don't you see the plan?

QUEEN KOSSOMAK: The plan? No.

HAWKINS: They are trying to cause you trouble, Your Majesty, and
by means of your royal person, it's His Highness your son they are
hoping to attack. To change his course of political action.

QUEEN KOSSOMAK: How?

HAWKINS: It's very simple. They create murky and dangerous incidents. What will the Queen's first move be, they tell themselves?
She'll recall His Highness. That's exactly what you ought not do.

QUEEN KOSSOMAK: You mean I *ought* to call my son back!

HAWKINS: No, no, no. Listen to me! They are doing everything they
can to have you to get His Highness your son to return, isn't that
obvious? Therefore it has to be a trap.

MOM SAVAY: What trap? They're murdering our Vietnamese. That's
all. His Highness must come back to stop the infamy, to punish
those responsible and to heal the people's wounds.

QUEEN KOSSOMAK: Continue, Mr. Hawkins. I'm listening.

HAWKINS: It shows they're prepared to do anything to stop the
Prince from going to Moscow. Believe me, Your Majesty, the
Prince is made for the heights. His place is on high, on the world
stage where peoples' destiny is played out, and not here in this
lowly domestic scene. By coming back just to do housework, he'd
be losing the last chance for peace.

QUEEN KOSSOMAK: You're looking to influence me, Mr. Hawkins.

HAWKINS: It would be an immense honor for me, if I accomplished
that, Your Majesty. You know I wish you only the best.

MOM SAVAY: I'm wondering who's paying him.

QUEEN KOSSOMAK: I'll think. Leave us.

HAWKINS: Your Majesty, I'll let you consult with your people.

QUEEN KOSSOMAK: Thank you, that's just what I'll do.

HAWKINS: *[leaving]* That Sirik Matak, he might have warned us that there was also the Queen's old bitch. I would have found some way to get her out of the picture. *[He exits.]*

MOM SAVAY: If I were in your shoes I wouldn't listen to this Hawkins. He's a CIA agent. A spy, a rumor monger. He's Sirik Matak's head prompter.

QUEEN KOSSOMAK: You're not in my shoes. Mr. Hawkins is simply *chargé d'affaires* at the embassy, and there's reason in his prompting.

MOM SAVAY: I'd rather the Prince came back.

QUEEN KOSSOMAK: Me too. . . . But what if it were a mistake. . . . Why, what's this. . . . *[The two old women try to go past without being seen.]* But who are you, my dear aunties?

MADAME LAMNÉ: *[to Khieu Samnol]* Have I fainted?

KHIEU SAMNOL: No!
Oh! Your very holy, merciful august Majesty, we're two poor women so filled with honor and with terror that I no longer have legs nor my neighbor either.
She is Madame Lamné, the fishmonger on my street who's Vietnamese which explains our shameful presence here completely by chance, adorable Majesty. Because you know all of the terrible misfortune that's happening to the Vietnamese in our city. And that's the cause of all this honor that we haven't merited on purpose.

QUEEN KOSSOMAK: And through whom have you gained this honor, my fair aunts?

KHIEU SAMNOL: Through the cousin of the son-in-law of my sister-in-law who's the fifth assistant four-spoon cook, Your Majesty, Mr. Dith Sophon.

MADAME LAMNÉ: But he told us that this terrace was not in use.

QUEEN KOSSOMAK: He's right. We never come here. And are you also Vietnamese?

KHIEU SAMNOL: Me?! Not on your life!

MADAME LAMNÉ: Her, she's Madame Khieu Samnol, the vendor of the best vegetables in my neighborhood. And she also knows how to cure the sick, birth twins, and bring back the dead.

MOM SAVAY: Bring back the dead? Can you really?

KHIEU SAMNOL: Really, but not everyone. Because they must return by way of the Bridge of Love. Now, if there's no love . . .

MADAME LAMNÉ: It's true, my husband, who betrayed me and forgot the poor, she never, never can with him.

KHIEU SAMNOL: But on the other hand, if Your Majesty wanted, our beloved dead King your husband His Majesty Suramarit . . .

MOM SAVAY: Our Suramarit . . .

QUEEN KOSSOMAK: Right now, it's a question of bringing His Highness my son back, Mom Savay.

KHIEU SAMNOL: Precisely, that's what I was talking about with Madame Lamné a moment ago: I think like Madame Savay, that His Highness Papa has to be brought back.

MADAME LAMNÉ: Me, too.

KHIEU SAMNOL: Well, what have you decided?

QUEEN KOSSOMAK: I must go telegram my son. See you later, my aunts. [leaving]

MOM SAVAY: Yes. What will you tell him?

QUEEN KOSSOMAK: I'll tell him . . .

MOM SAVAY: In your shoes, great Queen . . .

QUEEN KOSSOMAK: You're not in my shoes . . .

[Exit Queen Kossomak and Mom Savay.]

MADAME LAMNÉ: This Madame Savay pleases me. Right after Her Majesty the Queen, I think she's the most beautiful of all, don't you?

KHIEU SAMNOL: Our great Suramarit, when he was alive [she whispers to her . . .]

MADAME LAMNÉ: Oh! Well that's customary . . . *[Exit Khieu Samnol and Madame Lamné.]*

PART 1, ACT 3, SCENE 4

[Paris. Enter the Cambodian Ambassador to Paris.]

THE AMBASSADOR: Ugh! The Prince is a difficult, difficult man! Everyone is afraid of him. He's the King. He gets angry suddenly, and very violently. He has been known to get rid of Ministers with just one word, and without compensation. Fire them, yes. Thank them, no. He always wants to be the father. The world is changing; today it's all over for the father. But he doesn't realize it. The Prince is beloved, but only by the people. He is so well loved that he believes everyone likes him. But not at all! Not at all! Not everyone loves him that much! The Khmers are like that, they love a lot, but also not that much.
And the Prince, whom does he love?
First, he loves no one. Then he listens to no one. During meals, he talks all the time and never listens. He thinks that because I'm eating next to him I'm happy. Besides, he only listens to the Princess, his wife, just because she is his wife. She's a very beautiful woman. Very reserved. My wife likes her a great deal. As for public opinion, where the Princess is concerned, it's not so good. She's accused of having placed a brother in each Ministry. That's not true. The Princess has only one half-brother. But what the newspapers say . . . is nothing compared to what they're saying in Phnom Penh's high society. Such shocking rumors about the venality of the Princess's family are racing through the most honorable homes . . . ! Never, never could I repeat such shocking things. For several months now I see the Prince clearly threatened politically. Why am I still on his side? He's been very lucky since birth. He also has a genius for politics. He's very inventive. We never know what surprise he has in store for us.
He's very independent. Independence of mind is in truth a virtue. I'm all for independence. But the Prince has such independence of mind it's become a disease with him!
As a Khmer I think I'll never leave Sihanouk, for the time being, and despite all I'll remain on his side, for the time being.
And now, when I go announce the latest news to him, what will

happen again? I would have preferred a quiet embassy post where he never goes—Brussels, or even Bern. . . .

[Enter Sihanouk and Penn Nouth.]

SIHANOUK: Tomorrow, Moscow! In a week, Peking. Onward Penn Nouth, onward. *[He sees the Ambassador.]* What's the matter, Mr. Ambassador?

AMBASSADOR: A dispatch from Her Majesty the Queen arrived, Sir. The dispatch is still being deciphered but if you'll permit me, there's detailed news . . .

SIHANOUK: Have you read it? What does it say? Is it urgent?

AMBASSADOR: Her Majesty says that an angry crowd of soldiers and students gathered yesterday in front of the embassy in Hanoi.

SIHANOUK: Ah! Good! That's good. That's good.

AMBASSADOR: That's good? My Lord?

SIHANOUK: Go on. Go on. Then?

AMBASSADOR: And that another large gathering took place in front of the Viet Cong embassy.

SIHANOUK: Yes, Yes. That's right.

AMBASSADOR: What? Good? Her Majesty then says that she deplores having to report that the mobs stormed the two embassies.

SIHANOUK: Stormed? But no! No! Not that! What's this you're telling me?!

AMBASSADOR: Stormed and sacked them, Sir. Then—

PENN NOUTH AND SIHANOUK: Sacked them?

SIHANOUK: Where's this dispatch? Go get it for me right away.

AMBASSADOR: It's coming, it's coming, Your Highness. I didn't even have time to read it through to the end.

[Enter the secretary with the dispatch.]

SIHANOUK: Show me that! *[He reads.]* Oh! Penn Nouth! They stormed the embassies! Mama tells me that they tore it down, burnt, pillaged! Do you hear! Listen: "And finally they threw ten unfortunate Annamite employees out the window. And these savages dared to pronounce your sacred name while committing these acts of infamy!" Look! Here!

PENN NOUTH: I am overwhelmed!

SIHANOUK: Oh! Lon Nol! The snake! He went way beyond my instructions!

PENN NOUTH: I see, rather, Sirik Matak's signature beneath all these excesses!

SIHANOUK: It's Lon Nol! And it's Sirik Matak, too, of course. The whole basket of cobras! Oh! How naive I've been! My beautiful little strategy, they killed it off! I'm getting ready to demand a little restraint from the Vietnamese around our borders and here they're throwing them out the windows in the middle of the city! Oh! These venomous slugs want to force my hand! Lon Nol wants to make Sihanouk fight with the Vietnamese! How could this pig without balls believe that they could cuckold a Sihanouk! Did they think that Her Majesty my mother would not look out after my interests? Of course I could always count on your loyal services, Mr. Ambassador! How long did you forget to give me this dispatch?

AMBASSADOR: Forget!? My Lord?

SIHANOUK: It arrived three hours ago. Why? Were you letting it boil?

AMBASSADOR: The . . . the . . . the decoder . . .

SIHANOUK: You! They'd condemn me to death and you'd let me know about it after the execution!

PENN NOUTH: My Lord, listen to me. As justified as your fury is—

SIHANOUK: That squealing little pig!

AMBASSADOR: Your Highness!

SIHANOUK: These centipedes in uniform! These slugs with medals! This Lon Nol . . .

PENN NOUTH: May I speak to you, My Lord?

SIHANOUK: Go ahead and yell! You have to shout over my raging screams to be heard.

PENN NOUTH: Yelling is not my style. My Lord, Phnom Penh needs your presence. You must give up Moscow for the moment.

SIHANOUK: My trip! They're robbing me of my trip! They're taking Moscow from me! Peking! My diplomatic initiative! So be it! I'm going back! Mr. Ambassador: Have a telegram sent to Her Majesty the Queen. I'm returning to Phnom Penh. Immediately. And I am going to swoop down on these toads and cut out their gizzards. Go on! Don't look at me with those calf's eyes.

[The Ambassador exits.]

PENN NOUTH: My Lord, be wary of our ambassador. He hardly opened his mouth, but his ears were wide open.

SIHANOUK: Oh! I'm used to it. For ten years he's been giving me the fish eye and gluing his ear to my door.

PENN NOUTH: Nevertheless, you must hold your tongue. Your Grace. It will bring you misfortune!

SIHANOUK: Oh! My trip! And what will Moscow say? Make me go back to Phnom Penh!?! They'll pay for this! Lon Nol, the cooking pot and skewer are staring you in the face.

PENN NOUTH: I don't doubt that your words go beyond your intentions.

SIHANOUK: Not at all! I've wanted to have his kidneys roasted for a hundred years already! Traitor's kidneys! They must taste awful. Pe-uuh. Then I shall have him arrested and tried for sedition. Oh! I feel my anger is abating! What an attack! Dith Boun Suo! Go get me my vitamin-reinforced aspirin, the effervescent kind, please. When shall we leave, Your wise Excellency? Oh, my trip! What will Moscow say!

PENN NOUTH: Let's leave tomorrow, at dawn, Sir. Between now and then, I'll have been able to gather enough information on what awaits us in our capital.

SIHANOUK: That's that! I'm going back, putting everything in order, I'll strike, kill the flies, and leave again. Let's go inform the Princess of this little problem.

[Reenter the Ambassador.]

AMBASSADOR: A second dispatch has just arrived to go with the first.

SIHANOUK: Give it.

[*He reads the dispatch.*]

PENN NOUTH: What now, oh, Buddha!

SIHANOUK: The storm is over! The wind has fallen, the sea is calm! And we can again set sail for beautiful Moscow!

PENN NOUTH: My Lord, my spirits are still completely shriveled. If you would be so kind: translate, I beg you.

SIHANOUK: The dire message has been overtaken and annulled by this other one which is completely mollifying. A real dove. My mother assures me that the disorder in our capital is far from being as grave as my adversaries were hoping to make me fear. In other words: they wanted to stop me from going to Moscow! You get it?

PENN NOUTH: To stop you from going to Moscow . . .

SIHANOUK: Because once again if I were successful, heh? If thanks to my famous stubbornness I managed to extract a solid guarantee for our neutrality, heh? Sirik Matak, Lon Nol, the others—they'd die of spite!

PENN NOUTH: But of course, of course! Certainly!

SIHANOUK: And to think I almost let myself get caught! And you, too, Penn Nouth. What a turkey I've been. And you, too. Penn Nouth! heh? What a turkey? For once, your prudence . . .

PENN NOUTH: Hah! Hah! I admit it, my Lord, I went right along without the least suspicion. But you influenced me . . .

SIHANOUK: Excuse me! *You* influenced *me*. You're the one who told me to go back.

PENN NOUTH: I was so afraid, My Grace. I believed we were losing our Cambodia. I lost my head.

SIHANOUK: Luckily, our guardian spirits are watching over us. Sirik Matak *and company*[23] don't want me to go to Moscow. Well! I'm going!

---

[23]English in the original. TR

[They notice the Princess. The Ambassador exits.]

PRINCESS: I don't know who's reassured Her Majesty the Queen, but I'm less reassured than ever. This turn in the news. All these twists. My Lord, for once, I beg of you, listen to no one. Listen to prudence.

SIHANOUK: You mean listen to no one but you.

PRINCESS: Why not go back? Moscow can wait.

SIHANOUK: Then, every time I want to go to the Communists, Sirik Matak *and company* will set off a few bombs and Sihanouk will turn around?

PRINCESS: But at least let his Excellency Penn Nouth go see.

SIHANOUK: Don't even consider it! Penn Nouth and Sihanouk are the two sides of the same coin: No! No! We're off to Moscow. It's my history! My country! My decision! If I listened to you, I'd have found myself right back on the banks of the Mekong, but as a retired fisherman, with only his boat for a kingdom.

PRINCESS: Something tells me you're listening to your evil genie.

SIHANOUK: Why, that's incredible! For once Penn Nouth isn't being an obstacle, and it's my own wife who's contradicting me!
My nightingale is sulking this morning!
A little sadly, I close the window.
Come along, let's continue our dispute after we've left for Moscow.

PRINCESS: I'm not going. You go to Moscow without me. I'm going back to Phnom Penh.

SIHANOUK: Without me!? You! Turn your back on me? And you think that, seeing your sail go off, I'll run after you, giddily, and lose my battle, my fleet, and my honor?
Why, no! My angel! Sihanouk is not Anthony! You are not the Egyptian Queen Cleopatra, even if you do me the honor of being a world-famous beauty. And my story is not a terrible Shakespearean tragedy. Me, I adore you, but I won't follow you. Moscow and my victory will not escape me! And now, I'm going. Whoever loves me, follows me. Right? Well? Good, then, I'm leav-

ing alone with Penn Nouth? Will we see each other again in Moscow? In Peking? Perhaps never?

[*Sihanouk and Penn Nouth exit.*]

PRINCESS: I would love to be the bewitching Cleopatra. Unfortunately, it's I, I fear, who am Antony and who, despite the danger, cannot help throwing myself into the wake of this ruinous voyage.

[*She leaves. The Ambassador returns.*]

AMBASSADOR: "Whoever loves me, follows me . . . We'll see each other perhaps in Moscow? In Peking? Perhaps never?" He treated me like a calf brain. He dares to make the Ambassador of Cambodia lose face? Well, then, I, I reply: Ne-ver! You'll never treat me like a calf brain again!
I'll tell Prince Sirik Matak right away: I'll say: "Very respected Prince, the despotic dictator has dared to characterize you as toads, snakes, cobras, and pigs. As for me, he called me a calf brain. He also swore before me that he'd cut off the heads of your honorable persons and that he would have them prepared with tartar sauce. The moment he gets back."
So. After this message, I can be sure the Despot will never go back. And don't ever let them try to tell you that ambassadors don't make History.

[*He exits.*]

PART 1, ACT 4, SCENE 1
[*Saigon. Enter Kissinger, Laird, and Abrams.*]

KISSINGER: Let's get down to business. Take your seats, my friends. We're attacking the final chapter of our presence in Vietnam.

ABRAMS: If we have to be satisfied with just tickling the Cambodian borders, all discussion is pointless. We'll get nowhere. The Vietnamese have entrenched themselves in a vast zone in the northeastern frontier. That's where the secret General Headquarters is hidden. All the attacks are starting out there. Give me the Northeast, and I'll root the evil out.

LAIRD: General, a number of observers claim this famous General Headquarters doesn't exist.

ABRAMS: Ah! Just because they don't see it, they imagine it doesn't exist. But if they don't see it, it's because it's invisible, and if it's invisible it's because it's underground. If it didn't exist, there wouldn't be any guerrillas. It exists. It's an armed, concrete bunker buried eighty meters under the earth . . .

LAIRD: Eighty meters?!

ABRAMS: And it shelters about five thousand civil servants and as many technicians. It's difficult to locate because of a thick jungle covering the entire territory in the shape of a vault. But it's there, in the Hamecon region, I have absolutely no doubt about it.

LAIRD: Haven't you executed fifty-six raids in the Hamecon region on the pretext of destroying Vietnamese General Headquarters?

ABRAMS: Merely small raids, totally insufficient.

LAIRD: Twenty-nine thousand tons of bombs, that's not enough?

ABRAMS: Not hardly!

KISSINGER: Allow me? General Abrams, the President authorizes you to deploy the largest air offensive in Cambodia in order to finally wipe out the enemy everywhere they're hidden. This time we'll no longer allow the victors to require much persuading. The order is: Free fire.

ABRAMS: Free fire on Cambodia? Amazing! Why it's Christmas in July!

LAIRD: Mr. Advisor . . .

KISSINGER: I know what you're going to say, Mr. Laird.
Number 1: The Congress will shriek to high heaven.
Number 2: The Senate with all its adversarial strength will be opposed to our supplying Lon Nol suitable aid against the Communists.
And you know what answer I'll give you, once again, once again? Let everyone in our country do his own job. Let the Senate do the protesting, play the fine part. Let the President play the thankless, difficult, lonely role of the true head of state. For myself, I'll play the part of instilling a sense of America's lofty responsibilities in petty bureaucrats.

As for you, Mr. Laird, your only role is to diligently assure me of the resources for implementing our policy.

I don't want a single one of our giant bombers to remain dormant in a single one of our hangars in Asia. Our bombers are made for bombing. It's up to you to see to it.

You had something else to say?

LAIRD: Just this: to finance this huge project, we need a lot more money than what's left for the Cambodian project. There's not one dollar to hope for from Congress. They'd be quaking in their boots if they knew what you were getting ready to do.

KISSINGER: Whenever a financial project of such magnitude runs out at exactly the worst moment, the simplest thing is to expropriate the funds from neighboring projects then. The loans for Korea, for example, could certainly be tapped for the sake of Cambodia.

LAIRD: For the sake of . . . ! If Congress finds out about it . . .

KISSINGER: How would they find out except through your office?

LAIRD: Senators know how to count, Mr. Secretary. Besides, one could reasonably fear or hope that after the efforts of Senators Cooper and Church the next military budget will be severely cut and monitored. In a month, two at the most, sending troops to Cambodian territories will be prohibited.

KISSINGER: Oh, be quiet, you old goat! Two months? General? Agreed! We'll bomb day and night for two whole months including Sundays! Even Sundays and every other day! Two months from now we'll have found other resources, I'll see to that.

ABRAMS: Two months from now, we'll have won. Mr. Advisor, won! At last! I'll need fifty more B-52's.

KISSINGER: Find them for me, Laird.

LAIRD: And what else?

KISSINGER: Find me the planes, Laird, do you hear me? If necessary, strip Europe; I'll win peace for the President at any cost. What do all the dissent, protests, restrictions matter? We must cauterize Asia once and for all!

LAIRD: We'll kill the patient.

KISSINGER: Just how long is the President going to sit still for your treachery? Give me Cabinet members who are men! I want fifty more B-52's in Bangkok tomorrow, Laird, tomorrow, I want them! And fire on Cambodia, Abrams! Free fire!

ABRAMS: Fire! fire!

LAIRD: There's no room for even one single additional B-52 in the Bangkok airfield.

KISSINGER: Thailand can just drain a few rice paddies! Okay! Let's get the job done! Bombs away. Bombs away! That's it, stop up your little ears!

LAIRD: Cambodia's not Vietnam!

KISSINGER: Go ahead, Abrams! Bombs away on Laird! Bombs away on the traitors. Let's get the job done. Fini! Fini! *[Laird exits.]*

ABRAMS: Bang! Bang! Bang! Bang! And it's the end of the war in Vietnam! *The End!*[24]

[They exit.]

PART 1, ACT 4, SCENE 2

[Moscow. Enter Sihanouk, the Princess, and Chea San, the Cambodian Ambassador in Moscow.]

SIHANOUK: Let no one disturb our rest before our departure from Moscow. I don't want to see anything except my wife's face during this last hour. You too, Mr. Cambodian Ambassador to Moscow, leave us.

[The Ambassador exits.]

Have you noticed how everyone here has a distant but at the same time menacing air? They hide behind their brows like behind bars. And their teeth! These huge yellow, soulless teeth!

THE PRINCESS: I've never seen you so pale. Have they offended you?

SIHANOUK: No. Or, rather, yes. I say to them: "Couldn't you suggest

---

[24]English in the original. TR

a little restraint around my borders to your Vietnamese allies?"
... "Who? Us? The Soviets?" they protest, "intervene in the affairs of Vietnam? No! No! We'll never commit such an impropriety! Keep everyone in his own backyard. Vietnam's not our business."
They're the Olympic medalists of hypocrisy!

THE PRINCESS: I was sure they would be. But as for the rest, didn't they promise you anything?

SIHANOUK: Oh! Yes! They've coldly promised me posthumous aid. First off, I told them everything, frankly. That the army is on the point of no longer obeying me because our generals are nostalgic for the fine American weapons I disdained. But that, coming in the nick of time, superb Russian arms could console our military men and turn our guns in the right direction. Next I exaggerated, adding that with Prince Sihanouk's fate hanging by a single thread, this intelligent and generous aide had to reach us very quickly. I flattered, I puffed myself up, I humbled myself: they didn't respond to me. I started up my arguments again. A deaf bear. Finally, after a long silence, as long as a prison stretch, the Premier congratulated me on my frankness.

THE PRINCESS: Didn't they grant you anything?

SIHANOUK: Complete sympathy, respect, and friendship.

THE PRINCESS: And arms?

SIHANOUK: Ah! Yes, arms, trucks, equipment.

THE PRINCESS: When?

SIHANOUK: When? I asked that too: "When?"
"In six or eight months," he tells me.
"In six months, Your Excellency!" But it would already be too late in six weeks!
I start to yell: "And I might be dead in six days! I'm dying of thirst, I ask you for a drink and you tell me in six months! But in six months you'll be offering a drink to my skeleton!"

THE PRINCESS: Don't cry, my love, don't cry my love. Forget these Russians. We'll leave.

SIHANOUK: How I'd love to go back home. My Cambodia, my poor wondrous garden, encircled, my home so fragile, my little Asia . . .

THE PRINCESS: They've done you harm, my love. We'll never visit these savages again. They're only Russians. All is not lost. There is China.

SIHANOUK: There's still China. But should I rejoice or be worried about that?

[Re-enter Chea San.]

CHEA SAN: Your Imperial Highness, your official car has arrived. And Premier Kosygin is here to escort you to the airport.

SIHANOUK: Wipe away that sad face, San, and accompany us.

CHEA SAN: With joy, Your Highness.

SIHANOUK: Oh! Hurray China! *[Enter Kosygin and others.]* *[to the Princess]* The ghastly Kosygin. They might have chosen as Premier someone who gives you less of an urge to run away.

KOSYGIN: *[in Russian]* Your Highness, your plane is ready. I'll be brief, therefore: I have the misfortune to inform you that you've just been overthrown.

[The Interpreter translates.]

SIHANOUK: Overthrown!

THE PRINCESS: Overthrown! Don't be afraid! We are still alive!

SIHANOUK: Overthrown! Oh! My god! Rescue me from the shame. Kill me. Break my heart on the spot, I cannot live through this moment.
Overthrown, Excellency, it's impossible, it's completely illegal.

KOSYGIN: *[in Russian]:* Doubtless, Your Imperial Highness, but it is done, at the request of your government. And ratified by two houses of your Parliament.

[The Interpreter translates.]

SIHANOUK: When was this high treason perpetrated?

KOSYGIN: *[in Russian]:* Yesterday.

CHEA SAN: Yesterday morning, Your Highness.

SIHANOUK: You knew, Chea San? Then this hideous mask, it was the mask of my fate? You knew and you kept silent?

CHEA SAN: Yes, Your Highness. No, Your Grace, I was so unhappy . . .

SIHANOUK: You, too, have betrayed me. You hid the true face of my unhappiness from me. You left me in the dark—the darkness of your own cowardice. You blinded me and cut out my tongue. Everyone has lied to me. Who didn't know? Everyone knew?

CHEA SAN: We were so unhappy.

THE PRINCESS: Prince, let's not be overwhelmed.

SIHANOUK: Overwhelmed? I've never felt higher in pride nor in grief. Mr. Premier Kosygin, only a few instants remain before my departure for China. I'll be brief, therefore. What are you now going to do for my country?

KOSYGIN: Things have changed rapidly. We have not yet had the time to consult. We'll see what we will do. [The Interpreter translates.]

SIHANOUK: Will you answer me six or eight months from now? That is inadvisable. If you don't act quickly, you'll let China get the prestige of a friendly overture. You could even lose face before your allies. People would turn toward the Chinese sun like a field of sunflowers.

KOSYGIN: [in Russian] Lose face. That's one fear our people don't know. The Chinese were in favor of Sihanouk when Sihanouk reigned. But now that you've been overthrown . . .

[The Interpreter translates.]

SIHANOUK: Overthrown. We're not overthrown. Neither Sihanouk nor Cambodia. We've simply been separated.
But hear the words of a Prince whom neither fear nor hope masters. Nothing, neither treason, nor might could deter Sihanouk and Cambodia from finding each other again. Off to China.

[All exit.]

PART 1, ACT 4, SCENE 3

[The palace. Enter Queen Kossomak and Mom Savay.]

QUEEN KOSSOMAK: Left. My dream interpreter? My astrologer?

MOM SAVAY: He's no longer there. We've looked in all of his villas. Everything's been removed. Everything's empty. He's left for France, My Queen. And for good.
Forgive me, My Queen, forgive me.

QUEEN KOSSOMAK: Calm yourself, celestial bird. The fault is all mine, I ought to shave my head. Ah! They're rumbling now under our windows. Have you seen them, these heavy tanks, my poor wet sultry bird?

MOM SAVAY: They're all over, My Queen. They surround the government offices, ministries, public buildings, and then they stop and don't budge an inch more.

QUEEN KOSSOMAK: Ah! You! You! I shall always be bitter against you. You let me send that telegram and send my son away.

MOM SAVAY: The telegram! You never even spoke to me about it! I thought the Prince was coming back to us. In all honesty, I'd have advised you against this action, because by sending this message, you have, I'm afraid, obeyed not only the CIA, but once again this cursed astrologer who abandoned us today.

QUEEN KOSSOMAK: Ah! that's true! That's true! I don't even understand myself. I believed I was doing good, and the good turns and strikes back vindictively. But this morning, all I know is I adore my son and I'm sick with fright.

MOM SAVAY: Then call Our Highness back, perhaps it's not too late for a counterorder.

QUEEN KOSSOMAK: Call him back! O Yes! Yes! Yes! Yes! That's what I want! Ah! Go my love, do! Go to the French Embassy.

MOM SAVAY: I'll run!!

[Mom Savay exits.]

QUEEN KOSSOMAK: Oh! This clatter of tanks since dawn! The sound of destiny. These funerary rumblings in my city. My god! Have I done right to call my son back?

[A soldier enters.]

SOLDIER: Your Majesty, a messenger from Lon Nol. He requests audience with you even at this unseemly hour, and his face is completely gray.

QUEEN KOSSOMAK: I'll receive him.

[The soldier exits.]

> The flowers fall, the child goes off.
> In the deserted heart regret alone remains.
> Silent, afflicted, the old Queen
> Calmly receives the shameless enemy.

[Enter Captain Sim Narang, envoy of General Lon Nol, then Mom Savay.]

QUEEN KOSSOMAK: Who are you?

SIM NARANG: Captain Sim Narang, Your Venerable Majesty, aide-de-camp of General Lon Nol.

QUEEN KOSSOMAK: We'll hear Lon Nol's envoy.

SIM NARANG: If I've been sent so early, August Majesty, it's to implore your blessed pity for His Excellency General Lon Nol. This dethroning, to which he was constrained in order to save the country, causes him a very great moral suffering. Only the blessed forgiveness of Your Venerable Majesty could bring some relief to his devout soul. The General assures you of his loyalty.

MOM SAVAY: And so this toad sent your knees crawling instead of his?

SIM NARANG: The General understands a mother's anguish. But he thinks that once over your natural noble sorrow, and since His Highness is safe far away from here, Your August Majesty will understand where the true interest of the monarchy lies. Your Majesty says nothing?! Oh! I was afraid of that! Your Eminent Majesty, maybe it would be better . . . in the monarch's interest. . . . Pardon me, you understand? The General is counting on this pardon!

88

QUEEN KOSSOMAK: Captain, the Queen does not grant her pardon to the traitor Lon Nol. He has stolen this country, whose sap runs in my veins, not out love for our people but from rapacity. The Queen who has never taken sides has today taken her son's side.

SIM NARANG: Ah! Your Majesty, be careful of the words you speak in front of your servant. Any person who claims to side with our ex-chief of state's party is as of today outside of the law. Even your august person. Here's the rest of the message:
I am ordered to forewarn Your Majesty that in the case—dreaded—that you won't accord your favor, the General would be obliged to withdraw his own.

QUEEN KOSSOMAK: What does this mean?!

SIM NARANG: The General would be brought to abolish the monarchy despite himself.

MOM SAVAY: What! Let him try!

SIM NARANG: Madame, he is ready to try this evening.
He accuses you of siding with the Vietnamese. He'll have you arrested. You'll no longer see your son, nor your grandchildren. Ah! I most humbly ask your pardon. But I beg you, beloved Majesty, tell me something favorable to the General. Even if you tell the gods otherwise. I always revered Your Majesty. I have five sons and two daughters, Your Majesty . . .

QUEEN KOSSOMAK:
Captain, go deliver my prediction to your Master: Lon Nol!
Since you've turned against your master
All will turn against you.
If you have a dog, he will bite you.
If you have a knife, it will slice off your fingers.
If you have a friend, he will stab you.
You will be suspicious of Sirik Matak and you will sleep no
    more until you're dead.
One of you two will overthrow the other.
If you tell your legs to go, they will disobey you.

MOM SAVAY: Again! Again! My dear! Strike!

QUEEN KOSSOMAK: The gods, who noticed your tendency to grovel, will crumple your knees like paper and you'll no longer be able to stand up straight. Your bones will melt like wax in the sun. Go, Captain, and repeat each one of my words. Such is the final answer of the Queen.

SIM NARANG: Majesty . . . such misfortune! Such misfortune.

MOM SAVAY: Out! At once! For I am not Her Majesty! I haven't her goodness!

[Exit Sim Narang.]

MOM SAVAY: My beloved! How superb and terrifying you were! He'll never sleep again, I'm certain of that.

QUEEN KOSSOMAK: I've lost my son, through my own fault, I know it. I'll never see him again.

MOM SAVAY: Ah! No! My beloved. No false prophesies with Mom Savay. I don't believe in it.

QUEEN KOSSOMAK: I don't predict, I despair. And the telegram?

MOM SAVAY: I sent it just in time, My Queen.

QUEEN KOSSOMAK:
No. It went off too late . . .
My crown—I no longer want it!
The Queen had an only son.
I want my son I lost.
At her age with white hair,
The old woman wants her baby again,
Her withered breasts dream they are big and full of milk.
If they see the old woman's dream,
They must laugh at me.

[They exit.]

PART 1, ACT 4, SCENE 4

[In an airplane, above Asia, between Moscow and Peking. Sihanouk and the Princess.]

MUSICIAN:
The sun rose, I'm a dead man.
The sun has risen, the boat has foundered.
The sun is veiled. No one on the river.

SIHANOUK: Only yesterday, in front of Chea San, I was spinning out my next battles! I was winning! I would have won! I thought I was leading my country! I'll bring peace back to you! And in back of me, nobody! No more country, no more path, no more history! I'm gone! I see myself there, among my dead! They've not only taken away my throne, they've ridiculed me, wronged me! This Chea San, two weeks ago, I'd have had his severed head placed on his knees!

THE PRINCESS: Stop! I beg you! Get hold of yourself! You've got the wrong enemy. San's silence didn't betray you. He was drunk from holding back tears. Hang on, hang on preciously to all the good that still remains.

SIHANOUK: Keep talking to me, speak to me, lead me with your words to a river's edge and bathe my sick soul.

THE PRINCESS: Well, then let's live for this moment, right now in this plane. One day strictly for us, one day above all else, one day without ministries, without telephones, one whole day outside History!
Let yourself be rocked.
The sky under our hull[25] is full of flowers and fish.

SIHANOUK: Yes! Living with you in a plane and looking at the world with the eye of the gods suits my mood perfectly. Let's take our proper distance! Look! You see this monotonous, seemingly lifeless brown carpet. That's Mongolia. And it's on account of these more or less brightly colored carpets that, down below, with our noses about at the level of the banana trees, we cook over the fire of millennial hatreds, and dream our whole lives of killing our neighbors. And it's on account of the carpet they stole from me that I want to dissolve in a shower of tears.

THE PRINCESS: Ah! If we could really pull ourselves away from this history!

SIHANOUK: I've forgotten the inner ways of our Buddha too much. My misfortune was to have been chosen by the French to ascend the throne. The night before, I assure you, I was the happiest of

---

[25] *Coque:* lit. shell, but also the hull of an aircraft or boat. TR

children. My greatest worry in the world was the baccalaureate exam. And now how can I forget the great dream I turned into . . . I can no longer stop being Cambodia. I myself became these rivers. These rice fields, these mountains, and all these peasants who populate me. I'd like to forget myself and live another life. I would have to die. Would you come with me?

THE PRINCESS: Are you asking me to?

SIHANOUK: If you want, we'll be reborn together. What would you like to do or be, then, if we started over?

THE PRINCESS: Be? Still a woman, still your lover, yes, once again. I'd really like to paint.

SIHANOUK: Without this decision by the gods and the French, I'd have become a great saxophonist.

THE PRINCESS: Why not a soccer player?

SIHANOUK: Yes, why not?

THE PRINCESS: Why not a Chinese cook?

SIHANOUK: Chinese? . . .
I've fallen out of our dream. I can't pretend any more.

THE PRINCESS: Is it China you're afraid of? There's no reason. A smile from Chou En-lai will quickly cure you.

SIHANOUK: I'm anxious to see him. He's a sort of *homme fatal*,[26] incredible. He's a Greta Garbo, a real Circe. The first time I meet him, he invites me to lunch, I go. I'd never seen such a handsome man. Luckily I was also a man. We sit down to eat. By the time we get to the first course I'm bewitched. But what if he, too, were deceiving me? Oh! The traitors, they've crushed my heart!
Penn Nouth! Penn Nouth!? Where are we? What time is it?

PENN NOUTH: We'll be in Peking in an hour, Your Grace.

SIHANOUK: In an hour? As soon as we arrive in Peking, Penn Nouth, I'll address a dazzling message to our people. I'll say to them: Oh my people. Oh my children! . . .

---

[26]That is, like a *femme fatale*. TR

Ah! But where are my people?
Where are my people going?
And me, where am I going? When will I find it again?
These clouds are so dense. You'd think they were an icy land
  separating us from living earth.

[They exit and so do the clouds.]

PART 1, ACT 5, SCENE 1

[Peking Airport. Enter Chou En-lai, Liu Kiang, and then the Cambo-dian Ambassador in Peking.]

AMBASSADOR: Your Most High Excellency, yesterday I received the distressing order from the new government of Phnom Penh to send quite official word of Prince Sihanouk's overthrow.

CHOU EN-LAI: I am so sorry, Mr. Ambassador to Cambodia in Pe-king. But nothing obliges you to bring me these disgraceful mes-sages. You've nothing to fear. We haven't changed, that I can assure you. China remains the friend of my friend Sihanouk. Take some solace in that.

AMBASSADOR: Oh! Eminent Excellency, if only the Prince hadn't de-layed so long!

CHOU EN-LAI: In truth, I myself have felt distress this week, seeing how, with the inconceivable calm of a fisherman put to sleep by the swell, my friend Sihanouk let time, which these days is made more out of his kingdom's precious blood than out of moments, slip away.

AMBASSADOR: The Prince had always been so confident in his good luck that he's left the helm on several occasions to go write a song. But this time, his overconfidence, or else a strong current, drove the princely ship right onto the rocks.
Mr. Prime Minister, I have waited loyally as long as possible, but I must, this morning, take responsibility for the fate of my innocent personnel. I promised my devoted servants that none would be victims of these conflicts which do not concern them. Each one being free to decide his fate, all have decided to return to their country while there is still time.

CHOU EN-LAI: And you?

AMBASSADOR: And myself also, Mr. Prime Minister. Our love for our country pleaded against the hardship of undeserved exile.

CHOU EN-LAI: The Prince is arriving in an hour and you're fleeing? You're abandoning your master just before the battle?

AMBASSADOR: We reckon that it's he who has abandoned us.

CHOU EN-LAI: Hence it is Lon Nol's Ambassador who is presently addressing me?

AMBASSADOR: Himself, Your Excellency, as I tried to tell you on arrival.

CHOU EN-LAI: China does not receive Lon Nol's emissary, Sir. I thought I was lending an ear to Sihanouk's friend. Do you hear? How incredibly thick-skinned a human soul can be! He stands before me, metamorphosed into a shameless slug! I'm astounded! Yes and I want to be astounded again and again until I'm dead. I've seen so many men become slime before me these past few years, that if, by mischance, I stopped being astounded, who knows if I might not find myself oozing along on my belly on my couch one fine morning. Oh, my god! Make it so that when my death arrives, I'm still a man burning with indignation. Mr. Ambassador, you are unwelcome. Please remove all trace of yourself from this place.

AMBASSADOR: Magnanimity is easy when you're Chou En-lai. When you are treasonous, you call it revolution or just a new policy. We who are subject to leaders' whims should call fidelity pure servility.

[He exits.]

CHOU EN-LAI: Poor Prince! You've just lived out the final days of your life's childhood. Treason has begun to drive its tenacious harpoons into your side. I, too, have been betrayed and lacerated by some of those that I had elevated. Such wounds never completely heal. Once the sores close up, the poison remains.
And to think that just two days ago all could have been saved. I had procured a French plane that was ready to transport him regally. He would have arrived here only to set out again imme-

diately for his capital and once more take the reins of the runaway team in his legitimate hands.

Those two days, poor Prince, cost you two thousand years of monarchy and us the pleasure of a friendly alliance. You too, Liu Kiang, you have a warm affection for Prince Sihanouk.

LIU KIANG: An affection that has not diminished in twelve years.

CHOU EN-LAI: Well! Keeping the thought of this long affection in your heart, I beg you to undertake a delicate trip. Pay a visit to Lon Nol on China's behalf.

You must obtain everything, absolutely everything from him that our dear Prince granted us up to the present. First, protection for our Vietnamese friends, access to the port in Sihanoukville, secure transport for our convoys; everything we need, no changes. He'll resist, you'll persuade him.

LIU KIANG: That will be difficult. To make him do the same thing he overthrew Sihanouk for. I'll have to hypnotize him.

CHOU EN-LAI: Well, do so! Speak little and indirectly. But let him always see in your face and in your manner China's unfathomable prodigiousness and omnipotence. Strike his soul by the duration of your gaze. Curdle the spleen in his organs, fascinate his demons. But flatter him imperceptibly with false hopes and feigned respect.

And all the while maintain the discourse of cold political reason: Of course, we love Sihanouk, but that doesn't inhibit us from being realists and from knowing when to recognize change.

A SECRETARY: Mr. Prime Minister, the Prince's plane has landed.

CHOU EN-LAI: Go, Liu Kiang, bewitch elegantly for me this slave of phantoms.

[Liu Kiang exits. The plane lands.]
[Enter Sihanouk, Dith Boun Suo, and Ambassadors, including Etienne Manac'h, French Ambassador in Peking.]

MANAC'H: Take heart, Prince, you have friends.

SIHANOUK: I have enemies. But I have the courage of an elephant. So don't look sadder than I. I haven't lost a war. Only a little time that I'll regain. I'd like to see you very soon.

MANAC'H: Whenever you say, I'll be there. In the meantime, can I offer you any service?

SIHANOUK: Go revive my poor Penn Nouth who's over there almost unconscious. I didn't want to bear the heavy burden of despair so he's the one carrying it in my place. Later . . .

[Manac'h exits.]

Oh! Here's my powerful friend Chou En-lai, Prince of all the Ministers. But such seriousness on this venerable face! They're not all going to sulk just when I'm so happy to get here!

CHOU EN-LAI: Prince, may you find China, as always, pleasant and favorable. How are you taking this rather . . . overpowering[27] epoch?

SIHANOUK: My very precious, most revered friend, I assure you that I'll not fear these storms if you're not angry. I know what you're going to say, I'm late . . . and I don't even know why. But can one always explain everything? I don't know what came over me.

CHOU EN-LAI: Perhaps it was Sihanouk's strange destiny.

SIHANOUK: No doubt, yes . . . Oh! Finally you're smiling.
Mr. Prime Minister, I'm aware of the situation in which I find myself today, but I don't want any change nor any reflection of the violent anguish which stirs within me to appear on my face. There are too many vulture eyes around us. I'm not defeated. I won't remain in this night of exile long.

CHOU EN-LAI: I quite like your bravado, Prince. Can I have a few words with you? Would you please follow me?

SIHANOUK: I'll follow you. But not before you've promised me that you're not angry at me for . . . my destiny.

CHOU EN-LAI: I'm no longer angry with you.

SIHANOUK: I no longer fear anything terrible.

[All exit except Dith Boun Suo, the Musician, and Captain Ong Meang, the Prince's aide-de-camp. Enter Manac'h.]

---

[27]*Bouleversant: bouleverser* means both to be confusing and overthrow a ruler; hence Chou's hesitation in pronouncing the term. TR

ONG MEANG: So, there won't be any fanfare, no welcoming dances? And there won't be any national hymns? What a timid and melancholy welcome! One would think they were receiving a coffin.

MANAC'H: Our Chinese friends are having some difficulty in putting on a light-hearted face. The Prince's misfortune caused them not only surprise but pain and also worry.

DITH BOUN SUO: Poor Chinese!

MUSICIAN: Now I don't know which song would be suitable to compose. Should I do "Farewell, Cambodia" or "When I Return to Phnom Penh"?

MANAC'H: You're not going to betray His Highness, too?

MUSICIAN: How's that "too"? You're mistaken, Mr. Ambassador. Rama Mok is not one of those greedy civil servants who're always stateless before the fact. I'm a free citizen of Music and Sihanouk is my royal and beloved fellow citizen. You've bruised my soul, Mr. Ambassador.

MANAC'H: I ask all the forgiveness in the world from you, very dear and loyal friend. *[Sihanouk enters again.]* Prince, why such a dejected air? You were nevertheless so calm on arrival. I found you as great as the greatest.

SIHANOUK: And here I am, cut down to size once more? Yes. It's strange. But everyone is so strange since my fall. Everyone tries to make me fall even lower. Since this blow, everything I dream up falls into two opposing halves. Are you a friend? Chou En-lai, is he my faithful or my unfaithful friend?

MANAC'H: He's your faithful friend.

SIHANOUK: He's just spoken with me, and I understood nothing. He gave me a very friendly reception. But behind the exquisite and familiar courtesy, I sensed he was slightly withdrawn. He was standing one step behind himself. He made me speak nonstop about Russia, about my country, about Russia, but China was silent. In the course of the conversation, China said three words, but I understood nothing.

MANAC'H: What did he say to you?

SIHANOUK: He says to me: "What are your plans?" "And yours?" I say. "Do you intend to fight?" he asks me. I'm immediately out-raged: "Give me weapons and I'll show you." But he cools me down: "Don't answer me too quickly. Deliberate. We'll speak about it again in twenty-four hours." And he leaves. He leaves me alone in the woods. And him, not so long ago as tender and frank as a Virgil for his Dante. Where did he leave me? What beast awaits me? Whom am I going to meet on the dark path?

MANAC'H: I imagine he couldn't tell you more, without waiting to be directed by those he represents. The Prime Minister is no longer king. Behind him stands a large number of invisible authorities. Everything's changed, everything is changing nonstop from four years ago. Chou En-lai's word cannot be ventured without having been endorsed by twenty permissions.

SIHANOUK: He looked at me as if he was thinking of something else or of someone else.

MANAC'H: He was thinking perhaps of Lon Nol.

SIHANOUK: I thought so. But why?

MANAC'H: His obligation to send an emissary to Lon Nol must have caused him some distress.

SIHANOUK: To Lon Nol? An emissary? Ah! He hasn't wasted any time either! To him the office makes the Prince! I'll withdraw. Your France, will she accept me?

MANAC'H: France would certainly be happy to accept you, Your Highness.

SIHANOUK: Without kingdom, without state, without fatherland, without interest?

MANAC'H: But not without people, nor without glory . . .

SIHANOUK: And not without a past! Yes, I have a great past to take refuge in.

MANAC'H: The history of Sihanouk, his story[28] will not be finished

---

[28] *Histoire* is both history and story in French. TR

this year, I'm sure of that. It's the year that's bad. We must leap over it, in one bound, like an abyss.

SIHANOUK: No, I can no longer wait for anything. From now on, I belong to the past. I certainly do not intend to tell myself fairy tales about the eagle's return. Done for, I'm gone, I'm in the midst of erasing myself. What's the date?

MANAC'H: March 22, Your Highness.

SIHANOUK: On March 22 Sihanouk said his good-byes to the universe. Each year, in your country, while the Earth is beginning a new pregnancy, why, I'll celebrate the birthday of my disappearance. I'd love a little song for my exit, a funerary ballet, a cortege on the river. . . . But the end always comes costumed as it pleases.
Oh Chinese, implacable friend, You wear a straight jacket and gray slacks.
You extend a hand full of welcoming petals to me. In the other hand you hold out poison.
Manac'h, if you love me, see to my departure. As of today, I no longer want to be in this land. China killed me. Do everything for me, I am no more. I want to remove myself from everyone's eyes. Let me. And don't let anybody watch me leave.

MANAC'H: I'll secure you a safe leave, Your Highness.

[Exit Manac'h. Enter Penn Nouth.]

SIHANOUK:
We believe we're making our own History.
We labor, we fight, we fear, we hope.
For what? We're less than buffaloes.
Over our heads, masters who love us not
Barter us and sell us like cattle.
Oh my Cambodia, they're separating us, carrying me off, away from you.
They're exiling you from me, treating us like slaves.
What a sad expression you have, my friend. Must I sadden myself even more? Bad news?

PENN NOUTH: No, no. Don't be discouraged, Your Highness. There's nothing new.

99

SIHANOUK: Then there's still more of the same bad news. Oh! Tell me the worst quickly. They haven't by chance killed even my mother?

PENN NOUTH: Oh! No! No! Her Majesty is being held in the Palace. But she's in good health.

SIHANOUK: Then, that's good. There's nothing worse. You can tell me the rest.

[Exit Dith Boun Suo and Ong Meang.]

PENN NOUTH: What saddened me was to learn this morning that throughout the world our ambassadors rallied, one after the other, to Lon Nol.

SIHANOUK: Ah! They're already out changing the portraits. Not all of them, though? Not Kim Var?

PENN NOUTH: Him, too.

SIHANOUK: Him, too? And Sum Seng?

PENN NOUTH: Him also.

SIHANOUK: I believed they loved me.

PENN NOUTH: They didn't love you.

SIHANOUK: Then everyone, Penn Nouth? Not a single little ambassador capable of choosing honor?

PENN NOUTH: Yes, all the same, Your Grace. There is one, Chea San, in Moscow. He joins us. He announced his arrival here last evening.

SIHANOUK: San! San! Precisely, and he alone! Among them all, San, whom I treated so rudely. Penn Nouth, inside your bad news is hidden news so precious it almost reconciles me with humanity. One single glance suffices sometimes to snatch us from the jaws of Hell. In this instance, owing to someone I expected nothing from, I'm happy.
The good San. Out of forty-four traitors, one altogether faithful! If there were even four or five, Penn Nouth, I'd swear to you that as of tomorrow I'd leave to reconquer Phnom Penh. Doesn't it

only take five true knights united like the fingers of the hand to liberate a holy city?

PENN NOUTH: There's other news.

SIHANOUK: More painful news?!

PENN NOUTH: Your sons were arrested and all your supporters rendered powerless by prison or terror. But that doesn't satisfy them. You're so great in their imagination and so terrifying that, not content with having the doors of the country shut on you, they're now intent on wiping out all traces of your person. Because they think, if they allow your intact image to smolder in the people's heart, it might well one day ignite huge fires among the masses. That's why they've unleashed throughout the country a huge campaign of calumnies and lies. Millions of posters carrying accusations that I can not repeat, so revolting and shocking are their infamies and stupidities, have been affixed on the lampposts in even the tiniest villages. In the cities, obscene stories about your family and your private life are vomited on everyone's head by loudspeakers. Hate infects Phnom Penh. In the newspapers there were such atrociously grotesque articles, that reading them, I felt my soul overcome by dizziness, as if I had absorbed the violent poison of human stupidity through my eyes.

SIHANOUK: And no one responded? No one defends me?

PENN NOUTH: The people don't have loudspeakers, Your Grace.

SIHANOUK: Where are these newspapers?

PENN NOUTH: To tell you the truth, I had to burn them.

SIHANOUK:
    I want these newspapers, Penn Nouth.
    I want to read them with my own eyes.
    I want the blood in my veins to catch fire
    For henceforth I want, irreversibly, a superhuman rage to feed
       in me.
    They've stolen my land, my people, my power,
    They've hurled me to the bottom of the world
    And now they want to close people's hearts
    Where what remains of Sihanouk might take refuge.

It isn't only my place they desire,
Nor my death. They want me never to stop dying, buried under
   their excrement.
A horrible joy rises in my heart like a great purifying wind,
This joy is so very great a force,
It uplifts me! I am immense, I am alive!
Alive! alive!
It's decided. Penn Nouth! We shall take back the head of our
   people.

I want to see San on his arrival. He, you, and I shall hold council
this afternoon. Presently, I'll make my voice resound, over the
mountains of exile, in the ears of Cambodia. The whole world will
hear Sihanouk. I'll regain their hearts. I'll call my people to arms.
Today we're three, tomorrow we'll be millions.

PENN NOUTH: Your Highness, tomorrow, in order to be millions, we
must ineluctably hold counsel with the Communists.

SIHANOUK: Since it's unavoidable, let's make fatality our welcome
friend and embrace her courageously. Don't hold me back, Penn
Nouth, I must pounce on the enemy. I'm already galloping,
mounted on red Impatience. I herein form a Royal Government of
the National Union of Cambodia. Penn Nouth, don't hold me
back. I'm naming you my First Prime Minister. Do you accept?

PENN NOUTH: I embrace my fate, My Lord.

SIHANOUK: Go, Penn Nouth! Go find Chou En-lai, and tell him from
me that I have the answer.

[Exit Penn Nouth.]

Tomorrow, I was going to leave at dawn, an old man, I was going
to leave my nation to the vultures. I was going to feed my mor-
tification at pity's expense. And I would have spent the rest of my
existence asleep. What a nightmare!

[Dith Boun Sou enters.]

DITH BOUN SOU: The Cambodian Ambassador in Peking requests
audience with Your Highness.

SIHANOUK: Have Mr. Lon Nol's Ambassador in Peking come in.

102

[The Ambassador enters.]

Out! Back out, immediately, Sir. Now, come back in again the way you should before the Prince or I'll have you dismissed. Leave!

AMBASSADOR: I'm a Republican, now, Your Highness, I'm leaving.

SIHANOUK: Republican! You mean Lon Nol's shit eater! Reptile! Earthworm. Go, move! And on your knees!

AMBASSADOR: Your highness, I'm commissioned—

SIHANOUK: On your knees or I'll not listen to you. An ambassador must conform rigorously to the customs of the country he's in and to the person whom he has the honor to address. On your knees, always, before Sihanouk, whether you're red, yellow, green or gosling poo green, or whether you're Vietnamese or Khmer, now, on your knees or I'll make you feel that there's still strength in me. There. Now, stand up! I don't like looking at your behind.

AMBASSADOR: Your highness, I'm commissioned to notify you officially of Your Highness's overthrow.

SIHANOUK: What are you saying?! That's your message! Piece of cow-dung, rotten fish! Wait! I'll have you relay a direct message, without flourishes, myself. Have someone bring me the whips with eight knots, quickly! Wait, dog shit, wait for me to trample you. Quick, and also my hog knife! I'll chop you all up into little bits, I'll trim your bottom! Ah! Snake without head or tail, I'll cut you to bits.

AMBASSADOR: Your Highness, I am an ambassador, I'm only doing my job.

SIHANOUK: And a broom, so I can sweep him up when I've reduced him to fragments. Ambassador? I'll make you grovel in lion's urine. But wait till I strangle you a little first and tear your tongue out a bit.

AMBASSADOR: Your Majesty, I don't have the right to raise my hand against you. I'm a civil servant.

SIHANOUK: You're a torturer and, me, I'll torture you for—

[Enter Penn Nouth.]

Ah! Penn Nouth, there you are. Too bad! Or rather, no, what luck! Fortunately! I was just in the midst of asking myself if I should bleed him before strangling him. What do you think?

PENN NOUTH: Your Highness, what kind of state have they gotten you in? What's happened? You should let Mr. Ambassador go get dressed again.

SIHANOUK: No, not like that. It would be too easy to take advantage of a distraction. I authorize you to leave, but on all fours like a pig. All right, let me explain to you: this snake with a thousand legs came crawling from Lon Nol. Under the pretext of doing his duty, he read to me, perfectly calmly, to my living self, the announcement of my burial. I wanted to show him that the tiger was still alive.

[Ambassador finally leaves.]

I would have loved to have strangled him! But just the same it was an exquisite moment!
Now then, my friend through thick and thin, did you give my message to the Prince of Ministers?

PENN NOUTH: I hardly finished doing so, My Lord, when a true Chinese sun rose over his noble face. Instantly he has Hanoi called right in front of me and our August Siren persuades Mr. Pham Van Dong, the slippery Prime Minister of Vietnam, to come without delay, here, to meet Your Highness. In other words, My Lord, you're seeing Pham Van Dong right away. And he'll offer you the "spontaneous," friendly, revolutionary, and communist assistance of his powerful communist army.

SIHANOUK: I'll accept this communist aid. The Buddhist with a pure heart has no need to fear the Dragon's touch.
"Prince saved by Communists," that'll be a fine story: under the Chinese aegis, triumphantly supported by our cunning but subdued neighbors, Sihanouk put the Demon to flight.

> I owe you strange thanks, Lon Nol.
> I thank you serpents, newspapers, toads,
> For having awakened with your corrosive snarls

The tiger who was sleeping far away in the heart of my forest.
My pride almost consumed by the flames of disgust
A hundred thousand Sihanouks are reborn from my ashes
I become an army. My blood flows in a thousand rivers.
And you, ordinary Universe, so quick to mourn me,
Tomorrow I'll present a new Sihanouk to your astonishment.
And what a Sihanouk! An unheard of Sihanouk,
A Sihanouk perched on a communist elephant.
I'd very much like to make his acquaintance myself.

[Ong Meang enters.]

ONG MEANG: Your Highness, I have a very urgent message for you relayed by the Chinese Chancellor to us.

SIHANOUK: *[reading]* Declaration of total and unconditional support for H.R.H. Prince Norodom Sihanouk, head of state.
From the Khmer Rouge, capital K, capital R, Resistance, with a capital R, of the Interior.
Khmer Rouge, unconditional?!!

PENN NOUTH: There's some mistake!

SIHANOUK: But that's a surprise fall from the top of my elephant!
Look, Penn Nouth, look at these signatures, Messrs. Khieu Samphan, Hou Youn, my former red ministers . . . and someone called Mr. Pol Pot.

PENN NOUTH: Khieu Samphan and Hou Youn. And to think we thought they were dead! I can't get over it.

SIHANOUK: In any case, they, they're coming back and offering themselves body and soul to my cause.

PENN NOUTH: Fatality is assuming disturbing proportions!

SIHANOUK:
It's true! I never intended so much fatality.
Oh! for better or for worse! I accept!
Let us embrace fatality more widely still.
The end of my white neutrality!
Stupid America, blind and brainless ogre,
This is how you deliver people to the red Dragon for pasture,

people who only ask to graze peacefully in their own meadow.

The Khmer Rouge, Penn Nouth! I thought they hated me? They need me, Penn Nouth, did you see? If they need me, it's because they're just as weak as I am.

PENN NOUTH: The crocodile needs the Prince's skin to make himself more comely.

SIHANOUK: Oh Penn Nouth, don't show me a desolate face, at the very moment I'm taking a leap to bound from planet to planet, or else I'll let myself fall.

PENN NOUTH: Your Highness, it was a beautiful planet we are leaving behind. I fear we may have just this instant lived out the last scene of our history.

SIHANOUK: Perhaps it was the first scene of a new history which will end well, I hope so.

PENN NOUTH: Today, I can only hope that I'll be able to hope tomorrow.

SIHANOUK: All the paths that open before me are equally distressing. I'll take one anyway. I'm committing myself to a year of dark nights, full of traps.

Let's go, Sihanouk, forward, forward without turning back.
Forward, forward, the time for dancing is over.
There's no way to go back in time.
From atop my elephant, I can not see Phnom Penh.
Around me, the mist gathers,
Above me, the clouds.
Eyes veiled in tears, I ask the nightingale:
Will I myself, be back home under my own roof?
Let's go, Penn Nouth, light! Courage! Patience!
Boldness! And wiles!

[He exits and Manac'h has entered.]

PENN NOUTH: What does France say?

MANAC'H: I'll not lie to you, my government offers only evasive words.

PENN NOUTH: The Prince can't wait. Events, themselves, continue apace, and one must act without delay if one wants to hold on to a chance of being able one day to catch up with them. In the meantime you who aren't subjected to our fatality, you could, while we're sliding down the inevitable slope, attempt one more last recourse. Go plead the cause of neutrality. Shake France up. Touch America. Run to the West, friend, and while we're making our way East, we'll turn around often to see if, by chance, from faraway some glimmers of hope might reach us before our descent, having arrived at the ends of the earth, makes it already forever too late.

[Manac'h exits.]

> And in the meantime, you who watch over Cambodia,
> Spirits of the trees and waters,
> Spirits of the highways and trails,
> Don't go away, stay over there.
> Great and small powers,
> You who loved us so much
> When we were rich and happy,
> Don't forget to go at evening
> To the river's edge
> And call us back.
> We will come back, we will come back.

[He exits.]

End of the First Part

SECOND PERIOD, PART 2, PROLOGUE[29]

[Chorus enters.]

> What happens next in our story is dangerous.
> It is slippery and stupefying.
> The world rocks underfoot. The stars are fallen from the sky.

---

[29] This prologue does not appear in the actual production. AU

On high, the gods have gambled.
They gambled with Cambodia.
Some have won. Some have lost and are grieving.
We're of desolation's party.
Hearts are buried so far away from mouths,
That one can hardly hear what the characters are thinking.
It's a time of distrust. A cold sun is rising in the North.
There's no longer either Kingdom, or memory.
There's nothing anywhere but destiny.
Today the Prince Sihanouk's survival, the remains of his pride,
    the remains of his power, the remains of his honor,
And all the remains, from his roof to his food on the table,
He owes to the very ones he wanted never to owe anything to.
He is the debtor of China and Vietnam,
These two clever powers
Who move along the ground sideways, like crabs.
Do you understand?
Now the Prince is in Peking
And Cambodia is completely stupefied.
It no longer knows where it is,
Whether in Peking or Phnom Pehn,
Inside or outside of itself,
Nor who it is, nor on what side,
Nor of what species, what its name is,
If it is royalist or republican,
Nor where the wind which drives it mad comes from,
If it comes from China or America,
Nor in what foreign language and
To which gods to pray, appeal to which masters.
Which fathers to disobey from now on.
This era is shredded, this nation is cut into pieces.
Theater is charged with reassembling them
Let me not forget one single scrap.
When all is perfidy,
How hard it is for a narrative to be faithful.
One word of advice: if a character you respect
Swears to everyone that the dark night
Is a bright day, do not believe him,
Even if it's the noble Penn Nouth (whose part I have the honor
    to play again before you.)

Oh! May truth still cry out even faintly, so that you might hear
    it amidst the hubbub of evil tongues and bombings.
Put on your sharpest ears if you love it,
Because truth, exactly like falsehood,
Lives off those who listen to it.
Without ears, no truth.
Without truth, no theater.
Aren't we all here out of a desire to hear
And finally tear fragile Truth away from the furious tide of
    Falsehood?
Will we succeed? I do not know, I hope so, I believe so.
I, who am speaking to you, am myself an act of faith.
I believe truth hides amidst us all
Even if in my very human myopia
I do not always succeed in seeing it.
And if you'd like, it's to truth that I dedicate our entire
    performance including its errors and blindnesses.
As I speak to you, a conference of fateful importance for the
    country of Cambodia is being held here in Peking.
I leave you to judge it! The Prince is going to come in. . . . Oh!
What's happening? Excuse me. What I've just announced to
    you will be the second scene of the performance: the author
    has again changed her mind!

[Chorus exits.]

PART 2, ACT 1, SCENE 1

[Phnom Penh, Before the Sanctuary. The defunct King Suramarit enters.]

SURAMARIT:
    Evil days are here
    The sacred sword has rusted in the sheath.
    The sun rises trembling
    Today Sihanouk is driven from his ancestral lands
    By men who owe him riches, honor and loyalty.
    Yesterday evening I read the posters.
    All bear my august son's name
    All curse and vow the great Prince's death.

He is hunted like a stag.
Should I hope he'll return?
Our royal city has war sickness
The fugitives, with their wagons creaking in the streets, come
    seeking sanctuary.
Just now I saw our great river raging
Carrying on the breadth of its magnificent back
Hundreds of cadavers.
How sad it is for the dead man who comes back to his country
    with a timid joy
To find everyone in such a desolate state.
There's not a single child to console me
Mothers are terrorized. When curfew falls each gathers her
    little ones around her.
The sky is dead
The old Cambodia is drenched to the heart.

[Enter Khieu Samnol and Madame Lamné with their bicycle. They bow to the old King without recognizing him.]

MADAME LAMNÉ: Samnol, that's that, our bike's got another flat. You'd think we crossed paths with a snake. It's bit of a disaster, no?

KHIEU SAMNOL: Oh! My yes! Ever since they took away our Lord Papa from us we've been unlucky with this bike! When a bike breaks down three times in the same week, it's a bad sign. That means we must sell it to someone else to get rid of the evil spirits.
For myself, I think that we ought to sell it to the Chinese tinker. Because now that everyone from the villages is coming to live in Phnom Penh, on account of these accursed bombings, bikes are more valuable than gold.

MADAME LAMNÉ: To that Chinese bandit? Oh no! It would be better if you helped me fix it. Because you could make it come back to life[30] again, this bike, if you wanted to, I know you could.

KHIEU SAMNOL: Yes, that's true. Because I know how to make every-

---

[30] *Revenir:* we've used "come back to life" because Samnol is supposed to be able to raise the dead. TR

thing come back to life again brand new. Stained clothes, lost knives, pots, pans, and also the dead.

SURAMARIT: Oh! Yes?

MADAME LAMNÉ: Yes. She's the greatest at making things come back!

SURAMARIT: Oh! Good!?

KHIEU SAMNOL: But this bike, no! It's wrong to revive a bike that's bent on deserting us. This bike, now, it's fine for the Chinese fellow, because with the Chinese it's not the same. They're not afraid.

MADAME LAMNÉ: Well, me, I think I'd be happier if we gave the bike to my dear Father John of Jesus.

KHIEU SAMNOL: To give a bike as wicked as this one, which croaks every five minutes as soon as a good person climbs on, to your beloved Father Jesus! Say, you mustn't think of it!

MADAME LAMNÉ: Say, Samnol, our Prince Sihanouk who's no longer there since the accursed Lon Nol snatched him from us, couldn't you bring him back?

SURAMARIT: Oh, no, Madame Lamné, that is not possible.

KHIEU SAMNOL: Oh! Not that: because that isn't religion, it's politics. But on the other hand, our defunct King the great Suramarit, that last time at Her Majesty the Queen's, if it hadn't been for the bad luck of the Bigfoot, you'd have seen him return in flesh and bone, I could have done it.

MADAME LAMNÉ: You could?

KHIEU SAMNOL: I'm telling you.

SURAMARIT: You're really good.

MADAME LAMNÉ: Say Samnol, someday would you teach me the formulas for bringing them back, someday? Or some other?

KHIEU SAMNOL: And in return, what do I get?

MADAME LAMNÉ: I'd give in on the Chinese tinker.

KHIEU SAMNOL: Good. Well, then, you say:
Samtec Brah Suramarit varbodhipanna Mahabodhi sirisanganayak

tilak loka mahasangaraja paramapabitr. Subhamastu paramat-thubbavamangalajaiyyatirek pân. 1523 . . .

SURAMARIT: Precisely! That's it exactly!

MADAME LAMNÉ: I say: Samtec Brah Suramarit vabadhipou . . .

SURAMARIT AND KHIEU SAMNOL: What!
Not at all! Why, no! Absolutely not!

KHIEU SAMNOL: You say:
Samtec Brah Suramarit varbodhipanna Mahabodhi sirisanganayak tilak loka mahasangaraja paramapabitr. Subhamastu paramat-thubbavamangalajaiyyatirek pân. 1523 . . .

SURAMARIT: Just about. . . . If you tried just one little time more?

MADAME LAMNÉ: Are you going too fast on purpose? Or am I just stupid?

KHIEU SAMNOL: I'm doing it the way you have to, otherwise they don't hear, that's how it is.

SURAMARIT: Even a little bit faster . . .

KHIEU SAMNOL AND MADAME LAMNÉ: Samtec Brah Suramarit var-bodhipanna Mahabodhi sirisanganayak tilak loka mahasangaraja paramapabitr. Subhamastu paramatthubbavamangalajaiyytirek pân. 1523 . . .

SURAMARIT: 1523. There. There. There. We're there. It's no harder than that.

[shocked looks of the old ladies who recognize him]

My dear nieces, calm down, I beg you. It's not so terrible. You called me, I came.

KHIEU SAMNOL: Oh! What a frightful honor to have Your Majesty. Ah! Madame Lamné, how can I speak? What should I say to His Majesty? What should we be doing now?

SURAMARIT: My dear nieces—may I call you that?—take the kind liberty of calling me Uncle, it suits my new circumstance better.

KHIEU SAMNOL: Uncle? But it's an inexpressible honor you do us, myself and Madame Lamné, too. *[to Madame Lamné]* What? No? Why yes!

SURAMARIT: You were calling me and I was looking for you. Yes. Exactly, for several days I've been looking for the friendly assistance of a bike. And look how fate brought me to your door!

KHIEU SAMNOL: A bike, Your Augustness?

SURAMARIT: Call me Uncle. A bike or a small motorcycle. That is, anything that goes faster than my feet.
Because I want to go find my son again in Peking.

MADAME LAMNÉ: Peking? Over there?

KHIEU SAMNOL: Which son? Ours? Our Prince Sihanouk?

MADAME LAMNÉ: Evidently, Madame Lamné. We only have one, Our Uncle, one beloved son who's in Peking since they snatched him from us.

KHIEU SAMNOL: But let me be a little astounded all the same, going as far as Peking to see our beloved Lordship!

SURAMARIT: Yes, frankly, it's quite far away. The trip is perilous and excruciating. There are Americans with their B-52's, all the time, day and night, with the F105's, with their "helicopters," their "gunships."[31] The road is hard, you cannot see its end. On foot it's disheartening. I've been on the road a week, just like this, and already I'm not the same any more.

KHIEU SAMNOL: Why, it's true. You're quite a wreck!

SURAMARIT: I look like my poor people, I've lost my good spirits, my house, my buffaloes. I, too, have fled ahead of the war, on terrified roads, my head raised toward a sky massed with bombardier dragons. I wore out my sandals. New! I wore out my feet. I slept as my people did, in ditches, under cover of a small bit of blue plastic. And it's by hundreds of thousands that I arrived, tears in my eyes, at the city of Phnom Penh.
Ah! My heart is in the same state as my feet, completely flayed.

---

[31] "Helicopters" and "gunships" are English in the original. TR

However, I must continue on toward the North, the North.
That's why I want the gods to grant me a hike.
I thought on and on about it. It was just then that you invited me, dear Madame Khieu Samnol.
My dear sisters, dear Madame Lamné, I'd be very grateful to you for the favor if you'd like to lend me your bike. It will be completely secure with me. Otherwise, your bike, you know . . . with the brigands stripping all the poor people in our capital.

KHIEU SAMNOL: Yes, that's true.
Still, Your Majesty Uncle, check the brakes carefully. Madame Lamné rides slowly, so she never has to brake. But all the same, to go to Peking, pedaling?!

SURAMARIT: I thank you profusely, dear Madame Khieu Samnol. I'll take care.

KHIEU SAMNOL: If you see His Highness Papa, Your Majesty Uncle, tell him, for Samnol, mother of Khieu Samphan, to do the impossible, please?

SURAMARIT: Of course.
Now, my friends, I take to the road again. Guard your lives and each other well. I'd love to see you again on my return road.

KHIEU SAMNOL: Don't worry about us, Your Majesty Uncle. We know that you'll pray for us and that we'll see you again here or there.

MADAME LAMNÉ: And whatever the hour, My Uncle, in the heart of night, whatever moon it is or whatever the state of the world may be, just knock at our door.

SURAMARIT: Mountain after mountain, forest after forest, if I get to Peking, it's because the gods exist.

[He exits.]

MADAME LAMNÉ: Oh! My god, make the bike hold up all the way there!

KHIEU SAMNOL: A bike like that, Madame Lamné, if one's lucky, is indestructible.

[They exit.]

[Peking, Sihanouk enters, all alone.]

SIHANOUK: *[to the public]*

Well, where are we in this ill-fated month of March 1970? I
must direct my political counterattack from Peking, where
my destiny, fleeing the tempest of history, was to find refuge.

In Phnom Penh, Lon Nol, the extreme traitor, who I'd compare
to an Iago or, if you'd permit me, to your Ganelon, Lon Nol,
thus, handed over my proud and free kingdom to American
imperialism. But surely you must already know that.

Let me add that it's my own cousin, Sisowath Sirik Matak,
who's the MacBeth of this ignominy. I point him out to you
as being the same sort as Lon Nol.

And now, my Cambodia, which under my reign and under my
presidency always was independent, has become slave to the
dollar.

There's worse! My people will be used as cannon fodder for the
war America wages unsuccessfully but in great waves of
blood against the Vietnamese. And then the legs, arms, eyes,
children! The people will suffer enormously and twofold.
They've lost both Peace and My Lord Papa.

Well, what should I do?

Ah! Well, in the days and months that come, I shall have to use
methods that are very dangerous both for my soul and for
my body.

Yes, I won't hide it from you, I'm dreaming of submitting to
Vietnam, our enemy since the beginning of History, up until
last week.

Vietnam, this populous neighbor with a powerful army and
famous appetites.

You get the picture? You see what awaits me? The Cambodian kitten is going to hunt Bigfoot down with the Vietnamese tiger.
You know how Mr. Pham Van Dong, the Vietnamese Prime Minister, was until last year? Deaf to my prayers and enclosed in an
armor of indifference. Well! now, everything's changed. A phone
call from China, and he melted, he bowed down. It's not feeling
that creates these new friendships, it's situations. Peking's pleasure,
that's the key to these metamorphoses! Hanoi and I have in China

a common suzerain, in America, better still, a common enemy.
The Vietnamese are certainly rankled to have Lon Nol now instead of Sihanouk for a neighbor. Now America can boldly trample the combatants Hanoi was hiding in my territory.
All these good reasons are worth more than frail sincerity.

[Enter Penn Nouth.]

What time do we expect Pham Van Dong, Lordship Penn Nouth?

PENN NOUTH: You can expect him any time now, Your Grace. But
are you sure a virtuous honor rather than a shameful wrath and a
drunken thirst for revenge brings you to a meeting that is so . . .
perilous?

SIHANOUK: It wasn't me who set Vietnam totally against Cambodia,
it was destiny. Let us then dare to confront an ineluctable understanding between these two countries head on. The world map
says we're condemned to it.

PENN NOUTH: What if you gave destiny a little bit more time. Or if
you allowed Lon Nol time to rot naturally! [Captain Ong Meang
enters.]

ONG MEANG: Mr. Prime Minister of Vietnam, His Excellency Pham
Van Dong, is presented to us by the Chinese Chancellery. [He
exits.]

SIHANOUK: Hold back for my sake, Penn Nouth! Because the present
is galloping ahead of Sihanouk and I need to catch up with it.

Let's dare to do it! Let's dare to make such an unheard of union
    possible!
Let's celebrate the honeymoon of the tiger and the kitten
Under the half-closed and softening eye of the Peking Dragon.
Let's be extremely Chinese!
And let's not blush at embracing Hanoi.
But may my vibrant blue blending with their harsh red
Produce a divine saffron instead of a violet.
Onward Sihanouk! Onward Cambodia!

[Enter Pham Van Dong and his retinue.]

Mr. Prime Minister, welcome! Welcome! We're very touched by
your promptness.

PHAM VAN DONG: The Vietnamese never forget a wrong doing nor a kindness.

Your rivers, your forests, your mountains often welcomed our men pursued by the enemy. We can show them our gratitude.

SIHANOUK: Precisely, that's just what we'd like to talk about!

PHAM VAN DONG: China, who's inviting us to get together, is quite right: united we'll be freed twice as quickly.

SIHANOUK: Wait! Not so fast! Half of Cambodia will make a pitiful ally! We want to be entirely at your side. It is first of all fitting for my country to be in full possession of all its historic territory. You understand?

PHAM VAN DONG: May your new friendship have trust in our new friendship.

SIHANOUK: Sihanouk always has trust, Your Excellency. And it has just cost him his country. Frankly, I wouldn't want it cut from me a second time.

PHAM VAN DONG: I promise you that we'll always respect the configuration of your borders. I promised that, word for word, to His Excellency Chou En-lai yesterday.

PENN NOUTH: [to Sihanouk] And tomorrow, in front of an assembly of all the peoples of Indochina? Ask him, Your Highness.

SIHANOUK: And tomorrow, in front of an assembly bringing together—at my request—all the peoples of Indochina? As for myself, I have faith in you, but His Excellency Penn Nouth wants assurances.

PHAM VAN DONG: I swear to it, I'll swear to it again.

PENN NOUTH: And the islands, Your Highness, don't forget the islands.

PHAM VAN DONG: I swear we shall not touch your kingdom's beautiful coastal islands.

And to all these commitments, I'll add eternal respect your rightful desire for independence and neutrality.

Does this appease you, most prudent counsellor?

SIHANOUK:

> I believe that I believe you
> And oath for oath
> All I must forget
> So that the marriage of Angkor and Hanoi
> May be blessed and solemnized
> Sihanouk swears to forget.
> I'll forget that foreign Vietnam always coveted the land of
>   Cambodia. I'll forget that. I'll forget that after having
>   ravished our Cochin China last century, last year you
>   occupied my dear Ratanakiri province. I'll forget that.
>
> It's all in the past. Let's not speak about it. I've forgotten.
> I remember nothing but next year in Phnom Penh.
> Today I change hatreds, loves, and colors.
> I shall embrace with all my heart
> The one whom last year I reviled.
> I shall swear swamp garlic
> Is the intoxicating aroma of the carnation to my nose.
> For henceforth I admit "foul is fair."[32]
> And in order to retake my capital? My great friend, what are
>   we going to do?

PHAM VAN DONG: We'll assist to the full the Khmer and independent armies which you called up in your radio appeal. Whenever your people join up in your forests with the valiant handful of Khmer Rouge whom we've already been supporting for years with advice and arms, they'll find us there, by the numbers and full of resolve.

SIHANOUK: Then, I'll forget that I love music and hate war, guns, armor, medals, blood, explosions. And above all death. Yes! I'll forget that I hate sadness and death. And beginning tomorrow we'll attack!

PENN NOUTH: My god! Who could block this distressing marriage between the King of the Monkeys and the Crocodile now?

[Enter Ong Meang.]

ONG MEANG: Your Highness, Mr. Khieu Samphan, envoy of the

---

[32] English in the original. TR

Khmer Resistance of the Interior, earnestly requests the honor of delivering a most urgent and most important message to you.

SIHANOUK: Do you hear, Penn Nouth?! Khieu Samphan! The one who was kicked out, the insolent one, the red cock, the missing person! Khieu Samphan comes to see Sihanouk in Peking! Well, Ladies and Gentlemen, it seems like lightning we reached our history's next chapter! Go, my tiger! At a gallop! Onward, Sihanouk. Faster! Faster!

[to Pham Van Dong who makes as if to leave.]

Stay, stay, distinguished friend. Aren't we all brothers now?

[Enter Khieu Samphan and Hou Youn.]

KHIEU SAMPHAN: Your Highness! August President!

SIHANOUK: My dear Khieu Samphan! And Mr. Hou Youn too! What a nice surprise! But what a day! Everyone's back! And they said I had you assassinated! Yes, yes, Mr. Pham Van Dong. Isn't that right, Penn Nouth? When was it you disappeared? It's been three years? Four years?

KHIEU SAMPHAN: Three years, Your Highness.

SIHANOUK: Three years! A century! They were believed dead and suddenly there they are! You were well hidden, no? You're fantastic! How did you get here?

KHIEU SAMPHAN: Your Highness, as soon as we had the joy of hearing your voice broadcast this admirable call over Radio Peking to unite our nation against the traitors from Phnom Penh and American imperialism, our Command decided by unanimous acclamation to provide you with our complete and loyal support, unreservedly as soon as possible.

SIHANOUK: Unreservedly? But you know, my dear compatriots, that Sihanouk isn't a Communist. I'll never be one, nor a Maoist. However, I admire the kind President of this admirable China. I admire and love him. The way I love and admire the famous Maria Callas. You see, my wife and I never missed a single opportunity to go hear her at the Opera. What power! What grandeur! I adore her. I'd applaud her vehemently, standing there until I was exhausted, but afterward, when I came back home with my wife for supper, I didn't bring Callas with me! Ah! Now, with Mao, it's just the same, I don't want any part of him in my house! I'd rather let you know in advance! Sihanouk does not have a Chinese mind.

KHIEU SAMPHAN: We've never committed a sin against His Royal Highness the Prince Norodom Sihanouk. We bring our complete and unconditional support to the Prince and rightful leader of our country.

SIHANOUK: Let's be quite clear. Are you certain that as Communists you can also be monarchists?
Because I'll tell you right off that, after my return to our capital thanks to the union of all our Khmer forces and to the support of our Vietnamese friends, I shall establish a socialist regime Sihanouk-style—moderate, Buddhist and monarchist. So, let's have a clear understanding of these words.

KHIEU SAMPHAN: Everything's clear, Your Highness. We rally to you unconditionally, without ulterior motives.

SIHANOUK: But why?

KHIEU SAMPHAN: Out of patriotism. We hate the Americans and their Lon Nol-ian lackeys. Above all we love the whole Khmer people, for whom we are ready to sacrifice everything. Now the people love Your Highness Papa. Would we oppose the people's needs? No, we will serve them. And we'll assure them of the happiness they deserve. When the people see that the Prince is with us and that the Khmer Rouge are with the Prince, the news will be exhilarating for everyone.

PENN NOUTH: [aside, to Sihanouk] Clearly, they need you desperately to win over the peasants' hearts.

SIHANOUK: [aside, to Penn Nouth] I gathered that. [to Khieu Samphan] In short, you're adopting my program entirely and you renounce your own?

KHIEU SAMPHAN: Your Highness, we've established that our country isn't ripe for communism.

PENN NOUTH: Is that so?

KHIEU SAMPHAN: Your program is therefore at present the best one possible for our people.

SIHANOUK: OK. Good. Ph! Good . . . that's very good. Allow me. *[He takes Penn Nouth aside.]* Well, for the moment, I can't see any other any real barriers to the immediate constitution of a government of joint unification. What do you think, Penn Nouth?

PENN NOUTH: I don't see any concrete obstacles. Your Highness. I have only my distrust which has as many eyes as a peacock's tail. These Khmer Rouge . . .

SIHANOUK: They're reds but they're Khmers. And frankly, Penn Nouth, Lon Nol stole my entire army from me, so this is all I have left. If I must be surrounded by reds, I'd prefer that they aren't all Vietnamese.

PENN NOUTH: Of course, I know, they're Khmers, but they're reds all the same. I'll have to keep all my eyes open. And you'll have to move like lightning, Your Highness, so that these gentlemen don't have the time to use your popularity to swell their own ranks.

SIHANOUK: It's true that it will be a question of speed.
Oh Triple Jewel, give me the feet of a hare or the wings of an eagle, for the prophetic journey begins in five minutes!
Ah! So, Gentlemen, I see that everything encourages me to ratify my Royal Government of National Union here and now. Gentlemen, my former ministers, will you agree to be my new ministers? Mr. Khieu Samphan?

KHIEU SAMPHAN: Your Highness, I accept with excitement and pride.

SIHANOUK: And Mr. Hou Youn as well?

HOU YOUN: It's a great honor for me to be able to serve Your Highness and our people faithfully.

SIHANOUK: For my part, I'm also designating His Excellency Mr. Chea San, along with three other loyal companions during my exile. And naturally, Mr. Penn Nouth will as usual, if the gods are favorable to me, be our Prime Minister.

KHIEU SAMPHAN: *[to Penn Nouth]* My respectful congratulations, Your Highness.

SIHANOUK: We'll hold our first council tomorrow morning. The alliance with Vietnam and the plans for war will be the topics. Does that suit you?

KHIEU SAMPHAN: Tomorrow? Splendid, Your Highness. *[He takes Sihanouk aside.]*
We'll have a lot to say, Your Highness, about the alliance with Vietnam. Hanoi is only helping us in order to have an opportunity to steal our victory and our country from us.

SIHANOUK: No, no, no! We'll talk about it tomorrow, at ten o'clock.

KHIEU SAMPHAN: Tomorrow at ten o'clock. We'll be there, Your Highness!

SIHANOUK: But for the following council, it would be better for it to take place not on Chinese soil but on our own sacred ground.

KHIEU SAMPHAN: We shall report this day of historic union with pride to our Resistance's commander, comrade Pol Pot.

SIHANOUK: You may go, Gentlemen. Until tomorrow, my dear ghost ministers who have come back from the dead. Until tomorrow.

KHIEU SAMPHAN: Until tomorrow, Your Highness. And with joy, Your Highness!

HOU YOUN: Until tomorrow, Your Highness.

[Khieu Samphan and Hou Youn exit.]

SIHANOUK: But who is he, this Pol Pot?

PHAM VAN DONG: Your Highness, I respectfully take my leave. Time is burning up for Vietnam. Our war awaits me.

SIHANOUK: We'll see each other again soon?

PHAM VAN DONG: Will you do us the honor of coming to Hanoi, Your Highness?

SIHANOUK: With joy. *[Pham Van Dong exits.]*
With Jo-y. This word sounds today like a bell without a clapper. *[King Suramarit enters on his bike.]*

SURAMARIT: Cuckoo!

SIHANOUK: Venerable Papa! Great King, cherished among all living and dead! I'd have sworn that I would see you in this early winter of my life. I said to myself: I'm sure that beloved papa will arrange to find his son wherever he lies under the chilling moon.
Oh! My father, you look exhausted. What an interminable journey, from Phnom Penh to Peking! How did you do it?

SURAMARIT: By bike. Through our forests. I managed.

SIHANOUK: By bike!? My father, by bike?

SURAMARIT: A very good bike that two ladies from Phnom Penh lent me.

SIHANOUK: You awaken the highest hopes in me! If Your Majesty could come up by bike and on foot from Phnom Penh to Peking, why wouldn't it be possible to go from Peking to Phnom Penh under my own steam?

SURAMARIT: Indeed, why not?

SIHANOUK: My father, you're speaking so coldly, like a stone. Are you angry?

SURAMARIT: Angry? Not at all!

SIHANOUK: You are too, you're angry and you don't love me.

SURAMARIT: What I don't love are the people around you here. I travel through the whole world, mountains, rivers, forests full of tigers and guns to answer your prayer. And believe me, it wasn't easy. I collapsed ten times, and I collapsed from hunger and from thirst too. I arrive in this cold, treeless city where I'd never been caught dead when I was alive, walking streets that are so sad it's like being amongst skeleton bones, but, well, I'm looking forward to giving you a happy surprise. I reach the front of these foreigners' horrible house—it looks like a giant-size bar of soap. What was I saying? Yes, a house that seems to say to the passerby, "Don't come in or I'll bite you." I go in anyway, hear your voice ringing out like your saxophone, and find you at last. I find my son, Prince Sihanouk, the last vessel of our ancient sperm, surrounded by a crowd of Chinese and Vietnamese, and by these depraved Khmers you call Rouge. No, I'm not angry! But if I could have foreseen this, I wouldn't have exhausted myself coming to your rescue. Old fool that I am! You don't need me now that you have the Chinese and the Vietnamese to boot.

So, my poor child, you've come to this? Exiled and in the arms of our most hereditary enemies?

SIHANOUK: I have, and I don't regret it. Father, I have no other ground to plant my feet on any more. You would have thought, after my overthrow, that the entire world had become one-armed. When I knocked on doors, not one response, not a hand, except from China and, after that, on Chou En-lai's orders, from Vietnam, the Peking's powerful vassal.

SURAMARIT: But what's with the pajamas?

SIHANOUK: It is a polite gesture I'm making toward his eminence Chairman Mao.

SURAMARIT: Beware of this type of politeness. If you wear it for too long, it will turn your skin red right down to the bone marrow and poison your membranes. And, now, this fancy government you were announcing so joyously when I arrived, I don't like it at all. And I noticed that it isn't exactly to my dear Penn Nouth's taste either. I pity him, being head of a pack of red dogs!

SIHANOUK: We're rational subjects of fate. Our alliances are necessary but not eternal.

For that reason I embrace our Vietnamese friends with a very sincere heart, for, if they're willing in a few days time they can carry me triumphantly to the gates of Phnom Penh.

SURAMARIT: Well, then, what are you waiting for, you and Penn Nouth?

SIHANOUK: I can tell you the secret: we're hoping for a response from the West. If only I could avoid being obligated to the Communists! I really would have preferred to return to our city standing in a black Citroën. Or even a Cadillac.

SURAMARIT: This isn't the moment to be acting hoity-toity! Go back riding whatever you like. An elephant, a Vietnamese tank, or a bike, but get back immediately!

[Ong Meang enters.]

ONG MEANG: Mr. Manac'h, Ambassador to France in Peking, asks to see you, Your Highness.

SIHANOUK: Ah! Here finally our prophetic messenger. Pray for your son, beloved father.

[Manac'h enters.]

I beg you, Mr. Manac'h, speak frankly, sincerely and without evasiveness. Tell me the worst but in plain language. Were you able to vouch in favor of Sihanouk with the Americans? No?

MANAC'H: It's an absolutely out-and-out no, Your Highness. Washington did not deign to receive a single missive, on France's part, which was in your favor. Your name seems to act like an emetic. It's barely pronounced in the vicinity of the Oval Office than it's spit back up. Shall I stop?

SURAMARIT: No, continue! So that he learns the whole lesson!

SIHANOUK: No, continue, so that I learn the whole lesson.

MANAC'H: I've therefore gotten nothing. Security Advisor Kissinger claims the Prince is old hat. He's convinced you don't represent anyone but yourself.

PENN NOUTH: But he cannot be unaware of China's friendship for His Highness!

MANAC'H: Nothing proves that the Chinese really take the Prince seriously, he said. Advisor Kissinger will not meet with you. I beg your pardon, Your Highness.

SIHANOUK: And in your country, dear friend? At the Elysée Palace, what are the rumors?

MANAC'H: France does not want to break diplomatic relations with Phnom Penh.

SURAMARIT: What! What about your great friend, General de Gaulle, whom you love so much?!

SIHANOUK: It's Pompidou in Paris. Great friends leave us and their shadows are scant.

MANAC'H: So in the opinion of this France, you know, your friend Manac'h has even less credit than certain big rubber planters whose interests you've upset and who have the ear of President Pompidou and his friends.

PENN NOUTH: Helping Lon Nol! I would never have believed that France could be as stupid as America!

SIHANOUK: Ah! well, that's it. Our fight will be military and asiatic. I'll return to Cambodia. The Head of the Royal Government of the National Union must be found right alongside those who are fighting the traitors on their territory. Lord Penn Nouth, do you feel ready to accompany me into the zones occupied by Khmer Rouge?

PENN NOUTH: Your Highness, if I must die, I would prefer that it to be in one of our straw huts than in a Chinese hospital.

SIHANOUK: Captain Ong Meang, would you beseech all our Ministers of the Front, Messrs. Khieu Samphan, Hou Youn, Ieng Sary, and all the rest . . . , to call on me immediately. I want to choose the seat of our General Headquarters with them.

[Ong Meang exits.]

[to Manac'h] Your Excellency, I must leave you. We're entering a dangerous and arduous epoch.

MANAC'H: This summer I'll go to the little church of Pont-Aven and there I'll think about you, and about you, Your Excellency, with all my heart.

SURAMARIT: Thank you, thank you!

SIHANOUK: Thoughts of friendship are the most powerful prayers. Friend, farewell.

[Manac'h exits.]

What would you say to a government in Takeo, Penn Nouth? The struggling government in Takeo? Huh?

PENN NOUTH: I would prefer Kratie, Your Highness, its situation is nearer the heart of our country.

[Ong Meang reenters.]

ONG MEANG: Gone! Gone! Your Highness! Oh! Your Highness! They've left!

PENN NOUTH: Left?

SIHANOUK: Left?

SURAMARIT: This alliance is starting out well!

ONG MEANG: Oh! Your Highness, they were leaving, I swear it. I found them in front of the door. A shame, a rage swelled my heart, Your Highness. Well I took the liberty, excuse me, I took the liberty . . .

SIHANOUK: Liberty? Speak, dear Meang, speak.

ONG MEANG: I protested, Your Highness. I dared. I shouted: you don't have the right to go without asking to take leave of Your Highness, before the first council of ministers. It's illegal! It's dishonorable! I said that, Your Highness. And I said that I was opposed to such an unseemly action. I took the liberty, Your Highness.

PENN NOUTH: And so? What did they answer?

ONG MEANG: Lies. Khieu Samphan elaborated to me (you know how he talks) about how there are those who must fight in the heart of the people, and those who need to represent this fight abroad. But I, barring the door to them, I said that we'd take to the road tomorrow, and I ask your pardon for my audacity, Your Highness.

SIHANOUK: You did well! Your heart spoke for me.

PENN NOUTH: And so? And so?

ONG MEANG: So, they formally oppose it. They claim they fear for your life. And to make moving impossible on your part, they left the detestable Ieng Sary in Peking, this crocodile-hound, with a mission to dog your heels!
And all these ignominies were offered to me wrapped in politeness and sweetness, as if I was so stupid as to be hoodwinked. They don't wish you well, Your Highness, they don't fear for your life. They fear for their shabby prestige, which your presence would diminish.

SIHANOUK: Then I'm supposed to be the flag? I'm supposed to wave? Not even that! I'm supposed to be the postman.

[Suramarit sobs.]

ONG MEANG: *[to Sihanouk]* I beg you, Your Highness, don't cry. I beg you. I'll kill them, one day, I'll kill them.

SIHANOUK: My dear Meang! I won't shed a single tear on their account. And you will not kill them. The Khmer Rouge and us, we are not of the same civilization. But they're fighting our enemies all the same.

PENN NOUTH: Your highness, it's a great honor for me to be at your side in this rude epoch.

ONG MEANG: Wherever you go, Your Highness, on this Earth or another, I shall stay with you.

SIHANOUK: My Cambodia is moving away. Standing on the pier, I watch it moving out of view. The world grows immense.
I am becoming so small.
No, no! I shall overtake them!

[They exit.]

PART 2, ACT 1, SCENE 3[33]

[Washington. Kissinger and Watts enter.]

KISSINGER: Your eyes tell me that you haven't slept much!

WATTS: You asked me last night to look over the plans arranged by General Abrams for the invasion of Cambodia and to go over what happened yesterday morning in your staff meeting. I spent the night doing that. I've come to give you an account.

KISSINGER: I knew that you'd manage to do your job, even though the time was rather short.

WATTS: The invasion is set for tomorrow, then?

KISSINGER: Absolutely.

WATTS: Then here's my report. You could say that the Abrams's plan is brilliant in its pithiness. It contains no indispensable information, no instructions, in other words—no plan. No one knows

---

[33]Due to length, this scene does not appear in the performance. AU

how long the border is dividing Cambodia from Vietnam. No one has ever counted how many bridges cross the river from Cambodia. No one knows the number of villages situated in the zones that will be mopped up tomorrow.

KISSINGER: Given the urgency and the necessity for secrecy, the General hasn't had time to go into all of the details.

WATTS: No coordination with Lon Nol's army is provided for.

KISSINGER: This plan concerns an American-Saigonese attack.

WATTS: No one has sent an envoy to Phnom Penh to study the situation firsthand. No one knows what's happening in the western provinces. No one has any information on the movements of the communist troops in the interior of Cambodia. Tomorrow we're going to launch an aerial attack on Cambodia, but since our pilots don't have any precise maps of the country, they're going to be bombing with their eyes shut.

KISSINGER: I'll make a note of your remarks and send them forward.

WATTS: Note them, then. To sum up, we know nothing, we see nothing, and we're invading tomorrow. And you're asking me to write a one-page report on the consequences of this operation? Why not a one-word report?! Why not just do it in one word?

KISSINGER: Are you making a scene?[34]

WATTS: In one word, I resign.

KISSINGER: Your attitude mirrors the cowardice that consumes the entire pretentious East Coast establishment! Don't touch me!

WATTS: Until now, Sir, I thought the Security Advisor was ambitious, meticulous. But this evening, studying this plan, I saw you, as indifferent as a tyrant, committing a crime, a truly great crime which goes beyond the human gaze to become invisible. And you're committing it, right this moment, before my very eyes. You're in the process of assassinating Cambodia, you and this mad ventriloquist who governs us!

---

[34]See Shawcross, *Sideshow*, pp. 141–42, for some of the actual speeches by Kissinger. TR

KISSINGER: Don't lay a hand on me!

WATTS: You disgust me, Mr. Advisor!

[Watts exits.]

KISSINGER: My, such violence! Such violence! Why such violence?! *[He exits.]*

PART 2, ACT 1, SCENE 4[35]

[Phnom Penh. General Lon Nol enters, half-paralyzed; his servants.]

LON NOL:
> Eye of Buddha, you are on me
> Buddhaya namo, mo Buddhaya na.

[Captain In Sophat enters.]

IN SOPHAT: Your Excellency, General Seksaket, Governor of the Kompong Cham province.

LON NOL: Have him come in.

[In Sophat exits.]

> If the news is good, I'll say your name a hundred and eight times morning and night for a month. *[General Seksaket enters.]*

SEKSAKET: General, bad news!

LON NOL: Again!

SEKSAKET: A peasant uprising!

LON NOL: Another? Where?

SEKSAKET: My area, in Kompong Cham. Yesterday, at least fifty thousand rebels poured down on us from the west, from the north, from the east, from all sides, raging like flooding rivers. They're bearing down along three routes, in surging, fearsome columns. They're calling for Sihanouk. Intoxicated by rebellion, they're stopping traffic and forcibly handing out photos of Sihanouk.

---

[35] Due to length, this scene does not appear in the performance. AU

They reach the village shouting "Long live Sihanouk!" over-
whelming our feeble forces with their fierce numbers. The soldiers,
their rifles lowered, let the waves pass and in truth, unable to resist the current themselves, they let themselves be swept along,
shouting "Long live Sihanouk!"

LON NOL: And you, Sir, what did you do?

SEKSAKET: Well, as for me, seeing the furious wave growing minute
by minute, I retreated to my residence, organized my counterattack, and gave orders to my aide-de-camp.

LON NOL: Enough! Did you suppress them—yes or no?

SEKSAKET: Yes, yes.

LON NOL: Well, hop, hop! Let's get to your counterattack.

SEKSAKET: I'm getting to that, I'm getting there. Oh, My Buddha, if
only it were tomorrow! Meanwhile a hundred men under the
command of the man named Hou Youn scaled the pediment of the
Palace of Justice, others were busy pillaging, and I saw them from
my windows painting the word INJUSTICE in giant letters.

LON NOL: Hou Youn? Did you say Hou Youn?

SEKSAKET: Hou Youn, the former minister, the red, Your Honor. It
was he who painted the word INJUSTICE his own color.

LON NOL: Hou Youn? But he's dead. You know perfectly well! Executed, decapitated, buried, three years ago by Sihanouk's police.

SEKSAKET: I know. But I saw him with my own eyes and recognized
him.

LON NOL: And you're sure he was alive?

SEKSAKET: He was alive and he still is!

LON NOL: He still is? Congratulations, General. And now, the repression, when are we getting to that part?

SEKSAKET: I'm getting there, Your Excellency.
I waited for them, I told you. The troops were deployed around
my residence. My men raised their cannons. There they were,
these savages, armed with their toothpicks, stupidly heading for

their death. Three volleys. A brief burst of machine-gun fire. And it's F, I, N, ISHED!
Immediately the crowd disappears, dispersed by our cannonades like flowers by a great wind. There's nothing left in front of my door except cadavers.

LON NOL: How many?

SEKSAKET: A mere hundred. Well it's 6 P.M., Your Excellency; 6 P.M. alas! March 26, 1970.

LON NOL: What this "6 P.M., alas"?

SEKSAKET: 6 P.M. at that very instant, Your Excellency, at the very moment—6 P.M. precisely, at the airport. . . . No one has prepared you, then, Your Excellency? No one's told you anything?

LON NOL: Prepared? At the airport? Sihanouk in Kompong Cham? That's impossible! Don't tell me that! Such shocking news! I don't believe you!

SEKSAKET: Sihanouk? Why, no, no, Your Excellency. It was the anti-Sihanouk Deputies, your faithful companions, Mr. Sos Suon and Mr. Kim Phon as well as your extremely loyal and intrepid brother, the commander Lon Nil, who landed at 6 P.M., alas! at the airport in Kompong Cham.
Hardly had they time to set foot on the ground than they were instantly covered by a cloud of peasants under whose weight all three succumbed like a tree covered with locusts.

LON NOL: My brother! My brother! They . . . ? He is . . . ?

SEKSAKET: He is no more. In the blink of an eye, the wild beasts massacred him. And then, inspired by cruel superstition, the murderers tore out his liver and carried the tragic trophy to a Chinese chef. . . . There's nothing left of Lon Nil on this impure earth. But he didn't have time to suffer. Your Excellency. It was over in the blink of the eye.

LON NOL: And you? You're still living? You aren't dead?

SEKSAKET: It's by chance, Your Excellency, by chance . . . by mischance . . . I am sorry, Your Excellency, this is a loss for us all . . .

LON NOL: Don't try to comfort me, idiot! May Lon Nol draw divine
inspiration from his sorrow.

This crime is an atrocious homage to the greatness of my house.
What these bestial and jealous men hoped to acquire was my family's magical powers. But my brother's blazing force will henceforth dwell in me. I already feel his young maliciousness spreading
through my veins. My brother lives again in me! There he is,
breathing in my chest. Oh! There he is, my dearest! Now I will respond as befits my redoubled magnitude.

Governor-General, my air force will quickly conclude what you've
begun middlingly. That's not all. We shall blame all these events
upon a few well-chosen culprits. Who stirred up these peasants?

SEKSAKET: They heard Sihanouk calling them over the radio; you
know, Sihanouk has supporters high up in the police, even in your
army.

LON NOL: False!

First—No one listens to the radio.

Second—No one in this country is loyal to Sihanouk.

Third—These uprisings were planned and organized by the Vietcong.

It's the Vietnamese communists who are looking to ruin us. Are
you following me? What did I just say?

SEKSAKET: It's the Communists . . .

LON NOL: Thus, it's the Vietnamese. You follow me?

SEKSAKET: Vietnamese, Your Excellency.

LON NOL: From tomorrow on, therefore, I'm appealing to my Buddhist compatriots. I'll denounce the 400,000 Vietnamese enemies,
disguised as fishermen, mechanics, and Cambodian villagers who
live among us and infest our skin. A religious war will explode
this week. Besides, it's already raging in your province. According
to predictions established long ago, whenever there's a war, the
following events will occur: The appearance, in a gold or silver
palace, of a savior whose name begins with an L. Bloody battles
between infidels and nonbelievers, and the extermination of the
impious. Mysterious flight and disappearance of an infamous
prince, the appearance of comets.

133

I will profit from this occasion to announce that during this war martial law will maintain order throughout country. Anyone caught in the act of putting their ear to a transistor radio, with the sound turned down to the point that police one meter away cannot hear it, will be executed for high treason. After my police and my army have spilled the last drop of impious communist and Vietnamese blood, the holy war will end. I wish to reflect upon these predictions in religious solitude, Mr. Governor . . .

SEKSAKET: Your Excellency.
Oh Buddha, it wasn't as bad as I had feared.

[Seksaket exits.]

LON NOL: Once this purification of our land is accomplished we will take great strides in History. At the start of next month, I'll proclaim the Republic and promote myself to four-star General, to please you, my brother. I'll also have to grant Sirik Matak three stars. It's a shame, but it's hard to do otherwise, no?
And finally, we'll condemn Sihanouk to death for high treason. *[Lon Nol exits.]*

PART 2, ACT 1, SCENE 5[36]

[Phnom Penh. The Royal Palace. Queen Kossomak and Mom Savay enter.]

QUEEN KOSSOMAK: What day is it?

MOM SAVAY: May second, dear Queen.

QUEEN KOSSOMAK: This is the story of a queen who waits for the one she loves, the son of her breasts, the only son of her heart. A hundred suns rise. A hundred suns of ashes. The son doesn't come. Impelled by love's hunger, the Queen rises. No one. Clinging to the window, year after year, the Queen looks out. Her Palace is called a tomb. Her country is called banishment. She lifts her head. The sky has become a slab of shadows which darkens, darkens, darkens. And there, on the ground, I summon the sky to fall down on me and to bury me. What day is it?

---

[36]For reasons of length this scene does not appear in the production. AU

MOM SAVAY: May second, dear Queen.

QUEEN KOSSOMAK: Nothing comes. Not rain, not life, not death, not my son. No letter. Not a sign. The most miserable peasant is less miserable than the prisoner Queen.

[Captain Nissai enters.]

MOM SAVAY: At last! At last! At long last! The messenger! Well?

THE CAPTAIN: *[to Mom Savay]* Nothing.

MOM SAVAY: *[to the Captain]* Lie to her, out of pity. She no longer eats, she no longer sleeps, she's going to die . . . ! Captain, my dearest . . .

THE CAPTAIN: Venerable Majesty.

QUEEN KOSSOMAK: You've nothing for me.

THE CAPTAIN: Great beloved Queen, I have nothing yet, but I will, I'm hopeful, I'm . . .

QUEEN KOSSOMAK: Then go, brave messenger, don't hold me back.

THE CAPTAIN: Majesty, no, listen to me, I've succeeded, almost, in establishing contact.

MOM SAVAY: What contact? How's that? Speak, dear Nissai. Through the French Ambassador?

THE CAPTAIN: Yes, See! Through the French Ambassador. We'll soon have news of Your Highness, Your Majesty.

MOM SAVAY: My adorable one, we're going to have news, our Nissai promises us.

THE CAPTAIN: Yes, yes, I promise you. I beg you grant me a little bit more time, Your Majesty, I've had to overcome so many obstacles. First, I can only leave the Palace once a month. And then, the country, alas, being upside down, you can't find anyone.

MOM SAVAY: The country?

THE CAPTAIN: The country is fleeing madly in all directions, trying to take flight from the horrible mayhem.

QUEEN KOSSOMAK: Mayhem?

THE CAPTAIN: They're cutting the throats of poor Cambodian Vietnam, by whole villages. The Mekong with loathing has become a terrible tomb. With blind cruelty, Lon Nol's soldiers are murdering our fishermen, our mechanics, our garage keepers.

MOM SAVAY: Enough! Enough! Quiet! Spare poor human nature. Enough misery!! However gently a pagoda stands open for the people who crowd in, it can not take in more people than its walls can hold! You'll break her heart.

QUEEN KOSSOMAK: There's no news? Nothing comes. Not rain. Not a letter. Not a tear. The spring is dried up. My heart suffocates like a fish in a bowl.
No more patience, no more hope, no more love. No longer the strength to suffer.
There's no more room in my withered heart except for bitter and cruel necessity. I want my son. I want my son. I want him. I no longer love. I no longer hate. I no longer am.
I need. I want Sihanouk.

MOM SAVAY: Everything will come back, my dear beloved Queen, everything, love, pity, appetite, delicious life, as soon as you see His Highness again.

QUEEN KOSSOMAK: Poor little Savay, last tenderness. The strings of my heart are broken. Divine certainty itself could no longer hold me back. If you love me, let me pass away, my love.
Deep in my heart there's a door that opens onto nothing. My soul has arrived before this door. It wants to go on through it.
Oh! It wants to be delivered. Don't call me back, dear sister.

MOM SAVAY:
    Help, Buddha! Give me strength!
    What a struggle not to hold on to her!
    Ah! She's closing her eyes!
    Do you want me to draw the curtains, my love?

QUEEN KOSSOMAK: Yes.
    Savay, may I keep my eyes closed?

[Queen dies.]

MOM SAVAY:

> Sleep, my only love,
> Sleep peacefully, I'll watch over.

THE CAPTAIN: Her Majesty our mother?! August perfect mother!

MOM SAVAY: Go away for a bit, Captain. Let us rest.

> She was named Her Majesty, excellent and happy Princess
> Kossomak. Where is she?
> She goes to reign in the Other Country.
> Her noble severity and tender spite will now bathe the
> immortal dead in a royal light. Dead.
> Knees. My knees. Your absence before my knees. I'm jealous of
> the dead. O Kossomak, adorable heart.
> When you've arrived on the other side of the river, finally free
> and powerful and everywhere at once, call me soon, call me.

[The Captain and Mom Savay exit carrying the Queen.]

PART 2, ACT 2, SCENE 1

[Phnom Penh. Madame Lamné enters.]

MADAME LAMNÉ: Oh, great Saint Anthony! I beg you, bring back my
sister, Madame Khieu Samnol, to here, Number 4, Hibiscus Street,
where I'll die before she gets back, and knowing her as I do, I
know she wouldn't be able to endure this great sorrow of having
lost her poor sister, Madame Lamné. Then we'd both be disheart-
ened and without cure. Oh, my God, how you take pity on me because you know I'm Vietnamese, and it's still the same, I'm afraid,
and I can't go running around all over the district, to look for my
beloved Samnol in the streets or at the neighbor's, because of this
damned curfew which is robbing me of my legs just when I want
to go out.

[Khieu Samnol and Yukanthor enter.]

MADAME LAMNÉ: Well, well?! Where were you?! Huh?! Do you
know what time it is?

KHIEU SAMNOL: I was at the Pagoda. I'm late. But it was worth the
trouble.

MADAME LAMNÉ: It was worth the trouble?! What can be worth the trouble of causing your adored sister to die who thought you were dead and maybe even bombarded by bombs?

KHIEU SAMNOL: Sit down my son. This will blow over in five minutes. She's always like this since the curfew started, the poor dear, she even sees cutthroats in her cooking-pot.

MADAME LAMNÉ: And so you were at the Pagoda and you were at the Pagoda? Well?

KHIEU SAMNOL: Well, I was at the Pagoda and I was at the Pagoda.

MADAME LAMNÉ: And me, staying home, and I might as well just die, huh?

KHIEU SAMNOL: Oh, my, my! You're impossible tonight just because I am giving you such a pleasure. Okay.

MADAME LAMNÉ: Such a pleasure.

KHIEU SAMNOL: Don't think she doesn't see you, my son. She sees you but she's pretending not to in order to act smart. Yes, the very evening I bring you a present, you go and make a scene like never before!

MADAME LAMNÉ: And what gift, my sister, are you giving me?

KHIEU SAMNOL: [indicating Yukanthor] This one here.

MADAME LAMNÉ: What? Him? Ah! So now an unexpected guest whom we have nothing to offer to eat is called a gift?

KHIEU SAMNOL: This is not a guest. This is our son.

MADAME LAMNÉ: Our son? Ouch! Ouch! Wait. That takes the cake. What do you mean our son? Which one?

KHIEU SAMNOL: Ah! well, my dear, *that's* what happened to me at the Pagoda. He's a gift from His Majesty our Uncle, who was waiting for us all day already poor thing, because Our Uncle had the wrong address on the letter.

MADAME LAMNÉ: What letter? Who was waiting for us?

KHIEU SAMNOL: Let me at least start to explain it to you, otherwise I'll never finish! Well. Our Venerable Uncle thought of writing us to send us a letter and an extraordinary gift! So I read: "My dear nieces, in finding this single child the only one still living among all the dead who henceforward populate the unfortunate village of Mimot which was wiped out by American bombs, I immediately thought of you, alone and without protection, and without a bike, in the big city of Phnom Penh. Therefore I'm sending you by means of this letter this son whom I adopted. He has no one else on earth except you and me, but I am no one. But now that you've welcomed and adopted him, I'm more at peace. He'll do the shopping instead of your bike. He'll protect Madame Lamné against bandits and also, thanks to both your delicious cooking, he won't fail to grow up and become a hero worthy of both his lost and his adopted parents.

That's all the time I have to write you, but it doesn't matter, because you see even while I'm traveling along I am thinking of you. Your dear departed Suramarit, who understands your heart."

MADAME LAMNÉ: Ah! How beautiful that was! How beautiful that was! How finely His Majesty thinks!

KHIEU SAMNOL: Well, do you agree to accept the gift?

MADAME LAMNÉ: Why, of course! I'm sorry. It's staggering!! I say, a son! At our age! And coming from His Majesty! That's quite a miracle!

KHIEU SAMNOL: To me the miracle is that he wasn't killed along with the rest of the village and that he managed to stay alive, poor little waif.

MADAME LAMNÉ: That's what I was saying. And our son, my cherished sister, what's his name?

[American bombers pass above Phnom Penh.]

YUKANTHOR: I want to kill an American!

KHIEU SAMNOL: Ah! That's his line. All the way from the Pagoda that's the only thing he's said. Stop wriggling around, my son. Are you hungry? He's hungry. My dear, will you make us a bit of rice for the little fellow?

MADAME LAMNÉ: Right away. I'll even put in some sugar, no?

KHIEU SAMNOL: Sugar? But we don't have any more?!

MADAME LAMNÉ: I kept a little pound aside for Jesus and Mary.

KHIEU SAMNOL: Ah! You kept a little for Jesus! Good then you'll make a cake for our son and us.

MADAME LAMNÉ: But, so what shall we call him, my dear sister? Because I've thought of Anthony-Savior, maybe.

KHIEU SAMNOL: Anthony-Savior?!!!! Don't even dream of such a thing!! For me, I think his name should be Yukanthor, like our august Uncle's little cousin. You remember him, Madame Lamné, such a very pretty prince, brave and polite. I'm sure your saints would agree.

MADAME LAMNÉ: Oh! my yes, my yes, he's Prince Yukanthor to a tee. And say, my dear, while waiting for the rice, would you reread me His Majesty's letter?

KHIEU SAMNOL: I can recite it if you'd like. Frankly, I've read it so often I can say it by heart now:
"My dear nieces, in finding this single child the only one still living among all the dead who henceforward populate the unfortunate village . . ."

[They exit followed by Yukanthor. The bombings are heard again.]

PART 2, ACT 2, SCENE 2

[Phnom Penh. Sirik Matak and Cheng Heng enter.]

SIRIK MATAK: President of the National Assembly, Lon Nol must step down.

CHENG HENG: It's true that since his illness Lon Nol has neither the physical strength nor the nerve necessary to be head of a state so gravely menaced.

SIRIK MATAK: His paralysis paralyzes us. We're in great danger. Yesterday I saw our country's enemy calmly walking over our breast. Meeting no resistance, as if our country were their own garden, the Vietcong soldiers were able to get all the way to our airport, right up close to our heart. Even while the bombs were exploding, the President didn't budge. I asked him ten times: "What are we going to do? Give orders!" No answer. He was waiting for advice from the heavens. The attack lasted five hours. We no longer have a single plane. The fate of our country is at the mercy of a cloud. The day before yesterday he was deaf, today he's blind: I showed him on the map, and he still couldn't fathom our army's frightening retreat. We're holding only Phnom Penh and some tiny thongs of land across the country: All the rest is blood red. It all seemed sky blue to him. Tomorrow the enemy will be knocking at the door of our heart and he'll just let them in.

CHENG HENG: We should never have made him a Marshal. At noon, he acted as though he'd resign yet he came hobbling back this same evening.

SIRIK MATAK: He won't let go of anything unless we force him to; not one dollar, not one function, not the tiniest bit of power, not even Her Majesty Queen Kossomak whom he's detaining arbitrarily.

[Lon Nol enters, accompanied by In Sophat and his servants.]

LON NOL: What are you doing whispering in front of my door? I won't leave, I won't resign, I'm staying. If it's my departure you're discussing, you heard me.

SIRIK MATAK: Mr. Marshal, I was speaking to the President of the National Assembly about Her Majesty Queen Kossomak's departure. Since her imprisonment, Her Majesty declines, you know. The Republic doesn't need a queen. Let Her Majesty emigrate, that would be gracious . . .

LON NOL: I'll never let her leave. She cast a spell over me. She paralyzed me, she nailed down my limbs, so why would I let her stir about? As long as she won't give me back the use of my legs, there'll be no talk of your aunt. Mr. Prince. Let's go on. What was I saying? Have you readied our capital for the Kompong Thom victory celebration? My lovely victory!

CHENG HENG: Everything's ready. The pyrotechnicians are only waiting for your orders to fire, and the dancers await only your august presence to dance.

LON NOL: What are you whispering about? Is it not my victory? A battle I've been waging from my bed for more than a month now, hour by hour? And even step by step?

CHENG HENG: He can hear what we're thinking.

LON NOL: Beware, gentlemen, I hear everything you're thinking.

CHENG HENG: We're only missing Colonel Um Savuth, the one who led your men to Kompong Thom.

LON NOL: Oh! *My* Colonel! There's my man! Someone who understands me, who respects me and follows the movements of my inspiration to the utmost. He hears my ideas from five hundred kilometers off. He only has one ear but it's worth ten even all listening to me.

SIRIK MATAK: He's paid to do that!

[*Um Savuth enters. He only has one ear left and one arm, and he's drunk.*]

LON NOL: My Um Savuth! My dear one! My left arm!

UM SAVUTH: Your Majesty! I'm drunk with emotion!! Colonel.

IN SOPHAT: Not "Your Majesty," Your Excellency, Colonel. Your Excellency, I think the Colonel is a little giddy.

UM SAVUTH: I'm drunk with war, Your Excellent Majesty. The day was rough, rough, rough. It's still going on. But passionately. Such an expedition! What an experience! I'm overwhelmed! Advancing in rows, quiet as ants in transhumance! Traveling this entire route by the glimmer alone of your star, without stumbling over the shadow of the enemy's gun shot, it was a dream! Then Kompong Thom, coming on like springtime. And still not one Vietnamese, a milky sky, not a single hair in the soup . . . ! And overhead ta-ta-bang! What a harvest! The gods themselves went at it. So here's a provisional list, Your Marshal. For the villages alone of Baray and Kompong Thom: four tanks, twenty buses, four completely new armored vehicles, eight two-and-a-half-ton trucks, twenty-one vans. A 105 mm howitzer, less three hundred men in any case, but hundreds of machine guns. And at take-off, about fifty dead.

LON NOL: My, but what a magnificent victory, My dear Um Savuth! I understand very well why it's gone to your head!

UM SAVUTH: How well you take it, General! I'm completely deflated.

IN SOPHAT: Marshal!

UM SAVUTH: There it is, if you wish, the provisional tally of our losses, Mr. President-Marshal.

LON NOL: Of our losses? We lost the victory?

SIRIK MATAK: We didn't win?

UM SAVUTH: Hardly had we won the victory than we lost it. The Vietnamese launched a counterattack. It was an admirably planned shot! It's perfectly normal. I'd have done as much in their place.

SIRIK MATAK: And our men?

UM SAVUTH: Our soldiers fled like snakes in the swamp. They coped. I'd have done the same if I'd been a trooper. To be killed when you have your pockets stuffed and a full stomach is unpleasant. But if you haven't received pay for three months because you are under the command of my pig of an adjutant that thief Ith Suong, the most incompetent head of the entire peninsula, and moreover a half-breed and a wimp, it's utterly detestable! If they hadn't fled, we'd have lost three thousand. Fortunately the rout was complete. I stayed until the last minute, Marshal-President. So to conclude, I'm anxious to tell you I was very impressed by our adversaries! Those Vietnamese, what magnificent soldiers! And such equipment!

LON NOL: You're tired, Colonel. You may go.

[Um Savuth exits.]

CHENG HENG: Mr. Marshal, the task you have taken upon yourself is monumental. Ten men would not be equal to it. Carrying upon your venerable shoulders both internal and foreign affairs, war and peace, business and army. . . . Think of your health and that of our country. I beg you to place part of your burden on someone of your choice.

SIRIK MATAK: Give up the supreme command, Marshal. Allow your generals themselves to lead their campaigns. You can't fight on all fronts from your bedroom. Share the power before we've lost it entirely.

LON NOL: Share power! It's already divvied up too much. Everyone around me talks, but no one acts. You saw, you want to vote, you want to taste my cake. You presume to judge the supreme leader and to be wiser than the planets! I have difficulty enough already concentrating and you're hassling me. Taking away my army? You're only a flea in Cambodia's mane, and you think you're roaring!!

SIRIK MATAK: I'll bring the matter before the Assembly!

LON NOL: The roaring of a flea! I'm suspending your Assembly. I've had enough of playing at democracy and liberty. I'll suspend everything. We're at war, Gentlemen, and I'll lead this country with a firm hand until the end!

SIRIK MATAK: I don't doubt that you'll lead our unhappy country unswervingly straight to catastrophe. Suspend everything from your stars, they'll end up by breaking down, and the sky, collapsing on you, old scarecrow, will bury Cambodia along with its dictator! I'll no longer lend my name to your repugnant nation. I resign.

LON NOL: Finally! No more princes! The stars promised me this, but I was beginning to get impatient. For me this is the first true Republic purged of the royal garbage polluting our kingdom!

SIRIK MATAK: Lon Nol, I've watched you crawling toward our throne for a long time. Perhaps one day you'll succeed in ensconcing yourself there, but in our people's eyes you'll never be anything more than a slug with a crown.

[Sirik Matak exits.]

LON NOL: What? What? What did he say?

CHENG HENG: The Prince said you'd never be anything more than a slug with a crown.

LON NOL: And you, Mr. Cheng, whom I've set at the summit of the State, *you* dare to repeat that to me!

CHENG HENG: Well, Mr. Marshal, you're the one who asked . . .

LON NOL: Mr. Cheng, not only am I not deaf, but I can even hear your words before they've taken flight. Take this for example, at this very moment, I hear you saying: "And I, too, want to resign!" You were going to say these words, correct?

CHENG HENG: You're mistaken, Mr. Marshal, I won't resign!

LON NOL: Ah! You're not a prince, you. We'll have to resign you a little. So be it. A president of the Assembly without Assembly is an absurdity. I'm taking you down.

[Cheng Heng exits.]

Is he gone?

IN SOPHAT: A Message, Your Excellency.

LON NOL: Captain, take a letter.

IN SOPHAT: To the President of the United States? As usual?

LON NOL: As always.
"My dear brother Richard Nixon,
It's an honor for me to announce to you that I've just dissolved my Assembly, overthrown its president and proclaimed myself Head of my State, of my army, and Minister of all our Ministries. Henceforth, I alone assume the fate of my dear country. My health is very good. It's with admirable confidence that I can be assured that you and your country are entirely behind me. Together we will pulverize the Vietnamese armies.
Last night, I dreamed about you and cried with joy.
Dear Great President, single and absolute friend, I beg you to send me sixty B-52's or two hundred T-28's please, because all our planes have been destroyed . . ." *[They exit.]*

PART 2, ACT 2, SCENE 3

[Peking. Sihanouk and Ong Meang enter]

SIHANOUK: My heart is shriveled by anxiety.
The great Giap, the superb conqueror of Dien Bien Phu no longer comes to visit Sihanouk except to complain about the Khmer Rouge's latest misdeed or about Chinese treachery. My straitened path is narrowing, my sky is covered with clouds. Will we emerge someday from this dark passage? I strain my eyes, I cannot see light at the end of the tunnel.

ONG MEANG: Ah! Sir, I miss Cambodia terribly, I'd like to return, to fight for you on our soil!

SIHANOUK: Me too. For the moment, there is a lull on the Ho Chi Minh trail. I asked His Excellency Penn Nouth to take advantage of it to argue for our return in the service of the Khmer Rouge command. But it would be too good to be true if he succeeded. Three years, Meang, for three years already I've been navigating in exile. Three years already since we were supposed to have crushed Lon Nol. And my supposed allies the Khmer Rouge and the Vietnamese are spending more time cutting each other's throats than in smashing the usurper.
Lon Nol, you're fortunate. You owe three years of serene swindling to the bitter quarrels of my partners. We're flanked by tigers and snakes, Meang. If Hanoi drops us, we're left to the Khmer Rouge.

ONG MEANG: But Hanoi can't drop us, Sir!

SIHANOUK: If Vietnam can claim *urbi et orbi* to have been offended a thousand times by the Khmer Rouge, nothing will prevent them any longer from breaking off with us, and then turning against us, and then nothing nor anyone could stop them from pouncing on us. When Chou En-lai ceases to exist, when . . .

ONG MEANG: Ah! My god! If the august Chou En-lai disappeared, who would protect Your Lordship?

SIHANOUK: You see, you know more than you know! I'd be nothing all by myself. And to round out my description of the desolate landscape I see in my crystal ball, I'll tell you this:
If it's the Khmer Rouge tiger who regains Phnom Penh, he won't hesitate to hack me up if I look like I'm getting close.
If it's the Vietnamese snake, he'll devour my country under my eyes like a rabbit and I'll hear our piercing cries dying away in the reptile's jaws.

ONG MEANG: But, just now, I heard him, General Giap, he gave us his word again. Hanoi promises not to touch us. Don't you accept his word?

SIHANOUK: I still believe it. But everything fades away, youth, friendship, flowers, the river water, and one's word too.

146

ONG MEANG: But he has such an honest face.

SIHANOUK: It's true. But I've also seen him, with his eyes closed, Captain, before a map of Cambodia, putting his finger, unerringly, right on the smallest dots where our country's water is during the dry season.

ONG MEANG: Ah! I didn't realize your Lordship was so despairing! My blood wants to flow for you. Unused, it becomes bitter in my heart. *[Penn Nouth enters.]*

PENN NOUTH: Sir! Ah! Sir! I've just brought victory! Yes, such a beautiful victory!

SIHANOUK: Don't tell me Ieng Sary has surrendered!

PENN NOUTH: Why, yes! Yes! Yes! I swear it. I laughed and laughed about it while I was rushing to you. In short, I cried about it! I won, Sir! They've surrendered! You can return! Your Grace will be able to go to Cambodia, Captain! For once, the old crow's bringing you good news.

SIHANOUK: We're going back? When?! When? Oh! my god! We're going back! Oh! Meang! Oh! How happy I am! Forget it, Captain, forget everything I told you!

ONG MEANG: Yes, yes, yes, Sir! When are we returning, Your Excellency?

PENN NOUTH: Oh! My dear Captain, only his Lordship and the Princess are authorized to return! His Grace will leave tomorrow. But no one else for the moment. The leadership of our resistance, et cetera, et cetera . . . I told you, Sir, a little victory.

SIHANOUK: But it doesn't matter! It doesn't matter! Such beautiful news! Tomorrow! Your Excellency revives me, you lift me up, you . . . you delight me. I adore you!

PENN NOUTH: This will only be a short trip, Sir. A few weeks on the road. A brief month in Cambodia and you'll return to Peking.

SIHANOUK: Oh! I'm en route, I'm en route. All along the way I'll hear my heart repeat: Sihanouk's back! Sihanouk's back! In his country! It'll be the end of winter when I get there. Oh! Your Excellency! A thousand troubles vanish, and three years of mourning are erased like a dream. *[They exit. Giap enters.]*

GIAP:[37] Adieu, prince, full of illusions and doomed dreams! Cambodia's past has met its future, but it doesn't realize it.

While you are falling, we are being reborn. The Great Vietnamese Century is hereby heralded. This year, America, disgusted by our invincibility, at last lets Hanoi soar like an eagle over all Indochina.

Then, next year, who's to prevent us from swooping down on the South? From taking Hue, Danang, Phan Rang, and beautiful Saigon, the old Khmer city? And then, the day after that, why not Phnom Penh?

Yes, why not? I already see Hanoi reigning along the Mekong over fish-filled waters. Who could stop it? Who? China? No doubt old China would watch with displeasure our Vietnam plant her claws on vassal Cambodia.

But what does China's pleasure matter to us from now on? The old friendships are dead. Rings once exchanged are mislaid. Everything is but mockery and treachery.

The arms China opened to Hanoi yesterday are today embracing our American assassins. Peking is playing ping-pong with our enemy. Meanwhile the cunning old witch refuses General Giap henceforward necessary and friendly arms. Then, don't count on China's love, poor Prince. We no longer owe anything to the old monster, except hate, rancor, and spear thrusts.

As for Sihanouk, we retain only the memory of cold sentiments. Sihanouk is done for. Cambodia's new name is "Pol Pot—Ieng Sary," the hound with fangs steaming with Vietnamese blood.

Yes, yes, I already see our Phnom Penh closing toward us like the land slowly moving forward to meet the boat.

I'm sorry, kindly Prince, your season has passed. But I'll come often to share a good meal and stimulating conversation with you. *[He exits.]*

PART 2, ACT 2, SCENE 4

[Phnom Penh. Lon Nol enters followed by the Prime Minister Long Boret and Captain In Sophat, servants.]

---

[37]This speech did not appear in production. AU

LON NOL: And into the bargain, the author of this failed attempt is one of the most Sihanoukist son-in-laws of Sihanouk! Well? What do you have to say about it?

LONG BORET: The T-28 pilot a son-in-law of Sihanouk! But these Royalists are real monsters, cruel Cerberuses and loyal to the dictator.

LON NOL: Well, what do I do?
I'll arrest them all! Oh! Oh! All the princes, the princesses, and the tutti quanti who still dare to remain at liberty in our city. Go, go, my dear Prime Minister, arrest them all for me quickly.

LONG BORET: Everyone, Your Excellency?

LON NOL: Everyone! Everyone! Everyone!
The monarchy's dragon must be slaughtered and gutted to the last drop of his blood: long live the Republic! And don't forget Sirik Matak.

LONG BORET: Sirik Matak, Your Excellency!?! You really think so?! The Prince is a Republican, and sincerely so, I believe. Moreover, he's not involved in this atrocious attempt. Besides he's not in Phnom Penh. Ever since his resignation, he lives a very retired life.

LON NOL: Listen, Mr. Long Boret, you, you think and you have the impression that. . . . But I know, I see and I lead this state. "The Prince," huh?! You said: "The Prince!" You still have monarchy glued to your brain.
I order you to proceed with the arrest of Sisowath Sirik Matak, a traitor! An adversary!! He is saying all over, even to the Americans, that my regime is not viable. Be off!

LONG BORET: I'm going, Your Excellency. However, one more question, if you'd permit me. About the teacher and student strikes, which have been gaining momentum for several days now, what are we going to do?

LON NOL: That, well, that's easy. You've got the police, the army. Shoot!! I don't want any more disorder. Put everything in order today! The day is favorable. The newspapers, too! Suspend them. And decree a state of siege. And then stop worrying yourself about everything and nothing. I'm very well. I'll survive all my enemies. The Republic is not at risk. Captain! Accompany me!

LONG BORET: *[aside]* Not at risk! Never has our government's unpopularity been so strong. Everything is paralyzed. The road from Battambang is cut off. We can't get any more gasoline. We're entirely dependent on American aid. Oh! Triple Jewel, my soul is weighed down by anxiety. *[Long Boret exits followed by In Sophat.]*

LON NOL: The Republic is not at risk. Mo Boudhayana! Moreover, Phnom Penh is impenetrable since I surrounded the city with a cordon of holy sand. *[Captain In Sophat reenters.]*

IN SOPHAT: Mr. Ambassador of the United States, His Excellency John Gunther Dean.

LON NOL: Pfff . . .

[John Gunther Dean enters.]

DEAN: Another defeat, Mr. Marshal. If I invited myself in without dancing attendance, it's because it is for the last time.

LON NOL: Please, Mr. Ambassador . . .

DEAN: Your forces have just suffered an unacceptable, but unfortunately merited, defeat in Kampong Luon. I say defeat. I ought to say punishment.
I've come from your front. I went myself on an inspection tour of your army throughout the provinces.

LON NOL: That's too much! Too much, Mr. Ambassador! You'll exhaust yourself. An ambassador on the front. Has anyone ever heard of such a thing, Captain?

DEAN: And a commander in chief of the army who's never at the front, is that "heard of"?
You're courting disaster if you don't take the following immediate measures:
Make sure your battalions are made up of flesh-and-blood troops and not phantoms. You claimed to us that you had 500,000 men. There are no more than 200,000 men alive in or out of uniform! The 300,000 others are your own invention. I forbid you to pay wages to your phantoms. I order you to pay wages to your poor troops, each month and in the proper hands. I order you to forbid your officers to pocket their soldiers' pay.

LON NOL: What you mean, my officers?

DEAN: That's not all. This season we granted you three hundred sup-
plementary armored vehicles, hundreds of 88 mm mortars, a thousand grenade launchers . . .

LON NOL: Precisely! I was eager to say that General Haig . . .

DEAN: Forty thousand M16 rifles. What did you do with them?
You use them, you just don't fire them, right?!
You shower the enemy with bullets, hoping to cover him from a
distance! But do you fight? Oh! No, your officers are economizing
on their forces. So you fight once a week, let's say Tuesdays from
seven to eleven o'clock. Except if it rains or it's too hot!
But that is at least something. Since most of the time, there isn't
any war at all, at least on your side. Since your officers are unarmed. Unarmed? With all the arms our Congress has sent you?
Our guns are on the battlefield, but on the other side. Your officers
sell our shell cases to foreigners. To whom? To the Thais? That
would be too perfect, too fitting! No, no! You sell your ammuni-
tion to the Khmer Rouge! I know! Enough! The governor of Battambang, General Sek Sam Iet, doesn't have one single mortar. He
sold every one he had to the Khmer Rouge and doesn't even
bother to hide the fact. Because then he can boast of making a
good deal. After all, didn't he get, in exchange for this high deed,
the buyer's promise, that is to say General Hou Youn's, that these
anti-American arms, Marshal, would not be used against his own
city?! And he confided this to me, to me, smiling! Fortunately for
my faith in the human soul, I saw that one of his lieutenants was
crying. If America knew what she is supporting! What would a
commander in chief do if he learned of a such an infamous act? I
mean a normal commander. He'd have this monster shot by his
soldiers. What does Commander Lon Nol do? He has just added a
star to the breast of the fool. He decorates him. Well, Marshal,
what am I to tell America? What do you say?

LON NOL: I'm very, very sad, Mr. Ambassador. Sek Sam Iet is an old
friend who's had a magnificent career. Colonel at thirty, general
at . . .

DEAN: Fire him!

LON NOL: I'll summon him. Perhaps it's a misunderstanding. A bum rap.

DEAN: Dismiss him! Relieve him of his functions! He's an assassin! Relieve him of his duties, do you hear me!

LON NOL: I hear you! I hear you! You're yelling very loud!

DEAN: You're killing yourself! You're sick! sick! Do something for your Republic! In the face of some of these infamous acts, I who love this country, I who want to see the communist threat put down, I wept—I cried over your country and I cried over mine. We're arming the Khmer Rouge! We're the purveyors of baseness and corruption!

LON NOL: I, too, have cried sometimes, when I was exhausted— mostly in the evening. But believe me, Mr. Ambassador, all this is the fault of the war. All men are weak. Americans included. Sometimes we don't realize what we're doing. That's war.

DEAN: Well, then! Straighten up! Take the arms we're still offering you—and hurry up! Fight! Soon there won't be so many arms! Soon we won't be there any more there to prop you up again and again.

LON NOL: Hey, there! Wait! Are you speaking for Washington? Because I, I have the President's guarantee, you know!

DEAN: Oh, I am speaking for reality, Marshal Lon Nol.

LON NOL: [aside] It's no use trying to frighten me. . . . Mr. Ambassador, we'll retake the advantage after tomorrow. I'll make sure of this myself. . . . The month of March has always brought me luck.

DEAN: And the month of April, Marshal?
I've one more bit of advice to give you! You have to form a more representative government, gather around you men who've made this revolution with you, draw closer to Prince Sirik Matak . . .

LON NOL: Bring myself closer to Sirik Matak? But of course! But what good advice! I was thinking about him a moment ago. Very seriously. Isn't that right Captain?
Well, I'll busy myself with all of this. I'm off. See you soon, Mr. Ambassador. And thank you! Thank you!

[Dean exits.]

LON NOL: I didn't seize power to throw it out the window. This is Cambodia here! A country civilized long, long before yours! And don't forget it! Give us arms but keep your advice to yourself!

[They exit, the Captain, the porters, and Lon Nol.]

PART 2, ACT 2, SCENE 5

[Angkor. Sihanouk and the Princess enter.]

THE PRINCESS: My Lord, are you sad?

SIHANOUK: I'm sensitive. And I'm sad at being so tender. Youth, there's the secret. Prehistoric youth! Cave youth. Their army can pride itself on being the youngest, the most disciplined, the most illiterate, the most blind of any army in Asia. And even in the whole world. Have you seen them? Mouths closed, not a look, not a breath when we passed. Ghosts! Fifteen thousand ghosts in a row in the venerable forests of Angkor.

THE PRINCESS: And this Mr. Pol Pot! This smile overflowing with teeth! And that terrible speech! Such bloody words dancing for hours and hours like gleaming demons in front of these columns of fascinated child-soldiers. My heart recoils.

SIHANOUK: And to think this Pol Pot is only Saloth Sâr, the little geo-history professor!
Besides everyone's a professor here, except me. Have you seen? They're all professors: Mr. Khieu Samphan, Mr. Son Sen, Mr. Ieng Sary and his wife, Mrs. Ieng Thirit—I wouldn't want to meet up with her in a forest on a moonless night—Mr. Hou Youn, Mr. Sa-loth Pot . . .

THE PRINCESS: Mr. Saloth Pot! When you called him that, he made such a face! . . .

SIHANOUK: Oh! History has become intolerable to me! Pol Pot has the say and Sihanouk is muzzled.
He takes everything from me! The way of the giants, the way of the elephants, divine Angkor Wat, adorable Bantey Srey, the mil-lennial forest, the buffalo in water up to his nostrils, the child on

the elephant, the rain, stone, air, blessed earth, sugar palms, everything!

For a month I've seen only Khmer Rouge soldiers, Khmer Rouge staff, Khmer Rouge ministers, not one single peasant.

As close as I am to my people, I'm so far from their eyes and their ears I've kissed no one, I've blessed no one, I'm in my country and I'm an exile. And what if I'm wrong?!! What am I doing here? Should I fade out myself without delay?

The Khmer Rouge ministers want me to sign the cheap pamphlets they write. And I sign. They want to gild their face with my crown. I'll pulverize it into a face powder. I don't understand myself. Do you understand me?

THE PRINCESS: I understand you, Your Grace. Once the Khmer Rouge have crushed the Lon Nol-ians, you'll regain the position of head of the country. You'll raise it back up slowly, you'll console it and cure it of its long suffering.

SIHANOUK: Do you think so? Do you think so? Then let's leave this planet where Sihanouk is only a shadow of a head of state and let's return to Peking. Far from here, maybe I'll start to believe Sihanouk could one day bring springtime back to his country.

[An airplane is heard.]

THE PRINCESS: Ph! That's a T28.

[They exit. Saloth Sâr, henceforth called Pol Pot, Ieng Sary, Ieng Thirit, Khieu Samphan, and Hou Youn enter.]

IENG SARY: The Prince still has too much influence. After they saw him the peasants let their plows and hoes drop and ran behind the jeep forgetting their duties. Many yielded themselves up to superstition. They spread earth over the tire tracks and bullied the soldiers who couldn't fix the ruts.

IENG THIRIT: He's not yet in Peking. So many tragic accidents occur every day on the Ho Chi Minh trail!

POL POT: He'll get back safe and sound for the moment. The Prince is only an occasional cause. It's our peasants we must decisively enlighten.

Well, brother Hou Youn, where are you on the cooperatives? Is it the great leap forward?

HOU YOUN: The peasants are so passive. Buddha's forever on their lips, and there're always phantoms in their bundles. They're docile. They listen to us speak long into the night at political education meetings. Then they light up their cigarettes. And then there's always one who raises his head and says, "Oh! There he is! My Lord Papa, there's Sihanouk, I see him over there, in the moon, on the right!" and they put off all reflection till the next day. With our people it takes time.

IENG SARY: Or rather Hou Youn and his partisans let our peasants smoke during political hours. Because Hou Youn is watching out for his popularity more than for the Revolution.

POL POT: Let's keep united. Brother Hou Youn, the time for patience is over. We've been broad-minded and respectful toward the ancient forms.
The time has now come for the ultimate uprooting. Everything that resists the uplifting wind of our Revolution must be joyously rooted out. The aged Dragon still has three old venomous fangs. Let the young and the children help us to defang him. Let's root out Buddhism, monarchy, and egotistical property instincts.

IENG SARY: Let's defrock the monks, and make them have to work! Let them sweat a little like everyone else! We shall discover that their backs break like everyone else's and that they are perfectly mortal. No more yellow saffron. Let black unify and militarize our people under the single color of the peasant worker!

POL POT: Has the Prince met with the monks?

IENG SARY: I saw to it. He received the ones from Siem Reap.

IENG THIRIT: I took a picture of their audience.

POL POT: Perfect. Well! As for the monks, I see no objection to Ieng Sary's proposal.

KHIEU SAMPHAN: For a long time I've been asking for the collectives encrusted in the earth like parasites to be moved. I am asking again for all built-up areas to be wiped out, and for their personnel to be regrouped in numbered sections, in a collective settlement or encampment: a hundred people under the same roof is about right.

155

IENG THIRIT: Why not more?

HOU YOUN: We absolutely have to separate the young from the old who stupidize them and indoctrinate them. I request the separation of the two age groups.

POL POT: Let's get back to the Prince: he's no longer to be feared, as I said. On the other hand the remaining Sihanoukites alienate our ranks and cast a shadow over our cadres in the field. Our brother Ieng Sary could carry out this delicate mission.

IENG SARY: I need, given the importance of the work, the assistance of General Ta Mok and his elite troops as well as carte blanche for the suppression of the Sihanoukites.

POL POT: The Organization grants you full powers. Well! Wasn't I right to make you agree to this little visit from the Prince? His coming will have allowed us to make indispensable decisions much more quickly. And now, when will the next victory be? Mr. Commander in chief?

KHIEU SAMPHAN: I see us arriving in Phnom Penh in about six weeks.

POL POT: I am convinced we could be there in a month, by redoubling our will.

KHIEU SAMPHAN: Our army will be there, if it's humanly possible, Brother Pol Pot.

POL POT: The future is ours! Till tomorrow, beloved brothers!

[Pol Pot, Ieng Sary, and Ieng Thirit exit.]

HOU YOUN: We're overturning the world with such fervor that it seems to me sometimes we're going to cut all the roots of human reality off in one blow! Why haven't you ever married?

KHIEU SAMPHAN: I swore not to take a wife before our victory.

HOU YOUN: Me, it's because I wouldn't want children.

KHIEU SAMPHAN: What are we talking about? Come on.

[They exit.]

PART 2, ACT 3, SCENE 1

[Phnom Penh. Dean and Senator McCloskey enter.]

DEAN: The Khmer Rouge are going to win the war, it's inevitable. Us, all we can do is gain a little time! We've got to help our friends get through the dry season.
Then, during the truce dictated by these merciful rains they'll be able to try one last time for peace talks. It's only a little bit, and I haven't much faith in it, but we owe them this little bit.

MCCLOSKEY: Yes, of course, certainly. But there's this matter of Lon Nol. You know, in the long run it's hard to support a personality as unpopular as this rotten Marshal. You know he's completely cracked?

DEAN: But it's no longer a question of Lon Nol. It's a matter of the Khmer Rouge and Cambodia. Cambodia is not Lon Nol.

MCCLOSKEY: Yes, but from Washington's point of view, you might say. Couldn't you set that aside while I plead our case?

DEAN: I've been doing just that today, Senator McCloskey. Keeley! *[Secretary enters.]* Ask Mr. Long Boret to come see me at the Embassy right away. Mr. Saukham Khoy, too, even. He's an idiot, but he is Head of State at the moment.

KEELEY: Right away. *[He exits.]*

MCCLOSKEY: Good. But after May, when the rains start, The End! Huh? The United States shouldn't have a single man, a single dollar in Cambodia any longer beginning this summer.

DEAN: In any event, the Khmer Rouge aren't going to consult us, believe you me.

MCCLOSKEY: What will these famous Khmer Rouge do when they've won?

DEAN: Six months ago when they conquered the village of Sarsar Sdam, in the province of Siem Reap, they burned it, after having massacred its 300 inhabitants in the following way: the men were castrated and disemboweled; the young women were buried alive; the old women were nailed to the walls of their houses; the children dismembered with bare hands and domestic animals had their legs cut off.

MCCLOSKEY: Who told you these horror stories? A Cambodian?

DEAN: A French priest reported them to me. He was in the neighboring village. He took in the sole survivor of this carnage.

MCCLOSKEY: So a Cambodian all the same. Listen, John, for one reason or another, refugees always tell nightmare horror stories. Everyone knows that. No one ever believes them!

DEAN: You make me want to send you down there, Senator Mc-Closkey. You, and your confounded disbelief, and these fiendish journalists who only believe the facts when they're nipping at their own infernal heels! My priest, who's sixty, of sound mind, thirty years in Cambodia, neither a Cambodian nor a Lon Nol-ian, nor a nut, had to finish off the murderous work of the Khmer Rouge with his own hands and with fire because there were too many remains to bury.

MCCLOSKEY: Okay, Okay, agreed. But don't be so apocalyptic anyhow. There are always regrettable incidents in this kind of war. We ourselves . . .

DEAN: Incidents! No! Not incidents! And don't tell me, "regrettable!" "Apocalypse!" No words! No excuses! It's the truth! And these miserable men! The Khmer Rouge Revolution will be brutal, idiotic, and not incidental!

MCCLOSKEY: My, you're all worked up, John! Listen, how come the papers aren't reporting all this?

DEAN: I know a few journalists who've shouted out the truth, but who listens to them? Who's heard them? Is it because we haven't suffered enough that we don't recognize suffering? We deny it. We still need gas chambers before we can admit that Evil is always seeking to rule the world.

MCCLOSKEY: Are you Jewish, John?

DEAN: No, I'm not Jewish! I'm Cambodian. And you, you're a Senator. Come on, come on, do something for my Cambodia, that's all I ask.

[Keeley enters with Long Boret and Saukham Khoy.]

Come in, friends. Look, I've just been talking things over with
Senator McCloskey. He'll turn Congress around, but only if you
get rid of the General.

SAUKHAM KHOY: Rid of?

DEAN: He must be out of the country within twenty-four hours.

MCCLOSKEY: Tell them the truth! Either he goes, or Congress turns
off the tap.

SAUKHAM KHOY: He won't listen to us.

DEAN: Don't talk the good of the country to him. Talk dollars.
Money. Buy his departure! Put a price on it. And you'll still be getting a bargain.

LONG BORET: I'm off. How much should I start off with, Mr.
Saukham Khoy? 300,000 dollars?

SAUKHAM KHOY: 300,000, that's right.

DEAN: Don't be too stingy, we're in a hurry. You can call him from
my office, Mr. Prime Minister.

LONG BORET: Thank you. *[Long Boret exits.]*

SAUKHAM KHOY: Oh, Triple Jewel, may your graces be on our side, I
beg you, because we are all united, with the exception of Lon Nol,
on the side of our country.

MCCLOSKEY: And you, Mr. Saukham Khoy, what to think would
happen if the Khmer Rouge won? *[Long Boret reenters.]*

LONG BORET: Pardon me. I'm going up to 500,000. Okay?

SAUKHAM KHOY: Fine. *[Long Boret goes back out.]* Yes, Mr. Senator. When the Khmer Rouge have won, they'll do like the wild
buffalo does after rut, they'll calm down. You know, the Cambodians are like that. We disagree. We quarrel. And then we make
up. Besides, Mr. Khieu Samphan, vice-president of the Royal
Government, has declared that each Cambodian has his place in a
national society, whatever his past. Thus, when the Khmer Rouge
win, they'll have a policy of reconciliation.

MCCLOSKEY: Have you heard of the massacre of . . . of . . .

DEAN: Of Sarsar Sdam.

SAUKHAM KHOY: Of course. But, you know, the Khmers are like that. You mustn't get them excited. Afterward, it goes away.

MCCLOSKEY: And do you believe what Mr. Khieu Samphan says.

SAUKHAM KHOY: But of course. He was my colleague. I know him well you see, we're old buddies. *[Long Boret comes in again.]*

LONG BORET: Excuse me; I'm up to 700,000. And we have to give him the title of national hero who has brilliantly contributed to the support of his country. Okay?

SAUKHAM KHOY: Yes! Yes! That's a great idea. National hero! Very good! *[Long Boret goes back out.]*

MCCLOSKEY: But tell me. Mr. President, I thought the Republicans expected reprisals?

SAUKHAM KHOY: Well, not all of us expect them. You see, Prince Sihanouk announced clearly to us that only the seven super traitors would be killed. *[Long Boret comes in again.]*

LONG BORET: It's hard, but it's coming. He wants assurances from the Americans.

DEAN: To hell with him! Go up to one million and tell him that if in five minutes Senator McCloskey goes off without this deal being wrapped up, you're withdrawing the offer completely.

LONG BORET: Right! *[Long Boret goes back out.]*

MCCLOSKEY: You were saying the seven super traitors, meaning?

SAUKHAM KHOY: Lon Nol, Sirik Matak, In Tam, Sostène, Fernandez, Cheng Heng, Son Ngoc Thanh, and Mr. Long Boret who is on the telephone.

DEAN: Do you know, Mr. Saukham Khoy, that the list is up to twenty-one now?

SAUKHAM KHOY: Yes. Yes. Which means . . .

DEAN: But you, you're not on it . . . *[Long Boret comes in again.]*

LONG BORET: We did it, gentlemen! It's over. A million dollars and he's out of here.

DEAN: Congratulations. Mr. Prime Minister! Senator, are you leaving satisfied?

MCCLOSKEY: I promise you I'll fight to the utmost for your Cambodia. And for yours, Mr. Long Boret.

DEAN: May God help you, Senator. *[McCloskey exits.]*

LONG BORET: If only we could have waited for the rainy season! I wouldn't hesitate to beg Sihanouk to regain control.

SAUKHAM KHOY: Me neither.

LONG BORET: I'd be ready to pay for his return with my own head if it would save our country.

SAUKHAM KHOY: !!? *[Keeley enters.]*

KEELEY: Mr. Ambassador, Sirs, I am sorry to tell you I've come across a bad dispatch. The city of Neak Luong has fallen. The first and second Republican divisions have fled, abandoning their weapons. I'm very sorry.

LONG BORET: Neak Luong! Already! The lower Mekong is communist, Mr. Dean!

DEAN: My poor friends, this is the beginning of the end. But . . .

SAUKHAM KHOY: O my god! Mr. Prime Minister, go negotiate, quick, quick, tell them Lon Nol is gone, that . . .

DEAN: You've lost the war. I'm afraid that it's rather too late for a compromise.

LONG BORET: We've *all* lost the war. The Republic, Cambodia, America. But not everyone will pay equally for this failure.

DEAN: My friend, are you weeping? I'm still here. I'll watch over you. I'll watch over you.

LONG BORET: I am not crying for Long Boret. What's one Long Boret? I'm crying for my country, I'm crying for my country. [They all exit.]

PART 2, ACT 3, SCENE 2[38]

[Peking. Sihanouk, Penn Nouth, and Etienne Manac'h enter.]

SIHANOUK: Whoever gets to Phnom Penh first this month will be ruler of Cambodia. But if I beat the Khmer Rouge to the punch then everything's different. Together, we'll greet these Khmer Rouge together, my people and I, and I'll negotiate an equitable political solution for my country. Everything can still be saved. And everything still depends on the Americans. They just need to understand that for them, too, Sihanouk is the best bargain, and they should let me come back home this week. But that's precisely what they won't do.

PENN NOUTH: What if, for once, the Americans showed some intelligence, some generosity, some awareness of their own interests at the right moment? After all, Ford did replace Nixon.

SIHANOUK: But Kissinger replaced Kissinger. Nothing changed except for the worse. The Khmer Rouge are eating up the miles, and China loves us less and less.

MANAC'H: His Excellency Chou En-lai is still hoping to see you beat the reds to the punch. I'm sure of it. There's still some hope.

SIHANOUK: But old Mao Zedong, the eternal Mao, has preternatural leanings toward Pol Pot.

PENN NOUTH: We'd have to act quickly.

MANAC'H: Will you agree to let me take one last chance, Sir?

SIHANOUK: My dear friend, I'm entrusting my fortunes, my doubts, and my incurable hope to you. One nice little American airplane for Sihanouk; Mr. Dean waiting for me at the airport, and the whole face of Asia will have changed!
But don't forget in taking action that we're surrounded. The Chinese wall is full of Khmer Rouge microphones. So be careful! Don't go and compromise me . . .
[Ieng Sary enters.] Careful, here is Pol Pot's dog, his horrible brother-in-law Ieng Sary. . . . You know he always creeps up on

---

[38]Scene abridged for staging. AU

me like that, behind my back. Luckily I anticipated his arrival . . . by his smell. *[out loud]* You know I am against all negotiation. Even if Mr. Kissinger in person brought me back my crown on a silver platter I'd say, no, no, no! Negotiate, me? With Lon Nol! Let them bring that mangy cur before this lion of fire! One swipe of the paw, one bite and I swear all our problems would be eased. I'll never negotiate! Oh! Mr. Ieng Sary! You know Pol Pot's brother-in-law, Mr. Ambassador? Yes. There's an admirable couple. Sâr and Sary, like Castor and Pollux. Ha, ha, ha! There's none more faithful to Cambodia. Except Sihanouk!

IENG SARY: You're not going to betray us? No? No negotiations! No simulacra of peace! No divisions!

SIHANOUK: That's just what I was saying: no division. My government will fight to total victory. I'll never stop proclaiming it.

IENG SARY: Then, Sir, why don't they believe you, huh?

SIHANOUK: Why? Why because it displeases everyone that Sihanouk has joined with the Khmer Rouge. Nations are so egotistical! These Americans! They think I am a sorcerer. I had a white handkerchief. It's taken from me, dipped in a bucket of blood. My handkerchief is now all red. They'd like me to make it all white again, just like that?

IENG SARY: I've made five different attempts to negotiate since Nixon's resignation: September '74, October '74, December '74, January '75, February '75. Now, that's enough!

SIHANOUK: Aren't you forgetting November '74? I got there before you. Six attempts. But how tiresome! Always saying no, no, no!

IENG SARY: You know, Sir, if, taking advantage of his return to the partisans, Prince Sihanouk were to betray the Khmer Rouge . . .

SIHANOUK: One more word, Mr. Ieng Sary, and I'm telling President Mao everything. I'll tell him that Mr. Ieng Sary threatened to kill me in front of a witness!

IENG SARY: I said nothing.

SIHANOUK: Good day, Sir! *[Exit Ieng Sary.]* You see, Mr. Manac'h. All the time quarrels, divisiveness! Sometimes I want to withdraw!

But I cannot betray my country! I am faithful. I am faithful! *[They exit.]*

PART 2, ACT 3, SCENE 3

[On the banks of the Mekong. Enter Khieu Samphan, Ieng Sary, Ieng Thirit, Pol Pot, and Hou Youn, in combat dress.]

POL POT: What does taking Phnom Penh mean for us?

HOU YOUN: Final victory, success.

POL POT: First of all, the greatest victory in the world. But let's not be overwhelmed by the glitter of military triumph. Taking Phnom Penh is nothing. I take Phnom Penh, and afterward, what do I see?

KHIEU SAMPHAN: Two and a half million people starving.

HOU YOUN: A bordello. An immense chaotic brothel, starving, over-populated. Practically half the population is piled up in the capital. It's going to require a superhuman administrative effort.

POL POT: And I, what I see is that we shall administer nothing at all. I see a new war beginning immediately. I see our revolution being attacked by a counterrevolution.

IENG SARY: I was going to say that. What's Phnom Penh? Not only the gigantic museum of all corruptions, the stinking refuge for egotism, privilege, and cowardice, but also the general headquarters for American, Republican, and Sihanoukist spies.

IENG THIRIT: The whole city is crawling with double agents. Everything's mined, it's one big trap.

HOU YOUN: Most of the inhabitants of Phnom Penh are not really citizens, but refugees, peasants.

IENG THIRIT: Who swear only by Sihanouk and the Republic.

KHIEU SAMPHAN: Right. Phnom Penh is a Sodom that hates us. And I can't conceive how we could possibly administer it properly in the monstrous condition the war has left it in.

HOU YOUN: But how to proceed? What do you see?

POL POT: Do you think I want to administer the monstrosity? Do you think I want to nurture a crocodile who, barely on its feet again, will snap at us? No, I tell you!

KHIEU SAMPHAN: I agree. Feeding Phnom Penh is feeding our own death.

IENG THIRIT: Hou Youn doesn't agree.

HOU YOUN: No. . . . Yes. Only, I don't see what we can do?

POL POT: Do you think I want to maintain Phnom Penh? What does the Angkar say? The Organization says *No.*

IENG SARY: We must clean out Phnom Penh!

POL POT: That's it. That's the solution. It's correct. And it's the only answer.

HOU YOUN: What an idea! You think evacuating it will take less time than putting a new organization in place? Evacuate two and a half million inhabitants? Think about how much time it takes to get transports, provisions, a place to take them in . . . ?

IENG SARY: Who's speaking of somewhere to take them in? You have to clean out the abscess, lance it with one stroke. Dislodge one's enemies, pike out the rat's nests, and prevent any subversion by means of an unexpected, radical maneuvre. We're not going to move rats around in a limousine, and set them up in a palace!

IENG THIRIT: It doesn't take long to empty a trash can. All you have to do is turn it over.

IENG SARY: Everyone out! This had to be imagined!

HOU YOUN: But there's good grain mixed in with the fermented!

POL POT: We'll know how to sort it out, Hou Youn, we'll sort it out.

HOU YOUN: Where will all the garbage go?

POL POT: Out to the countryside, the fields; they'll build dikes, cultivate the rice.

IENG THIRIT: I want to ask Hou Youn . . .

HOU YOUN: But, really, two million people outside, on the road, in this season, with the country in ruins, what would they live on? What would they drink? It's inconceivable!

KHIEU SAMPHAN: *[to Hou Youn]* Be quiet now! Shut up!

IENG THIRIT: Hou Youn, have you no faith in the Organization?

HOU YOUN: I am opposed to this decision. Khieu Samphan, I beg you, some of our own people are in there. We have relatives, friends in Phnom Penh. Your mother's still there!

KHIEU SAMPHAN: Be quiet, Hou Youn! don't you see you displease us? My mother is in Phnom Penh, and I'm not hesitating for a moment.

HOU YOUN: It will be a hecatomb!

KHIEU SAMPHAN: Shut up. I've always wanted a new society to be born, of an inexpressible purity, without cities, without commerce, without any seeds of corruption. I wrote about it, and, moreover, you did, too, Hou Youn. Well, I'm not going back on any of my theories. I call for the exemplary evacuation of Phnom Penh and the total deurbanization of our Cambodia. I call for the censure of our brother Hou Youn for an indeterminate length of time.

IENG THIRIT: I was going to ask for the same thing.

POL POT: Done. Let's go on.

HOU YOUN: *[to Khieu Samphan]* I'm not the only one to miss Phnom Penh. I'm certain of it. I can't believe you're sincere. *[Exit Hou Youn.]*

POL POT: Khieu Samphan, you will lead the attack and direct the evacuation with Ieng Sary.

IENG THIRIT: Are we going to raze Phnom Penh and spare Hou Youn? For ten years he's been undermining us and sucking our blood. He's a CIA agent. I wonder which gods are protecting him?

KHIEU SAMPHAN: A CIA agent? I never thought of that.

IENG THIRIT: It's obvious. You like him too much.

IENG SARY: I did see him reading the *New York Times* in Peking.

POL POT: We'll eliminate him when we've won, Ieng Thirit, you'll see to it.

IENG SARY: Hou Youn was a very popular leader.

POL POT: We'll cross the river tomorrow. *[Exit all.]*

PART 2, ACT 3, SCENE 4

[Peking. Enter Penn Nouth, and the Special Envoy from the United States.]

SPECIAL ENVOY: Professor Kissinger and President Ford are now convinced that only Prince Sihanouk can put an end to the Cambodian drama. Our country wants him to return!

PENN NOUTH: Really, Mr. Special Envoy from Washington?

SPECIAL ENVOY: Really. They've realized! They look favorably on a national unity government, a sort of popular front. The Prince must get back to the capital *before* the Communists do. That's the way we see it. Everyone misses the Prince. Lon Nol's generals, most of the ambassadors, Prince Sirik Matak himself, have all let Washington know they yearn for his return.
The United States promises not to leave before his arrival. We will await him. This promise is unconditional. No conditions. Professor Kissinger wants to impose no conditions. You can trust him implicitly.

PENN NOUTH: That's very nice. But do you know what time it is? What day? What year? We are at the dawn of April 12, 1975. You can't take today for yesterday. Sihanouk was our hope. But the Khmer Rouge are our destiny. Do you know where they are? Yesterday they were within two kilometers of the Phnom Penh airport. Your air bridge is broken. Your rice and your arms will no longer get there.

SPECIAL ENVOY: Couldn't you ask the Chinese to put a plane at the Prince's disposal so he could return to Phnom Penh right away? *[The American Secretary enters.]*

SECRETARY: Mr. Special Envoy. A message from Mr. Ambassador Dean. The perimeter of Phnom Penh is getting visibly smaller. Our people are withdrawing immediately. Everyone's going off in helicopters. Toward the Gulf of Thailand.

SPECIAL ENVOY: They're leaving? We're going? Oh! Mr. Prime Minister, I am devastated, devastated. *[The Secretary and the Envoy exit.]*

PENN NOUTH:
> There's no going back.
> The old servant looks out the window. . . .
> The sun does not rise.
> Who will pick the chrysanthemums in the King's old
> palace? *[Exit Penn Nouth.]*

PART 2, ACT 3, SCENE 5

[Phnom Penh, beside the Mekong. Enter Sirik Matak, Saukham Khoy, and Long Boret.]

SAUKHAM KHOY: Oh! Your Excellency! They are on the other side of the river! They're getting closer, closer!

LONG BORET: Thank you for coming, Prince, thank you. I'm in great need of your counsel these days of . . . how should I say? . . . days of shipwreck. The boat is turning in every direction, and I'd like to save my passengers. How can I reach shore?

SIRIK MATAK: It is I who should be thanking Long Boret for your continuing confidence in the forgotten Sirik Matak. What's left of me belongs to Cambodia and to its noble Prime Minister. Nothing is harder, truly, than to lead a surrender into safe harbor. Let's do so without faltering and without submission.

SAUKHAM KHOY: It's up to us, Your Excellency!

SIRIK MATAK: And without yielding your adversary anything. They should pay as dearly as possible for the right of access to our royal city!

LONG BORET: The soldiers will fight to the last cartridge!

SAUKHAM KHOY: Since the Americans have stopped helping us, couldn't we turn to another great power?

SIRIK MATAK: Which one? China? You want to be Khmer Rouge?

SAUKHAM KHOY: No, no. But what about Russia? We could become socialists. She'd help us then.

LONG BORET: Hush! Even if no one heard us, such a stupidity is intolerable to me! Mr. President, get back to today right now and . . . *[Enter a secretary.]*

SECRETARY: His Excellency the American Ambassador. It's very urgent.

LONG BORET: Let him in! Let him in! *[Enter Dean].* Dear fellow!

DEAN: Thank God, you're all here! My friends, my dear friends, we must leave, we have to get out of here. I'll take you. Please go to the Embassy immediately. Don't pack, it's too late. There's no time left. Bring your families. No friends, no servants. Do you understand?
I'm absolutely heartbroken, my dear friends. But the instructions are formal. If, in three hours at the latest, my helicopters have not left Cambodian soil, they can no longer take off.
What's the matter with you? No time to delay. I know, I know, you feel you're abandoning your friends. I feel the same way. But we can't take everyone. It's too late, too late. It's not my fault you know! I begged you to leave much earlier.
Oh! Please, my friends, hurry! You have one good hour to get your precious things together. But no more.

SAUKHAM KHOY: One hour!

DEAN: We're going straight to Thailand. There's no risk there.

SIRIK MATAK: Excellency and dear friend. I thank you for offering to lead us to freedom. If I accepted it I'd die. Nothing but my death is left to me now, and I don't want to waste it. I want to save the beautiful death of Prince Sirik Matak. To die in the country where one saw the light is not to die, it is to find one's mother again. If you took me away, you would have only the failure and shame of Sirik Matak in your helicopter. As for you and your great country, Mr. Ambassador, it never occurred to me that you would have the sad courage to abandon a people who had chosen *your* freedom. I never doubted you for an instant.

DEAN: You're hard on me.

SIRIK MATAK: We never did understand each other. You refused us your protection, just like the pitiless gods of our religion. And we could do nothing about it.

DEAN: But I couldn't either! I couldn't either!

SIRIK MATAK: You're leaving. The Cambodians are watching you go. Their tears aren't flowing. The foreign friends turn back far away. They won't return. Smiling, the Cambodians contemplate the familiar faces one last time.
We hope you and your country find peace on the other edge of the sky.

DEAN: Prince, Your Excellency. . . . No. Words are useless. Mr. Prime Minister? Not you either?

LONG BORET: Thank you for wanting to understand, Mr. Ambassador. I will stay. I have a lot to do here. My heart has no room for the least regret. It's nothing but desire now. I want the happiness of being able to negotiate with the Communists suitably for the surrender of our army. Then I'll leave content. As for you, Mr. Dean, I hope you'll live to a hundred, happy in the bosom of your family under the starry sky of North America.

DEAN: And you, too, Mr. Saukham Khoy, you, too, want to do your duty, I suppose?

SAUKHAM KHOY: That's what I'd like to do, Mr. Ambassador.

DEAN: Gentlemen. . . . Sometimes the one going away is the one who feels abandoned. I'm leaving and I feel that a certain Ambassador Dean is watching me go, and refusing to follow.
Prince, because of you, your faces, your smiles, I leave a part of my heart in Phnom Penh. Goodbye. [Exit Dean.]

SAUKHAM KHOY: He's going, they're going! They're going!

SIRIK MATAK: They left a long time ago.

SAUKHAM KHOY: They'll be gone in an hour!

LONG BORET: Mr. President, you should hurry. You should go, shouldn't you, Your Excellency?

SIRIK MATAK: That's what I was thinking. You must accept Mr. Dean's offer. You don't have, as we do, powerful reasons for awaiting the Khmer Rouge.

SAUKHAM KHOY: You think so?

SIRIK MATAK: You're not condemned to death like Mr. Long Boret and me. You can take refuge without losing face.

LONG BORET: Do you really think so?

SIRIK MATAK: Go quickly, be off, say goodbye to your wife for me. Go. Go. Don't spoil this departure. Time is as precious as a wounded man's blood.

SAUKHAM KHOY: You think so? I'll ask my wife . . . I'd never have imagined that. . . . To abandon us like that after having pushed us into this war. [Saukham Khoy exits.]

LONG BORET: Poor Saukham Khoy.

SIRIK MATAK: Poor Cambodia. Victim of our cowardice and vanity. [Helicopter noises.] My friend, I am afraid. You?

LONG BORET: I am assuredly afraid too, your Highness, but a sort of passionate hope fights against my fear. Who knows? Where will we be tomorrow? In one week?

SIRIK MATAK: No. For me, I know it's over. May I embrace you?

LONG BORET: You're not leaving me??!!

SIRIK MATAK: No, I'll remain at your side as long . . . as possible. But perhaps when we leave later we'll be separated. Let's clasp each other here . . . in any case. [They hold each other.]

LONG BORET: Prince! At least our people soon will suffer no longer.

SIRIK MATAK: How odd! A very lovely song by my cousin, Prince Sihanouk, has just come back to me. Me, who laughed so much at his music! A good-bye song for Phnom Penh: [He sings the song.]

[The noise of the cannon and the bombs grows. They exit.]

PART 2, ACT 3, SCENE 6

[Phnom Penh. Enter Yukanthor, mad with joy, followed by Khieu Samnol and Madame Lamné.]

YUKANTHOR: I see them, I see them! Grandmother! Madame Lamné! The Khmer Rouge! There they are! There they are! It's the end of the war, Grandmother!

KHIEU SAMNOL: It's the end of the war if you're seeing them! What are they like?

YUKANTHOR: On top of trucks! Oh! They're on top of trucks! On top of trucks!

KHIEU SAMNOL: What on top of trucks? Can you tell us a little what the trucks are like?

YUKANTHOR: I'm coming, I'm coming!

KHIEU SAMNOL: My scarf! Give me back my scarf!

YUKANTHOR: It's to make a welcome flag. It's for Sir Papa! Grand-mother!

MADAME LAMNÉ: Prince Sihanouk? Is he coming?

KHIEU SAMNOL: His Highness Papa? Oh! Buddha! You saw him? And you didn't tell me? How is he?

YUKANTHOR: I didn't see him, Grandmother, but he's going to come because everyone's waiting for him. *[Suddenly they hear loud-speakers in the street.]*

LOUDSPEAKER: Inhabitants of Phnom Penh.
Our capital has just been liberated by our valiant and victorious armed national liberation forces, the Khmer Rouge.
The super traitors who ran away at top speed, crazed and dying, and who knocked on every door begging for help, have been smashed to pieces.
And now, listen! Inhabitants of Phnom Penh, the High Commander of the Revolution gives order for the whole population of the city to leave immediately. Immediately.
Leave the city, leave the city. The American imperialists are bombing tomorrow.
People of Phnom Penh, you must be out of here before nightfall. We are threatened with a bombardment by the American aggressors.
Leave the city!
Everyone must take the Monivong bridge.
Before nightfall. Before nightfall.

KHIEU SAMNOL: Everyone out? Aren't they a bit crazy? What about the sick? Are we going to leave the sick behind in the hospitals?

MADAME LAMNÉ: Do you think he's going to come?

KHIEU SAMNOL: Who?

MADAME LAMNÉ: His Lordship Papa.

LOUDSPEAKER: Everyone must leave. All buildings are to be evacuated. All buildings without exception. Without exception.
You may return in three days. In three days. When our brave forces have swept the city clean of all its arch-fascist traitors, the arch-rotten, the arch-traitors. Leave the city.
Then, as His Lordship Chief of State Norodom Sihanouk has said, we'll build a new Kampuchea.
All together. All together.
Everyone out. Leave the city. Follow the directives of the just and clairvoyant victorious leadership.
Go on routes 4, 5, and 6. Go on, go on. *[They exit with Yukanthor. Hou Youn enters dying.]*

HOU YOUN:
On route 6.
The carts squeal, the rough peasants are holding back their
    sobs.
In the automobiles the women with painted fingernails are
    crying.
Troubled and trembling with sorrow, the citizens sway like
    ghosts.
Children without parents wail
The red dust envelops the mournful route with a red veil.
With fruitless glances the parents look for their children.
Only the birds still think they're living in the world of before
The young girl will never find her mother again
Resigned, the old and weak lie down in the ditches
Beside the road some die without great regret.
Some give birth while hurling curses.
Head low, the passersby think: how sad it is to be born on
    April 17 in the year 1975.
The dead, full of compassion, will tell you that no infant born
    this day will be so unlucky as to survive.
They've broken my neck, they've run my belly through and my
    chest, with sharpened bamboo sticks.
But I'm dying of shame and hatred.

They cast me out of this land, but they could not exile my
  anger.
Floating on the crowd like two dead leaves on the water, two
  old women, holding each other up, go forward while turning
  back around: "Yukanthor, will he find us again?" says one.
"Where and when will he find us?" says the other.
This corpulent man in a black Mercedes, who goes through the
  haggard people smiling is the hateful Ieng Sary.
Seated behind him, Pol Pot remains unimaginable.
The two old women have seen the new Cambodian tyrants pass
  by.
How did they get so fat? they wonder.
On route 6
The slow, blind human river flows.
Phnom Penh was its source.
Where will its mouth be? *[He exits.]*

PART 2, ACT 4, SCENE 1

[Peking. Enter Chou En-lai, servants.]

CHOU EN-LAI:

At twenty, proudly, I set off to conquer the sun.
How short life is! I've kept on going fifty years.
My day is ending. My knees are bent.
Nightfall, and I'm done with nothing yet.
Neither victorious nor vanquished, I must quit.
You, however, my beloved China, you'll go on.
Beware of raw youth chafing under the rider.
Choose patient eternity instead. *[Enter Sihanouk.]*

SIHANOUK: Great friend! . . . You're going to fight! Right? If anyone
can conquer illness with the aid of the gods it's the great Chou En-
lai!

CHOU EN-LAI: Of course I'm struggling, my dear friend.
You're leaving, I hear, for Korea?

SIHANOUK: I don't wish to abuse China's hospitality endlessly.

CHOU EN-LAI: Friend, don't go to Korea. Go back to Cambodia, without dallying any longer. That's my advice and my wish. Your people need you.

SIHANOUK: And I need my people. But they've been stolen from me. I don't want to go off to Korea, but I really think I should.

CHOU EN-LAI: I know, dear Prince, that you're under some misapprehensions about the Kampuchean Communists, but I know above all that many generous as well as political reasons must help you overcome them.

SIHANOUK: Misapprehensions, Your Excellency? There are none. I apprehend everything they're telling me and everything they're keeping from me perfectly, because I have an absolute ear, you know. I'm not ill-informed, just non-informed. Silences as long as months without water, as long as the Great Wall of China. Here is what I have a right to in the so-called dialogue with my painful and unaccustomed so-called ministers.
If you knew what they've been doing to me, these last few weeks, you would not ask Sihanouk to go back to what is no longer his kingdom. The other day, by chance, I learned that Cambodia is no longer a Kingdom! Yes, by chance. Because now, by chance, I'm not being kept abreast of the state of my country by my government by chance. So, right in the middle of the embassy reception I found out that Phnom Penh, my capital, had been taken by the Khmer Rouge. They tell me that my city had been completely emptied. And I, what did I do then in front of everyone? I denied it! Another one of these fantastic tales, I proclaimed.

CHOU EN-LAI: I'm not sorry that you couldn't believe this news.

SIHANOUK: How did that make me look? Your Excellency, I looked like a liar and a fool! Right? And such humiliation when, traveling through Albania, they throw a big banquet for me to celebrate the new constitution of my country! Unhappy Sihanouk, what can he do? Well, he toasts the grandiose new constitution which he has approved, and which he has never heard of!
The Khmer Rouge, Your Excellency, don't use this term with me, they only plague me! So, I'm going to Korea, I withdraw, I cut the puppet strings, I free Sihanouk from his shameful posture. I'm no longer a player. I'm going to resign with pride and salvage my

own delicate health. The shame of it all would end by taking my skin. You understand?

CHOU EN-LAI: I understand, I suffer from whatever hurts you, and nevertheless, I insist: Go back to Phnom Penh. Cambodia's destiny is worth supreme patience.
By withdrawing now, you give your people over to men in whom neither you nor I can have any clear confidence.

SIHANOUK: Then you don't like them either!

CHOU EN-LAI: They lack refinement. If you leave them an entirely clear field they'll turn Cambodia into a prematurely and excessively communist country. Stay, stay with them, in order to be— amidst your people—as memory and as hope. I'm asking this for Cambodia's sake as well as China's. We would have preferred time to polish our compatriots' sharp teeth a bit.

[The Secretary enters.]

SECRETARY: Mr. and Mrs. Ieng Sary, Your Excellency.

CHOU EN-LAI: Well, what do you say, my son?

SIHANOUK: Could Sihanouk ever say no to Chou En-lai?

CHOU EN-LAI: Thank you. [to the Secretary] We await these visitors, his Highness and I. [Secretary goes out.]

SIHANOUK: [to the public] Cambodian gods, may Chou En-lai not be pushing down the wrong path! Don't let him leave this world too soon! And let me not find myself tomorrow at a . . . "dead end" (in a cul-de-sac, if you'll permit me this expression), all alone, without him. [Enter Ieng Sary and Ieng Thirit.]

CHOU EN-LAI: Welcome to the beloved communist comrade from noble, free Kampuchea. The Prince has just expressed his ardent desire to go back to his gloriously liberated country, so that he can serve his people there in the heart of a government over which he has the honor to preside. This exemplary government rejoices the heart of China.

IENG SARY: We are quite aware of this, Mr. Prime Minister, and very honored by it.

176

SIHANOUK: I'm most anxious to see my country again, my friends . . . those who are left. And my very esteemed government, in full power, including Mr. Saloth Sâr Pol Pot whom I so rarely have the pleasure of greeting, and the honest Mr. Hou Youn whom I never see anymore.

IENG SARY: His Grace will be able to find out what extraordinary transformations that we have wrought in record time in our war-ravaged country.

CHOU EN-LAI: It's precisely in this spirit of record time that I wanted to impart my slowly ripening thoughts to you. You're young, you're beginning to plant communism in your venerable land. You will thus have a chance we Chinese did not: benefitting from the experience of your elders.
Dizzy impatience cost China many a disastrous failure.
Men must be turned around with gentleness and slowness. Proceed delicately. Treat your country like a baby, or better yet, like an aged mother. Above all, no Great Leap Forward. Walk like a gardener, taking care not to crush young plants. People must grow toward communism like flowers toward the sun. There are seasons. Don't skip them. That's my thought.

IENG THIRIT: *[to Ieng Sary]* You'd think we were in the Pagoda.

IENG SARY: Your Excellency . . .

SIHANOUK: Our government is moved and profoundly cognizant of your clairvoyant solicitude. Yes? Yes, aren't you quite moved, Madame Ieng Sary?

IENG THIRIT: Quite.

IENG SARY: The Chinese experience is precious for the whole universe. We'll draw the proper conclusions from it.

CHOU EN-LAI: I must leave you. My unfaithful legs are willing to support me no longer. You see what happens when one has been too quick.

SIHANOUK: May I accompany you, dear friend?

CHOU EN-LAI: I was going to beg you to do just that. *[Sihanouk and Chou En-lai exit.]*

IENG SARY: I'm looking at the past, going off on tottering little footsteps, leaning on the past.

IENG THIRIT: It's incredible! The old Chinese is jealous! Slow down! He wants us to slow down!

IENG SARY: Our Revolution is going to give the world proof that one can achieve perfect communism in a single blow, and without mealy-mouthed hesitations. As Pol Pot says, it's Cambodia that's going to win the trophy in the Revolutions competition. We just have to stick with it.

IENG THIRIT: What will the old monk say tomorrow when we are all alone at the peak of this century?

IENG SARY: Nothing at all any more. He'll be dead tomorrow. And then we'll have China's full support without all this reticence and all these codicils.

IENG THIRIT: And Sihanouk? Will we have to go on keeping him at our expense?

IENG SARY: Let him go back to Cambodia. Caged, a lion is no more worrisome than a bird. [Exeunt.]

PART 2, ACT 4, SCENE 2

[Night. Camp of Veal Vong. Enter Khieu Samnol and Madame Lamné.]

KHIEU SAMNOL: Here is where the dead disembark when they cross the river to look for the living. You have the candle?

MADAME LAMNÉ: Are you sure, Samnol?

KHIEU SAMNOL: Sure? It cost me three boxes of rice for the old holy woman who has the forest genie in her body. They start passing by when the first star comes out. But if you don't have faith, they won't want to stop.

MADAME LAMNÉ: But I do believe, I do believe. I swear to you. The second son of my neighbor lady died today and she no longer had the strength to cry. Her father was expiring at the same moment. Sadness itself hasn't tears enough for everyone.

KHIEU SAMNOL: One dead every day! Three dead! Five dead! But they want the end of everyone!

MADAME LAMNÉ: Yes, it took me some time to comprehend that. But if they cut down the rations, it's because they really do want us to disappear.

KHIEU SAMNOL: Well, I'm going to ask the great cadre chief Khieu Samphan: "Comrade, how can we live without eating? work without strength? sow without grain? populate without children? believe without hope? This is what the Revolution is, then? The transformation of poor Cambodians into beasts who no longer have any human qualities but memory?

MADAME LAMNÉ: My dear sister, you should have saved your own life, you with your son so highly placed.

KHIEU SAMNOL: Don't speak to me of that, ever, Madame Lamné! I have wiped my son from my memory, and remember him only to curse him. I would rather be dead than mother to such a son. Are you watching the sky with your good eyes?

MADAME LAMNÉ: I'm watching. But where is our Sihanouk? What's he waiting for before coming to save us?

KHIEU SAMNOL: It seems that he is going to come back to our country and retake the reins at New Year's.

MADAME LAMNÉ: At New Year's? Then we'll not see him. It's already October, and I think we'll die in November if no one saves us.

KHIEU SAMNOL: October? But, my dear, it's already late in November.

MADAME LAMNÉ: Don't tell me November?! Then I'm losing track of time too.

KHIEU SAMNOL: You see, that's better. We're already to November and we're not dead yet.

MADAME LAMNÉ: Yes, but they told me that Sihanouk already came to deliver us, and that they locked him in prison.

KHIEU SAMNOL: That's not true. He is coming back, he'll reopen the pagodas, the schools, and he is giving the Khmer Rouge orders to let us go back home immediately. That's what he said. In five points. That's what I've been told.

MADAME LAMNÉ: Who told you that?

KHIEU SAMNOL: The village chief. He's a red, but he used to be a monk.

MADAME LAMNÉ: And he told me: "You'll be here your whole life. The Angkar said so."

KHIEU SAMNOL: He told you that? But me, I was told by a new fellow that Commander Kong Siloah has become a partisan to combat the Khmer Rouge and get rid of them.

MADAME LAMNÉ: Kong Siloah? Captain Kong Siloah? But he died before April 17. The Khmer Rouge killed him because he loved the Prince too much.

KHIEU SAMNOL: The captain, perhaps, but not the commander.

MADAME LAMNÉ: They say! They say! They say! They say! Instead of rice we live on "they say" now.

KHIEU SAMNOL: We're grasping at straws.

MADAME LAMNÉ: The Star! the Star!

KHIEU SAMNOL: Quick! the candle! Pray to your gods. I'm going to call on Her Majesty the Queen, because I know that she cannot have forgotten us.
"My very dear August Majesty, how are you today? Speak!" I hear nothing!

MADAME LAMNÉ: Not like that! "Above all, August Majesty, if you haven't time to answer us, take your august time."

KHIEU SAMNOL: Let me say it!
"My very dear Majesty, I will never forget your face, your smile, your gentle action of embracing me, your gentle words with me."

MADAME LAMNÉ: "And do you remember us?" Is she going to come?

KHIEU SAMNOL: Pray, it's better to do that.
"Madame Lamné and I, we believe that you're asking the gods to protect us." [The Queen has come in. Only Madame Lamné sees her.] "I know, dear Queen, that I'm wasting your precious time,

but it is because I'm placing my greatest confidence in you due to your very strong royal power and your holiness."

MADAME LAMNÉ: Your Majesty! Your Majesty!

KHIEU SAMNOL: Our Majesty!

QUEEN KOSSOMAK: My beloved aunts! At last! I heard you, I heard you and I was having trouble finding you in the dark!

KHIEU SAMNOL: This is all we have for a candle. Oh! my beloved saint, I adore you! To have come here! How are you? Oh! You're making me laugh.

QUEEN KOSSOMAK: I have been looking for friends for a long time and finding no one. I meet up with an old peasant woman on the route to Takeo. She is looking for her children. I carry her on my back. At the entrance to the city, she grows very heavy and she is dead. I find no loving. I meet the dead everywhere. All my old ones, all my beloved young—I find them thrown by the thousands to the vultures in ditches. I find them decomposing all alone in forests.

KHIEU SAMNOL: They forbid us to burn the bodies. Our poor dead remain raw and disturbed.

QUEEN KOSSOMAK: I find Prince Monireth, my beloved brother, my aunts, my cousins, my Bothum Popha too. And all her children! My own grandchildren and their children. I can save no one, not a one! Finally the gods grant me the favor of finding you, my dear aunts.

KHIEU SAMNOL: And how is Madame Mom Savay? We can absolutely never forget the moment of our first meeting.

MADAME LAMNÉ: And her photo, we look at it every day!

MOM SAVAY: [who has entered] Not every day, Madame Lamné. I've been here for a week, and you didn't look at me once!

KHIEU SAMNOL: For a week! Madame Mom Savay?! But where are you staying? In whose house?! I didn't come across you either!

QUEEN KOSSOMAK: My dear sisters, don't you see that my beloved sister has passed to the other side?

KHIEU SAMNOL: You, too, are dead, Madame Mom Savay? Oh! Oh yet one more sorrow! Madame Lamné, yet one more sorrow!

MOM SAVAY: Above all, don't cry for me, my dear friends, I'm fine now, I'm saved.

QUEEN KOSSOMAK: My beloved little Mom Savay, they. . . .

MOM SAVAY: Say nothing! I don't want you to speak of it! Don't think about it any more, my love. And you, poor friends, what about you? It's you whom we have come to see, you who are suffering and still fear dying.

MADAME LAMNÉ: We fear living most of all. Since we were expelled from Phnom Penh we are still in poverty and feeling terrible. On Friday the eleventh I suffered a malaria attack.
And Madame Khieu Samnol is always taken with the colic and is practically emptied out. Happily, it's not too serious because we're together, we're not apart. But we're both despairing of life.

KHIEU SAMNOL:
    One day without rice, life goes
    A lump of sugar is paradise.

MADAME LAMNÉ: But there is never any.

KHIEU SAMNOL: Dear Queen, you who are so intelligent and wise, what can I do to find a little rice before dying?

MOM SAVAY: Have you no jewels? I've noticed the Khmer Rouge don't disdain the jingle of coins.

KHIEU SAMNOL: We had the great sorrow of being robbed of the ring Madame Lamné inherited from her mother which was banded by twelve little diamonds. And now we have nothing more, except these one hundred miserable dollars.

QUEEN KOSSOMAK: A hundred dollars! But that's better than a jewel!

KHIEU SAMNOL: You can see you're no longer from here, Great Majesty. They're throwing dollars into the river. And not only American money; all currencies: riels, francs. . . . Everything. Money has been suppressed.

182

MADAME LAMNÉ: Now, to get rice you'd have to buy it with rice.

MOM SAVAY: Careful! Someone is at the end of the path! Leave!

MADAME LAMNÉ: The village chief! Quick! Let's get out of here!

KHIEU SAMNOL: Pardon us, my very dear Majesty!

QUEEN KOSSOMAK: No, dear aunts. We won't abandon you. We're staying here. We await you.

KHIEU SAMNOL: No! Don't stay! Don't stay! I beg you. They are so evil, they'll even assassinate the dead!

QUEEN KOSSOMAK: We'll go back to the other side of the river. We shall return. *[The two old women exit.]* But go quickly. *[Enter Hou Youn, dead.]*

QUEEN KOSSOMAK: Oh! It was only Mr. Hou Youn! Mr. Hou Youn! Are you also looking for someone?

HOU YOUN: I seek my brother throughout the forests, the rivers, the villages. I do not find my brother.

MOM SAVAY: When you were in the maquis, how many brothers did you kill before they cut out your tongue and cut off your hands?

HOU YOUN: I've never killed anyone with my own hands.

QUEEN KOSSOMAK: Don't argue, Mom Savay. He's never understood. He never understands.

HOU YOUN: May I walk along with you?

MOM SAVAY: Please, come.

QUEEN KOSSOMAK:
How strange it is
We are in extreme misfortune
The river that separated the worlds
Has become as thin as a wand
The living, each day, are closer to the dead.
And just as one passes from life to death in one step
So, too, one passes from hatred to pity. *[They exit.]*

PART 2, ACT 4, SCENE 3

[Siem Reap. Outskirts of Angkor. Enter Sihanouk, the Princess, Penn Nouth]

SIHANOUK: No. I don't want to take one more step. I want to lie down right here under this fig tree and go to sleep. My dear Penn Nouth, you will tell his Excellency Comrade Khieu Samphan that Sihanouk fainted under the fig tree.

THE PRINCESS: Just one more work site, Your Grace, and it's over!

PENN NOUTH: I beg you to show patience.

SIHANOUK: I can't stand it any longer! The visit to Battambang yesterday exhausted me. Today Siem Reap finishes me off with the final blow. I want to die immediately and to find myself safe and sound in Peking.
Besides—aren't we already ghosts? I found you strange, yesterday, dear friend, while we were passing through the deserted streets of our cities which were once so animated.

PENN NOUTH: It's true, Your Grace, hearing the Khmer Rouge resound in these muted boulevards, I was struck dumb as if by an evil lightning bolt, I was streaming with a cold sweat. Nevertheless, My Lord. . . .

SIHANOUK: Pagodas razed, mosques full of pigs, mountains of automobiles cut up like beef and pyramids of rusty air conditioners. They could at least have sold them in Thailand! But no! no!
And my children, my poor children who dig and dig day and night as if the kings of Hell had given them the order to dig a single, immense tomb for my Cambodia. And here I am on a guided tour of this tomb! I'm a guest in Hell! I pass, and from afar they see Sihanouk going by, and, digging and digging, they watch him passing, and they smile with so sad a joy, so faraway, so desolate. And the air between us is filled with mute appeals, with good-byes and regrets. No! No! I can't stand this spectacle any longer! I must resign immediately, immediately!

THE PRINCESS: No, not right away. If they can no longer use Sihanouk, they will be completely without scruples.

PENN NOUTH: My Lord, I beg you to keep your calm. Let us present a smooth face.

SIHANOUK: But I'm not, Penn Nouth, I'm not! I don't know how to put a calm coating over my face when I'm racked with sobs. If I can't show my feelings, I'll turn into a Chinese monkey! I don't want to wear false smiles. I want to cry! I want to cry! I want to weep! I want to be a man again!

PENN NOUTH: You're not the only one!

THE PRINCESS: Your impatience not only endangers Sihanouk, but also all those who, because of their extreme fidelity, didn't want to refuse to come back with you.

PENN NOUTH: Your Grace, I see Mr. Khieu Samphan coming back.

[Enter Khieu Samphan and some Khmer Rouge guards.]

THE PRINCESS: For Buddha's sake, say nothing! Nothing!

SIHANOUK: *[to Khieu Samphan]* Ah! My dear Vice-President! I have awaited you with impatience. As the head of state of Democratic Kampuchea, I want to make a few remarks to you.

PENN NOUTH: *[to the Princess]* He's going to get us killed, Madame.

KHIEU SAMPHAN: What remarks, Your Grace?

THE PRINCESS: No. It is I, My Lord. Mr. Vice-President, it is I who have a few petty complaints, to tell you the truth. I found the condition of the Shelter of the Temples of Siem Reap left a lot to be desired; and I tell you we're haunted by toilets that don't flush. Frankly, the New Cambodia could not receive foreign visitors under such conditions. I advise you to repair your bathrooms.

KHIEU SAMPHAN: Thank you. I'll see to it. Now if you want to climb up to the parapet. From here we see the work sites over the horizon.

SIHANOUK: I want to very much. Since my return I want very much to do what I don't want to do.

KHIEU SAMPHAN: Look at these thousands of workers digging the canal with faces flooded with pride.

SIHANOUK: Completely. Flooded.

KHIEU SAMPHAN: Who would believe that they were, but a few months ago, unfortunate hostages locked by force into the concentration camps of Phnom Penh and the other cities.

THE PRINCESS: What do you mean concentration camps??

KHIEU SAMPHAN: Our compatriots were dying by the millions of hunger and mistreatment. Families were painfully separated. Women were given over to prostitution. Children were kidnapped and sold by tens of thousands to American slave traders.

THE PRINCESS: [to Sihanouk] What's he telling us?

SIHANOUK: One of us must be mad! Merciful Buddha, guard Sihanouk's sanity!

KHIEU SAMPHAN: Finally, the seventeenth of April arrived. Then began an era of happiness, prosperity, dignity, whose radiant image you can, after only a few months, already see reflected in all these shining glances.

SIHANOUK: [to Penn Nouth] Your Excellency, do you see this reflection?

PENN NOUTH: I see it My Lord, I see it.

SIHANOUK: Don't you find it looks a bit like a camel?

PENN NOUTH: Like a camel, Sir?

SIHANOUK: Or, perhaps not, rather like a weasel? No?

PENN NOUTH: A weasel?

THE PRINCESS: A weasel, yes! Your Excellency! Yes, assuredly, a weasel!

PENN NOUTH: Ah hah! Like a weasel, of course! It's just like that! "Or like a whale!"[39]

SIHANOUK: Why, yes! Like a whale! This image "is very like a whale," Mr. Vice-President.

---

[39]English original, quote from *Hamlet*. TR

KHIEU SAMPHAN: Excuse me? I don't understand.

PENN NOUTH: It's a quotation.

SIHANOUK: *Hamlet.* Act three, scene two. Do you like William Shakespeare, Mr. Vice-President?

KHIEU SAMPHAN: Each evening the workers say that every day's a holiday now. In the old society, life was very sad. People worked side by side without ever meeting each other. No one knew happiness.

SIHANOUK: I have a rather different memory of it. And you, Mr. Penn Nouth?

PENN NOUTH: My Lord, the extraordinary zeal of these new Cambodians fills me with wonder. *[Enter Yukanthor.]*

YUKANTHOR: Oh! My Lord Papa! You came back and I'm seeing you for myself, with your own feet and in your own sandals on this land which was so sad and desolate only five minutes ago, and also for so many years. O your hands, Your Grace! Your hands, all your fingers, and your palms. Oh! It's really you, My Lord Papa, and it is really me, Yukanthor, who you see again and who am myself!
Without you, My Lord, for months and months when I was working under the cruel sun, I was an orphan. But I dreamed of when My Lord Papa will find out, when My Lord Papa will come back by way of the path through the bamboos, with his round face, tender as the moon, coming to save us desperate ones!

SIHANOUK: Any you never stop thinking about the shining future, I know.

YUKANTHOR: Oh! It's really your voice! I hear you and my ears drink in the cool water of your voice! Oh! Your Grace, today I see my dream popping out of my head and coming true right in front of me, in reality.

SIHANOUK: My dear child, we see our dreams being realized too. Since our country, thanks to the Angkar of which His Excellency here present is an eminent member, is recovering its sovereignty and all the Khmer patriots are reunited at last. You understand

deeply the path to follow for the country's recovery. You also love
and admire intensely the Angkar who sees everything and has
more eyes than a pineapple.

YUKANTHOR: But, My Lord. . . .

THE PRINCESS: I see by the shining radiance of your eyes that you've
understood, my child? Right?

YUKANTHOR: Yes, I understand down deep, Sir, I see right through![40]
May our revolutionary Angkar be celebrated! He liberated us
from rotten, corrupt regimes and . . . and . . .

PRINCESS: Thanks to the Angkar, peace . . .

YUKANTHOR: Thanks to the Angkar peace and justice reign over the
whole country. In short, I've never been so happy.

SIHANOUK: I congratulate you on it. And now go back to the work
yard and continue digging this admirable canal, with your heart
full of radiant optimism, your eyes full of tears of pride.

YUKANTHOR: Yes, My Lord, I'm going back. *[He exits.]*

KHIEU SAMPHAN: *[to a guard]* Follow him and keep him under sur-
veillance. Now, My Lord, we're going to visit the crocodile farm.

SIHANOUK: Oh, no! Your Excellency, no! I've already seen them.

KHIEU SAMPHAN: How? No you haven't.

SIHANOUK: Oh, but I have! Crocodiles as big as whales. Right my
love?

PENN NOUTH: Buddha, have mercy!

THE PRINCESS: Your Excellency, My Lord is weary.

SIHANOUK: No? Yet I could swear I did. Since the death of my precious mother my memory is somewhat whimsical. What is it I was
starting to say a moment ago? Oh yes! Your Excellency, the visit
to this province, the work done under the enlightened Angkar, has

<hr />

[40] *Profondément* and *clairement* would usually be translated as "profoundly" or
"deeply," but might not ordinarily be spoken by a youth. Yukanthor is trying to convey to Sihanouk that he "gets" that he's being overheard by Khieu Samphan. TR

made me understand my duty fully. I, who belong to the ancien régime, must not tarnish the brightness of the Revolution, so pure, by encrusting myself like a leech in the state apparatus.

Yes, I'm convinced: there must be "fair play."[41] Sihanouk must step down. And let "bygones be bygones."[42] I'm going to announce it to the people.

PENN NOUTH: Your Lordship!

KHIEU SAMPHAN: No, no, your Grace! In front of Mr. Chou En-lai we promised to keep you as Chief of State of the Kampuchean Democracy in perpetuity. And we'll keep our promises.

SIHANOUK: Oh, but it's so excellent! I'll announce it to the people.

PENN NOUTH: His Lordship has a fever.

PRINCESS: Your Excellency, we're really tired out, His Grace and I. Permit us to go lie down.

SIHANOUK: Yes, that's it! That's what I wanted to say! Let's put the crocodiles away! I'll announce it to the people.

KHIEU SAMPHAN: If you like, I'll escort you to the hotel right away.

SIHANOUK: No! Not right away! I want to talk to the people!

KHIEU SAMPHAN: No! No! We're leaving, we're leaving right now.

PRINCESS: Let's go back! Let's go back, Your Grace!

PENN NOUTH: All this will be taken care of, Your Grace! Everything will be settled, Your Excellency. This will pass.

SIHANOUK: "Let bygones be bygones"![43] *[They lead him off. Everyone exits but Khieu Samphan.]*

KHIEU SAMPHAN: Beware, insolent residue of tyranny! If, through the scandal of a heedless resignation, you dare degrade our glorious image in the eyes of the world, we'll carry ruin and mourning into your cowardly retreat. We'll create a mortal void before your eyes.

---

[41] English in the original. TR
[42] English in the original. TR
[43] English in the original. TR

189

And you'll end by being surrounded with the icy phantoms of your parents, your friends, your whole court of servile parasites.
Messrs Ong Meang, Chea San, Sarin Chak, Norodom Phurissara, Norodom Naradipo, Sisowath Methavi:
Shave your heads and complain to the gods, because Sihanouk, your father, has abandoned you and condemned you to death.

PART 2, ACT 4, SCENE 4

[Night: Camp of Veal Vong. Enter Khieu Samnol and Madame Lamné]

MADAME LAMNÉ: But why is she taking so long? I wouldn't like to go away without saying my good-byes to her.

KHIEU SAMNOL: If she is not yet here, it's surely because she knows that there's no emergency, my dearie. She'll come see us, as usual. O Great Adored Queen! Hurry! I'm so afraid, so afraid for my little sister. Oh my god! Here she is.

MADAME LAMNÉ: Where! Where?

KHIEU SAMNOL: Over there. She's coming. But, but, she's not at all hurried. Oh! No. She's taking slow steps as if she were thinking. *[Enter Queen Kossomak.]*

MADAME LAMNÉ: Great Queen, I'm so happy to see you again because I think I'm going to go away today!

QUEEN KOSSOMAK: Madame Lamné, my dear, if you can wait until tomorrow still without eating, I'll save you both.

KHIEU SAMNOL: Why, of course we'll wait, My Queen, right? Save her for me, August and Powerful Lady, save her for me!

MADAME LAMNÉ: I'd really like to know your idea.

QUEEN KOSSOMAK: Buddha has granted me an idea! Your dollars, we are going to revive them. When Mr. Tchang, the Chinese man, goes by, you, Madame Samnol, you will beg Madame Lamné to sell you her dollars.

MADAME LAMNÉ: Sell my dollars? To my sister?

QUEEN KOSSOMAK: She begs you very hard. In front of Mr. Tchang the Chinese man. Very, very hard. She says to you: "I'm buying your dollars, Madame Lamné."

MADAME LAMNÉ: But dollars—

KHIEU SAMNOL: Listen to her Majesty! So, I buy her dollars. But with what?

QUEEN KOSSOMAK: With whatever you have: with your last boxes of rice. You say: "I'm prepared to pay you three boxes of rice for your dollars."

KHIEU SAMNOL: I say three boxes of rice.

QUEEN KOSSOMAK: In front of the Chinese, Mr. Tchang.

KHIEU SAMNOL: In front of the Chinese.

MADAME LAMNÉ: Three boxes of rice, what?? But she doesn't even have one box of rice left!

QUEEN KOSSOMAK: Madame Lamné! Don't be so impatient. Listen carefully. She proposes three boxes of rice to you. Then you refuse.

KHIEU SAMNOL: She refuses? Three boxes of rice? But you're mad, my sister!

QUEEN KOSSOMAK: Be quiet while I speak!

MADAME LAMNÉ: Yes, let me hear!

QUEEN KOSSOMAK: All this is *in front of the Chinese man*. The Chinese man sees everything. He hears everything. He sees that you are ready to give up rice in order to get these dollars. He, who till then had thought that the dollar was dead.

KHIEU SAMNOL: Wait, wait! Oh! I see!

MADAME LAMNÉ: Why, what do you see, say it!

KHIEU SAMNOL: Why, I see the Chinese man!

MADAME LAMNÉ: You see the Chinese man? Oh, my god! My eyes are already giving out, then.

KHIEU SAMNOL: No, no. I see the Chinese man in my head. He's watching us like so, while I, I'm buying dollars from you, and he's saying to himself: "So, dollars are still currency?" Is that it, your Majesty?

QUEEN KOSSOMAK: That's it, that's it, Madame Khieu Samnol.

KHIEU SAMNOL: Then you, you don't want to sell me your dollars, not even to me, your friend you love like a sister.

MADAME LAMNÉ: Me, I don't want to? Great Queen!?

KHIEU SAMNOL: One wouldn't believe she's Vietnamese!

QUEEN KOSSOMAK: You let her beg and beg, Madame Lamné, up to the point where Madame Samnol proposes seven boxes to you.

KHIEU SAMNOL: Seven boxes!

QUEEN KOSSOMAK: Then the Chinese man gets more and more interested.

MADAME LAMNÉ: Oh! Yes! Oh! Yes! Oh! That's it! That's it! Oh, my god! I think I'm about to understand! Yes, yes. . . . Oh! no. . . .

KHIEU SAMNOL: Buddha! Jesus! Everyone! Help her!

QUEEN KOSSOMAK: Hurry, dear Madame Lamné, because I see the Chinese man leaving his house.

MADAME LAMNÉ: Wait! Wait! And then, then, the Chinese man will . . . get interested in my dollars? Is that it?

QUEEN KOSSOMAK: That's it! Bravo, my dear.

MADAME LAMNÉ: Oh! How tired I am! Oh! How happy I am!

QUEEN KOSSOMAK: Here he is. Get going, Madame Samnol. Go on. [She goes off a little way.]

KHIEU SAMNOL: I beg of you, Madame Lamné, dear Madame Lamné. You have no need of all these dollars. I'll bring you three more boxes of rice next week.

MADAME LAMNÉ: Next week . . . ?

QUEEN KOSSOMAK: [whispering] "No! I shan't let go of my dollars at that price!"

MADAME LAMNÉ: No! I'll not let go of my dollars at that price. And I'll be dead by next week!

KHIEU SAMNOL: Don't speak of misfortune! What if I swear to you I'll bring you five more boxes tomorrow?

MADAME LAMNÉ: Tomorrow? Five boxes?

QUEEN KOSSOMAK: "No, no."

MADAME LAMNÉ: Five? Tomorrow? No, no, no!

KHIEU SAMNOL: Six boxes. Will you make me an offer? Me, your Samnol whom you so dearly love?

MADAME LAMNÉ: You know, I've already been offered more than that just now and I didn't budge! Because . . .

QUEEN KOSSOMAK: Yes, yes, yes, Madame Lamné!

MADAME LAMNÉ: Because dollars, they're stronger than everything right now. The word is getting around.

QUEEN KOSSOMAK: Yes! Yes!

MADAME LAMNÉ: And you know . . . if I weren't afraid to go over there before the frontier's opened I wouldn't part with a single dollar.

QUEEN KOSSOMAK: Magnificent! Magnificent!

CHINESE MAN: [aside] The frontier's opening?

KHIEU SAMNOL: I don't want to profit from your condition, my poor Madame Lamné. I love you so, I'd give you all the rice in the world if I had it.

MADAME LAMNÉ: I know my dear, I know. Now, how much can you really pay?

KHIEU SAMNOL: Really? Six right away, and then I still have a pretty golden Buddha. I could get six boxes out of it and then. . . .

QUEEN KOSSOMAK: Good! Good! Go on!

MADAME LAMNÉ: Good. Okay. But for that amount, I'm giving you only one fifty-dollar bill, right? [The Chinese man draws closer.]

KHIEU SAMNOL: Many thanks, Madame Lamné.

MADAME LAMNÉ: Unless I'm dead: then I'll leave you everything.

CHINESE MAN: I see that you're interested in dollars, Ladies?

KHIEU SAMNOL: Of course. When our country reestablishes relations with Thailand, next week, and the Khmer Rouge reinstate currency, which one's going to be strong? The dollar!

MADAME LAMNÉ: Especially now that there's none left. I've seen people lighting fires with them, and even wiping themselves.

CHINESE MAN: Relations with Thailand? Who told you that?

KHIEU SAMNOL: Go ask the village chief. He told my nephew so. His uncle is a Khmer Rouge cadre very highly placed is the one who told him so. The village chief. This morning.

MADAME LAMNÉ: You're talking too much, Madame Khieu. Now it's going to go through the camp like lightning. Everyone is going to want some.

KHIEU SAMNOL: What do you mean I talk too much? What about you?

CHINESE MAN: In any case, I'll say nothing about it. But will you do me a little favor then? Do you still have some dollars?

MADAME LAMNÉ: Well, yes.

KHIEU SAMNOL: [to Madame Lamné] You're not going to sell your dollars to a person who has everything he needs and rice to boot and all?

MADAME LAMNÉ: Oh! Listen, Madame Samnol. I already made you a price.

CHINESE MAN: How much do you have left?

MADAME LAMNÉ: Two fifty-dollar bills.

CHINESE MAN: That's not much. But I'll give you twenty boxes of rice for it.

MADAME LAMNÉ: Twenty!

KHIEU SAMNOL: You see! I would have given you fifty!

CHINESE MAN: Fifty? Ha! ho! ho! No! No! I'll give you twenty-five.

MADAME LAMNÉ: Twenty-five! Ha, ha, ha! No! No!

CHINESE MAN: No! Ho, ho, hee! Well, I'm off!

MADAME LAMNÉ: You're going?

QUEEN KOSSOMAK: Let him go.

MADAME LAMNÉ: Good. Hey! great. Good-bye. Anyway, I prefer to keep them for Madame Khieu Samnol.

CHINESE MAN: All right. Forty.

MADAME LAMNÉ: *[to the Queen]* What do I do? Is it worth it?

QUEEN KOSSOMAK: Fine.

MADAME LAMNÉ: Fine. Go on, Madame Samnol, don't be sad, I still have one bill left. I'll save it for you. Now hurry up, Mr. Tchang, I'll wait for you. Because if others go by, eh. . . .

CHINESE MAN: I'll be back, I'll be back. *[to the audience]* The old lady must have others up her sleeve. She's wicked. These Vietnamese are wicked. *[He exits.]*

KHIEU SAMNOL: Forty boxes Madame Lamné! Next week your cheeks will be fat! Oh! Beloved Power, truly you're brilliant!

MADAME LAMNÉ: Oh! High and Mighty! I suddenly caught on, I got it! I understood so well I'm giddy. I tell you, Samnol, when the Chinese man gives us the forty boxes, put thirty aside, then take ten and run and sell them to . . . who's got dollars around here?

KHIEU SAMNOL: Mr. Peang. I sell him how many?

MADAME LAMNÉ: Oh! Well, you can go as high as twenty boxes for two hundred dollars. On account of the friendship you bear him. But no more, okay?

KHIEU SAMNOL: Twenty boxes. Two hundred dollars. Then I come back.

MADAME LAMNÉ: Why no! No! You run over to the Chinese man's with the two hundred dollars.

KHIEU SAMNOL: Oh, of course! How silly I am. Then I'll sell him the two hundred dollars. For forty boxes!

MADAME LAMNÉ: You could try for fifty, right?

KHIEU SAMNOL: Fifty!

MADAME LAMNÉ: Whereupon you take ten boxes and you . . .

KHIEU SAMNOL: But tell me, Madame Lamné, how far are you going with this? You think the Chinese man still has his warehouses filled to the roof with rice?

QUEEN KOSSOMAK: It's true there'll come an end to the rice, Madame Lamné. For Mr. Tchang, too. But you'll have what it takes to survive on for a while. And then I'll see, I'll look around.

MADAME LAMNÉ: I know, I know, but anyhow. It gives me so much pleasure to think of all that rice.

KHIEU SAMNOL: Look at her sticking up like a flower that's been well watered!

MADAME LAMNÉ: It's only because I'm so amused. *[They exit.]*

PART 2, ACT 4, SCENE 5

[Enter Princess and Sihanouk.]

SIHANOUK: Not even one little smile?

THE PRINCESS: I cannot, My Lord.

SIHANOUK: Three days without smiling, it's hard! You've closed the doors of your face to me.

THE PRINCESS: Since you sent this fatal resignation letter, my mad thoughts betray me and no longer obey anything but my fear.

SIHANOUK: And yet I maintain that the Earth is still spinning, and that I did the right thing to resign. For a year now, I have been lying with every breath. No, I don't breathe at all: I lie, I lie, I lie red. Each time I open my mouth, I turn red up to my teeth. But the worst is not the shame of it. By lying I'm constructing the Tower of Lies, I'm creating the Hell of False Truths myself. And by dint of calling darkness "radiant" and prison "sweet liberty" I'll end by forgetting what the true light is, the true truth. Then one day, I too, will call the silence of death "music." All I have borne in order not to die and not have others killed is

196

worse than death. And do you really believe if I hadn't resigned that all those for whom I fear Khmer Rouge vengeance, would have been spared?

THE PRINCESS: I do.

SIHANOUK: I don't any longer. The minute Khieu Samphan says to me: "So and so is doing very well" I translate: "he has just died." *[Enter Ong Meang.]*

ONG MEANG: My Lord, His Excellency Penn Nouth, all by himself!

SIHANOUK: All alone! Quick, let him in! *[Enter Penn Nouth.]* My dear old crow, my millennial tree! How did you manage to shake them?

PENN NOUTH: I didn't shake them, My Lord. I obtained only the favor of one last interview with your Highness.

THE PRINCESS: One *last*!?

PENN NOUTH: No, no. I mean: one last private interview before all the measures entailed by the final decision are taken by the "beloved" Angkar.
Renounce, My Lord, renounce. The Angkar holds on to you so furiously that it can not do without Your Highness without . . . great damage.

SIHANOUK: You mean without reprisals?

THE PRINCESS: My Lord is under the protection of China!

PENN NOUTH: Only under that of the late Chou En-lai, Your Highness. But since his demise . . . My Lord, you'll be arrested.

SIHANOUK: Did they tell you that to frighten me?

PENN NOUTH: They begged me to deter you from your project. But at this moment, it's Penn Nouth begging you.

THE PRINCESS: And you think they'll carry out their threats?

PENN NOUTH: I do.

SIHANOUK: Well, then, I'll carry out my threat today, too. My resignation and I are no longer separate.

I've finally found the necessary courage.
True, such courage frightens me. I have gooseflesh, but I'm in ecstasy.

PENN NOUTH: My Lord, I fear that many people who are dear to you—and near—will be paying a cruel price for such courage.

SIHANOUK: I beg you, Lord Penn Nouth, help me resign.

PENN NOUTH: How could I, My Lord?!

SIHANOUK: Don't follow my path. Remain safely on the red Khmer bank. I don't have the strength to be guilty of every anguish. Abandon me! And safeguard thus your venerable person.

PENN NOUTH: And if, My Lord, if I. . . . If I told you that . . . I agree to stay . . . in the Angkar . . . you'd pardon me?

SIHANOUK: I'd thank you, dear Penn Nouth. This is what I dare ask of you!

PENN NOUTH: Well, My Lord, yesterday I did accept the position of High Councillor to the Khmer Rouge Commander. You forgive me?

SIHANOUK: Yesterday!

THE PRINCESS: How well you've done. Your Excellency! You have a duty to protect your family, and your political future as well. One day, god willing, we'll all be delivered. And then My Lord will need you, as before, as ever.

PENN NOUTH: My Lord, will you pardon me?

SIHANOUK: Why speak of pardon? You merit only my confidence and my thanks. You have done well, My Lord. Had I had the chance, like you I would have chosen the path of prudence. But that takes a courage I did not have. Don't contradict me. Only pride gives me courage. You get yours from a miraculous humility!

PENN NOUTH: Do you really mean what you're saying?

SIHANOUK: I swear it. Don't cry.

PENN NOUTH: My Lord, permit me to take my leave. If I take too long in your dear and august presence, if I keep listening to you, I'll no longer be able to go back, over the sad red bank.

SIHANOUK: Go, go, venerable friend.

THE PRINCESS: Your Excellency, when will we have the joy of seeing you again?

PENN NOUTH: Your Highness, I'll never again have the pleasure of greeting My Lord.

SIHANOUK: What? I'll never see Penn Nouth again?

PENN NOUTH: Only "disinterested visitors" will be admitted from now on to Your Highnesses, that is, only Khmer Rouge commissars.

SIHANOUK: Only kamaphibals for Sihanouk?

THE PRINCESS: But since you'll be High Councillor?

PENN NOUTH: One will assume that I am not "disinterested."

SIHANOUK: And, no phone, of course, I suppose?

PENN NOUTH: No communication, My Lord.

SIHANOUK: Good. Well! We'll communicate by the stars. I no longer have the land, but I still have the sky. I grant you a meeting each evening, Penn Nouth, at the first star. Be there, I beg of you. From my prison I'll send you my most secret thoughts "air mail."[44]

PENN NOUTH: My Lord, I'll be there at the rendezvous every night.

SIHANOUK: Then, farewell old friend. The gods will be our messengers henceforth. The Angkar tried to separate Penn Nouth and Sihanouk, but in vain. *[Penn Nouth exits.] [to Ong Meang]* Captain, you heard Penn Nouth's words. My Lord is a wise and honorable man.

ONG MEANG: As aide-de-camp to Your Majesty, I have the honor of expressing my warmest approval of your resignation.

THE PRINCESS: Nevertheless, Captain, you should perhaps follow the example. . . .

ONG MEANG: The day My Lord was crowned I made him the gift of my whole life, including my death. What's given is given. I am My Lord's.

---

[44]English in the original. TR

SIHANOUK: I'll keep all of you, Ong Meang. We'll not leave each other. And when I'm dead among the dead, we'll find each other again. Then, I'll prostrate myself before you, in my turn. Come, let's go to prison together. We'll remember the hours of silver and of sun along the Mekong. *[to the Princess]* "When you smile at me, I'll sing like a caged bird. When you're angry at me I'll kneel and beg your pardon." And what will we speak of?

THE PRINCESS: Of those who think they're losing and of those who think they're winning. *[Exeunt.]*

PART 2, ACT 5, SCENE 1

[Night. Camp of Veal Vong. Enter Khieu Samnol and Madame Lamné.]

MADAME LAMNÉ: Now recite everything to me the way it's supposed to go, okay, since if you're the way you were last week tonight at the political education meeting, not knowing a single lesson, then the mustachioed kamaphibal is going to send you into the forest, and since I'll be going with you, we'll both be crushed under the Wheel of History. And our vertebrae likewise broken to pieces. My little dear, you're tired but do your best all the same because I'm against death and for life. So we start with the Chinese and then, we do the Vietnamese, alright?

KHIEU SAMNOL: Alright. So I say, "assuredly," like Pol Pot, right?

MADAME LAMNÉ: Assuredly.

KHIEU SAMNOL: Then give me the question, please, for the Chinese?

MADAME LAMNÉ: Who is it we are far outstripping?

KHIEU SAMNOL: We are outstripping the Chinese who admire us. They buy sewing machines for their wives, since they're still attached to the family and to their comfort, through feelings that lack greatness.
We, we have come to abolish all feeling toward the family, and our family is the Angkar.
And for comfort we love above all to work for the Revolution with both hands.

MADAME LAMNÉ: In the service of our glorious Revolution! Try!

KHIEU SAMNOL: Our glorious Revolution and our beloved Angkar, to which everything, even our children, belongs, even our spoons. Do you hear what I hear?

MADAME LAMNÉ: Our children and our spoons. Assuredly we surpass the Chinese by a lot. They try to imitate us. Will they succeed?

KHIEU SAMNOL: Assuredly, not. Don't you hear that music?

MADAME LAMNÉ: What music? I hear only the night birds crying "Pol Pot, Pol Pot" in the trees. Because now everything in the country is political, even blowing one's nose. Go on my dear, now recite the Vietnamese. So, what is our duty?

KHIEU SAMNOL: Our duty is to hate with all our hearts the Vietnamese invaders and leap up with hatred at the mere mention of these savages, but my own, my very own heart, the real one in my chest, is leaping all over my lungs.

MADAME LAMNÉ: Weakness is causing a total heart failure in us both. Go on, finish the Vietnamese: "Our duty is to teach hatred to each of our children: Let's kill: . . ."

KHIEU SAMNOL: Let's each kill ten Vietnamese, let's teach our children and grandchildren that much. Assuredly.

MADAME LAMNÉ: Now do the "You see this ox" for me.

KHIEU SAMNOL: You see this ox pulling the cart? He pulls. He never thinks of his wife and his children. The ox never refuses to work. He follows blindly the directives of the Angkar. He never complains. He eats where he is tied up. Let's model ourselves on the ox. I'm an ox. . . .
The taste of pork, do you remember it? I don't.

MADAME LAMNÉ: The taste of pork? Come on, Samnol, do the seven "*Long Lives*" for me quickly and then we're done. It's not so hard.

KHIEU SAMNOL: It's not hard, but today it's impossible. Because my lips no longer want to move. And my head is like an abandoned straw hut where a little girl squats crying Mama, Mama, Mama, Mama.

MADAME LAMNÉ: That's the fever. Okay. I'll do the seven "*Long Lives*" once and then we'll go to sleep.

> Long live the just and clairvoyant revolutionary Angkar!
> Long live the great Kampuchean Revolution!
> Long live the great people of Kampuchea!
> Long live the Glorious Democratic Kampuchea!
> Long live powerful and valiant revolutionary army!
> Long live Marxism-Leninism.

KHIEU SAMNOL: Shhh! But what's that music? Oh! My Buddha! It's your bells. Of course! Pardon me! It's this political education! What's happened to my brain?

MADAME LAMNÉ: Weren't you listening?

KHIEU SAMNOL: Oh! my dear! Excuse me for the seven "*Long Lives*" but the dead are calling me because, unfortunately, I have to go away and leave, right now! Oh! Pardon me for leaving you so suddenly without having warned you, nor me either, because it is only just now this instant that I got the warning.

MADAME LAMNÉ: Oh! no! Don't leave! No! It's too much! No! Stay! Wait! Wait! Yukanthor!
Don't leave me! I beg you. Wait a day! I'll take care of you! I'll heal you! Oh! My god! *[Enter Yukanthor.]*

YUKANTHOR: What's happening?

MADAME LAMNÉ: She's going off, my son, she's going.

KHIEU SAMNOL: My dear, if you could only see all the high personages waiting for me! There's his August Majesty. Madame Mom Savay, too. Oh, how terribly honored I am.
And there's also a man, tell me . . . but without your good eyesight I can't see . . .

MADAME LAMNÉ: A man?

KHIEU SAMNOL: Wait! Wait! It's Mr. Hou Youn!

MADAME LAMNÉ: Mr. Hou Youn! What! Hou Youn and not Madame Lamné! No! It's too unjust, this injustice!

KHIEU SAMNOL: My adored dear one, you think I'm leaving you, but I'll never leave you because on the other side I'll think about you all the time, up to the moment I come to get you. Amen.

MADAME LAMNÉ: Amen. Oh! Don't go! My dove, don't leave me all alone in this desert exile where nothing grows but despair.

YUKANTHOR: Shh! Grandmother.

KHIEU SAMNOL: Shush! My dear, because you'll wake up the mustachioed kamaphibal if he hears you. Oh! That did it! Here he is coming along the path. Now my dears, it's better for me to go right now. Leave me. Leave me now. Take my hand and say no more. Shhh. . . . I adore you. Amen. Silence. . . . *[Silence]*

MADAME LAMNÉ: Samnol! Take me away! Help! I don't want to stay in Pol Pot's infernal misery! She's gone, my bird! She's gone back to the nest!

YUKANTHOR: Shh! Grandmother! Shh!

MADAME LAMNÉ: Oh! How peaceful you'll be now in your new dwelling!
And I, left alone, without rest, I'll walk without forgetting under a starless night.
Life kills us, death separates us. I'm thinking of those I love. *[Enter the Kamaphibal.]*

KAMAPHIBAL: What is it now? Who's disturbing the village at night, huh? Oh! you again, comrade witch! You every time . . .

MADAME LAMNÉ: Oh, venerable comrade! It's my sister! My sister has just left me! Oh! Let me cry for five minutes, I beg you, let me cry for my sister!

THE KAMAPHIBAL: Cry! Cry! That's all you know how to do! Go on, let her be, comrade. We'll throw her in a ditch tomorrow.
Go on, rest now. She'll make grade two fertilizer. We don't give a damn for these old rotten bones, in the end!

MADAME LAMNÉ: Don't touch my sister! Help! Help!

YUKANTHOR: Comrade! That's my grandmother! *[Enter Hou Youn.]*

THE KAMAPHIBAL: *[to Yukanthor]* Come closer. You want me to make your grandmother shut up?

YUKANTHOR: I beg of you!

HOU YOUN: Don't touch the grandmother, comrade.

THE KAMAPHIBAL: What?! Huh? Who's there?

HOU YOUN: *[seizing the Kamaphibal from behind]* It's Hou Youn!
The General Hou Youn! Go on, Yukanthor! Hurry! I've got him.
Go on! Go on! Kill him! Kill him!

YUKANTHOR: Ah! Ah! Eat that, comrade! Die, die!

MADAME LAMNÉ: Kill him! Kill him!

HOU YOUN: Eat that, Pol Pot! Die Ieng Sary! Die Khieu Samphan!
Excuse . . .

MADAME LAMNÉ: Not at all.

YUKANTHOR: He's dead? I've killed him?

HOU YOUN: You've killed him.

YUKANTHOR: Me? I've killed a Khmer Rouge? I've really killed one
of them?!
Oh Merciful Buddha! And to think that once I prayed to kill an
American! Oh! I've killed a Khmer Rouge, Grandmother!

MADAME LAMNÉ: But my god, what are we going to do with him?

HOU YOUN: I'll take him away, Madame Lamné. Don't you worry. I
leave you with the deceased. And if you pray, take pity on Hou
Youn, too, in your invocations.

YUKANTHOR: Mr. Hou Youn, I thank you, it's been an honor and a
joy.

HOU YOUN: It's I who thanks you, my son, for your present. You
know, we who are dead, we have desires, but not the
strength. *[He leaves, carrying the Khmer Rouge.]*

MADAME LAMNÉ: *[to the tune of "My Dear Doll"]*
"My dear little dolly, doesn't want to sleep all alone.
Sleep dolly, sleep. Sleep or I'll die. When day comes I'll wash
you
And I'll dress you in your clothes,
Such beautiful clothes . . ."

I crouch all alone in the depths of my deserted heart.
An icy wind blows through the country.
Even the dead have fled far away from this bitter season.
I beg my bird to come back, but I don't know if she hears me.
Vietnam, Cambodia. How I feel for you.
Life is going out, night gains on infinity,
As high as its wings carry it, hope can not perceive the promise
of day.

PART 2, ACT 5, SCENE 2[45]

[Phnom Penh. The Royal Palace. Enter the Queen.]

QUEEN KOSSOMAK:
Now three years pass. One year, two years. Three years.
And during these three years, nothing but dying takes place in
Cambodia.
Here dies Cambodia, dies, dies, dies, dies.
We are falling, falling.
We are planting our skulls in the earth.
If a friend came
If he came to Cambodia, a friend today
If a friend came to meet the little child Cambodia
The child with the smile and the little clasped hands
If he came and saw,
The Age of Pol Pot, Pol Potted Cambodia,
He'd have to cry out, cry out, cry out
Until the World with stone-deaf ears
Finally heard Cambodia crying out, crying out.
But no one comes to Cambodia.
Not one friend for a thousand days
And during all this time, where is the Prince my son?
Thirty months under arrest with the Princess.
On the radio, he listens to the Voice of America
He listens to the voice of Pol Pot
He hopes, he despairs
The radio announces to him that Sihanouk is dead, that he is
deaf, that he is mad, that he is writing his memoirs.

---

[45] Abridged for the performance. AU

He rereads the works of Victor Hugo three times.

He does not write.

Three times he weeps

Every day he is afraid

Every evening, from his window, he watches the birds flying off in flocks, crying, far away from Phnom Penh. *[She exits. Enter Sihanouk.]*

SIHANOUK: Bird! bird! Sàt Slaap! "Bird!"[46] *Sàt Slaap!*[47] Bird! Bird! Faster still! Higher still! Be careful! Of the Pol Pots. Higher! Fly higher!

Shh! Mice! Mice! My little mice! My little dearies! Little, little, little. Come my little pretties.

O! My Lord Buddha!

Thank you, Lord, for having left me the mice. *[Enter Princess.]* Come see the little family. I believe there are others!

THE PRINCESS: Our people no longer give birth. No more Khmer babies are being born. Oh, my god, in order to admire your Creation now, we must rejoice in the birth of baby mice!

SIHANOUK: I want to see my children! I want to see my children! Mr. Chorn Hay! Mr. Chorn Hay! *[Enter Chorn Hay.]* What's going on? It's been three weeks since I wrote to Khieu Samphan! Did you give him my letter?

CHORN HAY: I gave Mr. President of the Presidium your letter that very day, My Lord. He'll assuredly come to pay you a visit, Your Grace, assuredly.

SIHANOUK: I don't want to see Mr. Khieu Samphan! I want to see my children! My children! My nice children! For two years all I've seen are gray lizards, snakes, geckoes, mosquitoes, mice! And then I see Mr. Chorn Hay, my mother-in-law, my old aunt. Then next I see Mr. Chorn Hay, my mother-in-law, my old aunt, every day, every day, since the month of April in 1976.

---

[46] English in the original. TR

[47] *Sàt* means a being, human or animal, in Cambodian, though it also sometimes means "lion"—one of the meanings of Sihanouk's own name; *Slaap* may be close to *Sla:p* meaning wing; hence "winged being." TR

Well, it's too much! I don't want to see anyone anymore. I want to die. I want to see Her Majesty again, my Majestic Mother. I want to see my dead again. There are a lot of people in the hereafter that I'd like to see right now. I want to leave this place, I want to make my escape. Thank you, Mr. Chorn Hay. *[Exit Chorn Hay.]* Shh. I hear the gecko.

GECKO: Tokkai!

SIHANOUK: Liberated!

GECKO: Tokkai!

SIHANOUK: Liquidated.

GECKO: Tokkai!

SIHANOUK: Liberated.

GECKO: Tokkai!

SIHANOUK: Liquidated.

GECKO: Tokkai!

SIHANOUK: Liberated.

GECKO: Tokkai!

SIHANOUK: Liquidated.

GECKO: . . .

SIHANOUK: Come on!

THE PRINCESS: Tokkai!

SIHANOUK: Liberated then? Do you believe that?

THE PRINCESS: I believe in Lord Buddha, I believe . . . *[Reenter Chorn Hay.]*

CHORN HAY: Your Grace! Your Grace! Mr. President of the Presidium. He's here! You see, My Grace, what did I tell you? You see! *[Exit Chorn Hay again.]*

THE PRINCESS: He must have loved you once, this Mr. Chorn Hay, you can still see it. *[Enter Khieu Samphan and Chorn Hay who carries a basket of apples.]*

KHIEU SAMPHAN: Your Highness, Princess, allow me to set these here for you. It's a gift from the very Revered Comrade, the Prime Minister, Mr. Pol Pot.

SIHANOUK: A gift from Pol Pot. But why?

THE PRINCESS: What is it?

KHIEU SAMPHAN: They're apples, Your Highness.

THE PRINCESS: Apples! It's been at least three years . . .

SIHANOUK: Apples? They're assuredly poisoned. Don't touch them! And what's the Angkar's response to my letter, Mr. Vice-Prime Minister?

KHIEU SAMPHAN: What letter, My Grace?

THE PRINCESS: Mr. Chorn Hay?

CHORN HAY: Princess, I swear to you . . .

SIHANOUK: The letter where I asked for the authorization to see, on the occasion of my birthday and for one day only, my children, my grandchildren and relatives, who are presently scattered throughout the glorious and extraordinary cooperatives in the country. I would like to see my children:

> Prince Naradipo
> Prince Khemanourak,
> Princess Botham Bopha,
> Princess Sorya Roeungsy,
> Princess Sujata,
> as well as their families.
> I would like to see my fourteen grandchildren.
> I would also like to see my cousin Norodom Phurissara and my
>   cousin Sisowath Methavi and their families.
> I want to see my beloved captain, Ong Meang.
> I want to see my friend Chea San, and I want to see His Grace
>   Penn Nouth and his wife.

KHIEU SAMPHAN: I'm sorry, Your Highness, I didn't receive this letter, but I can assure you that all of your family is in good health.

SIHANOUK: Then you refuse! You refuse?

KHIEU SAMPHAN: Please resubmit your request in writing. I'll refer the case to the Presidium.

SIHANOUK: Your Excellency, I have the privilege of being treated like a caged lion, which is to say, that I have the immense privilege of being fed. But apart from the right of pittance, I don't have a single one of the rights of man. I don't have the right to receive a letter, a visit, a newspaper, a parcel, except this parcel of poisoned apples from Pol Pot. Now then, permit me to ask you a question: why does the extraordinarily clairvoyant Angkar keep a caged lion with his wife and his old aunt? Since he no longer displays them in public anymore? It's idiotic. Since I'm already dead, put me to death! As a former head of state, I am demanding the right to a public trial and to a capital execution. Show me to the people and shoot me outside, standing up, and in front of everyone! I want to be shot! I want to be shot!

KHIEU SAMPHAN: My Grace, the Angkar has no intention of keeping you a prisoner for life. Our comrade Pol Pot thinks a lot of you, I can assure you. Mr. Chorn Hay, follow me. *[Khieu Samphan and Chorn Hay exit.]*

THE PRINCESS: My god! My god! Buddha! Have pity!
Great compassionate Jesus! Shot. . . . Help!

SIHANOUK: Bang! Bang! Bang! Bang!

[Chorn Hay returns.]

CHORN HAY: Your Grace, the Angkar has ordered me to leave Your Highnesses immediately. All palace personnel must leave the compound definitively before nightfall.

THE PRINCESS: Are they coming tonight?

SIHANOUK: Well! Good-bye, Mr. Chorn Hay! Good-bye! Leave quickly. It's almost night already. *[Chorn Hay leaves.]*

GECKO: Tokkai . . . Tokkai . . . Tokkai.

SIHANOUK: Liquidated! *[Chorn Hay returns with flowers.]*

CHORN HAY: For Buddha . . . *[He exits.]*

GECKO: Tokkai!

SIHANOUK: Liberated! He's crazy, this gecko!

THE PRINCESS: Oh! It's night, My Lord! Night! Closing in!

SIHANOUK: I would have wanted to meet Alfred Hitchcock before my own ending . . .

THE PRINCESS: They won't . . . shoot you?

SIHANOUK: Why, if they don't shoot me! Oh My Buddha! What if they torture me! What if they wrest bestial cries from me. . . . What if they spit in my face! *[fearsome noises]* Oh! Already! Is it midnight? Quick, a kiss! A kiss! It's not the nightingale, my love, our story, our hell, is over. We'll meet again. *[Tokkai! noises]* Hold them off a few moments. Tell them I have violent diarrhea. Make them wait in the salon. They'll not take me alive. Leave me! Come, Zodiac, my beautiful horse!

THE PRINCESS: I won't let you go! No! No! It is forbidden! I beg you, I beg of you. You have no right. I forbid it! *[Enter Suramarit.]*

SURAMARIT: And so do I! I forbid it! How pitiful! How shameful! So you're getting on your horse and hop! leaving your wife on this side of the world, all alone and in this sinister palace. A suicide in our family! The rumor came to us among the dead that you were losing your mind! So, is it true, my daughter? Wait! Can you see me?

THE PRINCESS: Oh! Yes, great King. I'm extraordinarily overjoyed to see you!

SURAMARIT: But your eyes are all pale.

SIHANOUK: We are dead with fear, beloved Papa.

SURAMARIT: I, too, seeing your vacant palace—sinister, tight-lipped—I get a cold chill, too.
Well. Let's see. What was it I was coming to tell you? It was very important! Oh! With your craziness, you made me lose the thread! It's all your fault! Oh! And yet, it was such important news that I walked from Kompong Cham all the way to the Palace without stopping a moment to piss, I was in such a hurry to bring it.

THE PRINCESS: *[seized with wild laughter]* To piss! Pardon me, Your Majesty! It's been so long since I laughed!

210

SURAMARIT: Obviously. You look as deflated as a couple of gray lizards, both of you.

SIHANOUK: A couple of gray lizards? You're not fair to the animals, father. Lizards are like rabbits in heat!! Sometimes the male jumps the female like a wild beast and penetrates her for a whole hour. While we, we are so overwhelmed with anxiety and pain, it's been two years since we . . .

THE PRINCESS: That, My Lord, is imprecise! It's only been since your removal from office, that we . . .

SIHANOUK: What do you mean, since my destitution! Have you forgotten in Peking?

SURAMARIT: It will come back. When you're set free. But be quiet a moment. Let me think.

SIHANOUK: Liberated!

SURAMARIT: Liberated. Wait. . . . It was something of that sort.

THE PRINCESS: Liberated, father? Oh, merciful Buddha, please help our August King bring back his memory.

SURAMARIT: Permit me. [He goes out to do peepee, comes back.] Done. Yes! That's it! My son, Cambodia is in the process of throwing off its yoke.
The Khmer Rouge cadres in the eastern region are in revolt. They meet secretly to plot against Pol Pot. Out there, there's someone named So Phim, a certain Hen Samrin, and others who seem as wicked as Pol Pot and who really want to do away with him. What? You're disappointed?

SIHANOUK: Pol Pot, So Phim, Heng Samrin, one Khmer Rouge or another, one demon or another, change of dictators, that's all.

SURAMARIT: But wait, wait, I'm not so naive, let me finish! If I told you that the Vietnamese are on our borders like tigers in search of prey?

SIHANOUK: The Vietnamese, my father? The Vietnamese? Where? How many? Have you seen them? Are there many?

SURAMARIT: There must be some thirty divisions already. And you'll

211

be happy no doubt to learn that it is your friend, General Giap, who's in command.

SIHANOUK: Giap! So, Mr. Pol Pot, Ieng Sary, Khieu Samphan—you can pride yourselves on having precipitated my Cambodia into the very mouth of the very Vietnam who has gaped before us and been waiting now two centuries for us! Giap! He'll crush the serpents! No! This gives me no reason to rejoice! No!

SURAMARIT: As you wish. Don't be happy. But in the meantime, don't go kill yourself.

THE PRINCESS: I'm rejoicing anyway, Your Majesty. For all the Cambodians who are in the work yards, I'm rejoicing. For today.

SIHANOUK: Father, I have no news of my children.

SURAMARIT: Nor have I either, my dear, nor have I. I'll go ask. I'll scour the country. They're surely somewhere. I'm off. See you later. [Suramarit exits.]

SIHANOUK: Good-bye, dear father.
Oh! To be unable to pray with a light heart for the extermination of wild beasts! To fear what one hopes for! Not to be able to greet joyfully one's sweet deliverance.
Will we one day be able to smile without shedding tears? How will life taste if it is offered to us by bitter Vietnam? [A great explosion is heard. All the lights go out. Suddenly we see the light of a pocket flashlight.]

KHIEU SAMPHAN: Where are you, Your Majesty?

SIHANOUK: Who's there?

KHIEU SAMPHAN: Khieu Samphan, Your Majesty.

SIHANOUK: Again! We're here. In the darkness of History! Was it you who cut the lights?

KHIEU SAMPHAN: No, no the whole city is out tonight! Your Majesty, Mr. Pol Pot would be pleased to receive you in the new General Headquarters of the Presidency, beside the river.

SIHANOUK: At this time of night, after so many years of . . . disinterest!

KHIEU SAMPHAN: Will you do me the honor of following me, Your Majesty? By your leave, we'll go on foot. It's at the Monivong bridge.

SIHANOUK: On foot! Go a kilometer on foot! Oh, delicious exercise after three years of a snail's life. [to the Princess] Samphan seems as relaxed as a fish in a frying pan. He's calling me "Your Majesty." [They start out.]

KHIEU SAMPHAN: Over here . . . shhh . . .

THE PRINCESS: Your hand, your hand, My Lord. [Exeunt.]

PART 2, ACT 5, SCENE 3

[On the other side of the Mekong. Enter General Nguyen Giap and General Van Tien Dung.]

DUNG: Taking Phnom Penh—it's the realization of our nation's oldest collective childhood dream for our soldiers. The prettiest piece of Indochina is ours from now on, General!

GIAP: So the map of Asia finally changes its face! What a lovely war! Everything is on our side: law, the requisite international approbation, and the strange mildness of these nights made for invasion.

DUNG: This little dark man who slipped out of your tent, was that him? Commander Heng Samrin?

GIAP: It certainly was, the future Cambodian Marshal Pétain in person. There are all kinds of monsters in the Khmer Rouge, and there are also timid and furtive monsters like Commander Heng Samrin. Doesn't he inspire you?

DUNG: With disgust. He inspires me with disgust. He massacred not only his own compatriots, but also thousands of our villagers.

GIAP: He is ideal, you'll see how useful. He thinks Indian file. One thought. Then another thought. This follows that. It goes its little way, head down like a humped ox, till it gets to us. We'll easily slip the Annamite yoke over him.
Come on, comrade, what exactly do we want? To give Cambodia up, once it's liberated? No.

DUNG: Of course not.

GIAP: To correct the unbelievable injustice of History, which gave all the meat to Little Cambodia, and nothing but the bones to Great Big Vietnam? Yes. Then, it's Heng Samrin.

DUNG: I agree.

GIAP: Let's think only of Vietnam and of our happy victory. For centuries and centuries my memory, which has inherited our oldest desires, has been burning to see this day finally arrive. This evening your army will bring the rest of Cambodia into our nets. Tomorrow will bring us Phnom Penh and the rich Mekong. *[They exit.]*

PART 2, ACT 5, SCENE 4

[Beside the Mekong. Enter Khieu Samphan, still followed by Sihanouk and the Princess.]

SIHANOUK: *[He looks like he is going to throw himself on Khieu Samphan to strangle him.]* Did you come alone, Mr. Khieu Samphan?

KHIEU SAMPHAN: Of course not, My Lord. The Honor Guard is awaiting us.

SIHANOUK: Too bad, too bad!

KHIEU SAMPHAN: I'll go inform His Excellency Mr. Pol Pot. *[He exits.]*

THE PRINCESS: How nice to see you again, great river, innocent and full of stars! Can you smell this odor of dormant trees in the water? *[A cannon is heard.]*

SIHANOUK: And without doubt behind this beautiful starry silence, Vietnam, disguised as a forest, is readying for the fatal assault.

THE PRINCESS: What are they going to do to us?

SIHANOUK: Which ones?

THE PRINCESS: I dreamed that the Vietnamese attacked the Palace and that a snake, who was Pol Pot, tightened around us in a band, and the touch of its skin was the most frightening sensation that—

214

SIHANOUK: Here he is!

[Enter Penn Nouth.]

Penn Nouth! My Penn Nouth! My dear friend! My god! What good fortune!

PENN NOUTH: Your Grace . . . *[to the Princess]* Your Highness.

SIHANOUK: Three years! You've hardly changed. He hasn't changed a bit, has he? You don't look like you've been altered too much by these long ordeals!

PENN NOUTH: Nor you, My Grace!

SIHANOUK: What! What is it?

PENN NOUTH: Oh, nothing, nothing, My Grace. It's nothing.

THE PRINCESS: But yes. There is something.

PENN NOUTH: Well, yes there is, Your Highness. I cannot, with a wink of the eye, rekindle a heart that you have cooled so much.

SIHANOUK: Cooled? Meaning?

PENN NOUTH: I believed that thirty years of fidelity, thirty years, My Grace, at your side, through many adventures, risks, storms, thirty years of my life that I gave you, and during which so many times I had taken Sihanouk's part against my better judgment—would have earned me the only reward I desired: your confidence.

THE PRINCESS: Your Excellency, you speak very unjustly.

SIHANOUK: No, no. Let His Excellency finish this pretty little speech. Now then, Your Excellency, how exactly did Sihanouk reward your thirty marvelous years of common pilgrimage?

PENN NOUTH: What do you call it when you suspect an innocent friend of intrigue, ambition, jealousy?
How could you believe that I tried to take your place in the people's heart which your resignation had thrown into mourning? Penn Nouth, Sihanouk's rival? What a revolting accusation! And when, refusing at first to believe that my revered master could maintain such an unjust opinion of me, I tried hard to obtain an audience, begging, humbling myself, ten times I'm about to knock on your door, not to give me even once a chance to justify myself!

Answering me that Sihanouk doesn't receive traitors, returning my
letters without having opened them, but marked with a "No"
penned in your furious hand?!

SIHANOUK: And did the subtle Penn Nouth, friend of thirty years,
ever notice anything suspicious? Did the honorable Penn Nouth
ever doubt the bearer of these messages? No? Did the cunning
Penn Nouth ever put on his glasses to look a little closer at these
"No's" penned in such a furious hand, as you put it?
No! No! Penn Nouth chose to believe the worst. Did you want it
to be that way, honorable friend? What, thirty years of my friendship didn't carry any weight at all?

PENN NOUTH: Your Grace—

SIHANOUK: Let me finish! Penn Nouth, after thirty years of confidence, took the slippery slope to mistrust. You chose to doubt
Sihanouk.

PENN NOUTH: My Lord, don't turn everything around . . .

THE PRINCESS: Oh! Your Excellency, how could you possibly believe
it? His Highness never received the slightest sign of your concern.

SIHANOUK: Oh! No! No! Don't exonerate me. Don't give proofs to
this false friend. But let me make a confession, dear old honorable
friend: here, in prison they told me that the Lord Penn Nouth
didn't complain too much about my withdrawal, that he found
many advantages in it.

PENN NOUTH: Oh! . . .

SIHANOUK: But luckily, luckily, I never wanted to believe such remarks! No. You see, I preferred to keep, safe in my heart, the
sweet memory of your unwavering friendship. Yes, I pity you. You,
you had lost Sihanouk. But me, for three years, I looked forward
to seeing Penn Nouth again.

[Enter Pol Pot, followed by Khieu Samphan, Ieng Sary, and their fol-
lowers.]

POL POT: Your Majesty! Your Highness! I'm grateful to you for
doing me the honor of accepting my invitation. [to Penn
Nouth] Mr. Top Advisor. . . .

Pardon me, My Grace, for not having had time to see you. We postpone. Time passes. We never notice how time just flies.

SIHANOUK: Mr. President, I know you're a man overburdened with responsibilities. In contrast, I, for three years unburdened by cares of state, used to watch time pass, from my window, over the roofs of my Palace, in the sky.

POL POT: The sky is above the roof, so blue, so pure. Verlaine.

SIHANOUK: If you'll permit me, it is: The sky is above the roof, so blue, so calm. Verlaine. Wisdom.

POL POT: Your Majesty, you know that we have declared war on the Vietnamese. We have launched, a month ago, a formidable offensive against the enemy. And I have the honor of telling you that we are dec-i-mating them!

SIHANOUK: You are dec-i-mating them?

[Penn Nouth makes a sign that suggests otherwise.]

POL POT: If you don't mind, I'll paint, in a few words, our war picture. The Vietnamese are over by Koki at this moment.

SIHANOUK: Koki? But that's right next door! You said an offensive!

POL POT: Follow me, I beg you. I am letting the horde enter very deeply into the country. They advance. I fall back, I retreat, I retreat. There! And suddenly, I bear down upon them from all sides; I encircle them, I have them! Clack! We close our jaws upon them. And then, there, I grind them up, you see, I'll cut them to pieces; minced, crushed, crumbled, and, finally, pulverized. There you are. In two months, your Majesty, there won't be any more of them left.
Meanwhile, you, Your Majesty, with the Princess, are going to explain the situation a bit everywhere abroad.

SIHANOUK: What? I'm "going"? I'm leaving Cambodia?

POL POT: That's what I have the pleasure of proposing to you. You will draw the attention of nations to the expansionist Vietnamese aggression. You will go first to China, naturally. Then to the U.N. Afterward, to Western Europe. And in two months you'll come back.

THE PRINCESS: In two months? . . .

SIHANOUK: *[to the Princess]* In two months. . . . As soon as Mr. Pol Pot has eliminated, annihilated, and crushed the Vietnamese. And His Excellency, Penn Nouth?

POL POT: His Excellency Penn Nouth goes with you. The mission leaves at dawn for Peking.

THE PRINCESS: We're leaving for Peking?

SIHANOUK: *[to the Princess]* Mr. Pol Pot has been explaining the urgency of this patriotic tour to us for half an hour. We leave right away, and return in two months. *[Khieu Samphan whispers a word to Pol Pot.]*

POL POT: A limousine will be coming to get you here in two hours. Permit me to take my leave. Long live the Democratic, Eternally Victorious Kampuchea. *[The Khmer Rouge exit.]*

SIHANOUK: What an exit! They slither off like snakes among the ruins.

THE PRINCESS: What do you mean?

PENN NOUTH: The Vietnamese are already at the gates of Phnom Penh. The red commanders are in the process of fading into an underground movement.

THE PRINCESS: And the plane? Will there really be a plane?

PENN NOUTH: Your Highness, we'll be in Peking, tomorrow. The Khmer Rouge will do everything to prevent Your Grace from meeting the Vietnamese.

SIHANOUK: And why wouldn't they just kill us?

PENN NOUTH: They must have thought of it, My Grace. But international opinion . . .

[The Vietnamese bombardment upon Phnom Penh intensifies.]

SIHANOUK: Yet another exile. Nine years already. Nine years of separation. How many times nine years? Everything is swept away by pitiless destiny, children, grandchildren, hope, dignity, honor. Even down to the last friend.

PENN NOUTH: My Grace, it's because I believed that you were holding an implacable grudge against me.

SIHANOUK: I told you in April 1976 that I understood you. No. No! There are no excuses. And tell me, Lord Penn Nouth, exactly what you did on your own side while I was whiling away the time counting my mice?

PENN NOUTH: Ah! I'm not mistaken! You do hold a grudge against me!

SIHANOUK: But no, not at all. It's just that I am *so* curious.

THE PRINCESS: Let's go now. I can't bear the idea that the Khmer Rouge have also succeeded in driving friends apart.

SIHANOUK: It isn't the Khmer Rouge who have separated us. It is he who has separated himself from me!

THE PRINCESS: Get a hold of yourself. Don't cut off your nose to spite your face. My Grace, it would be so great a victory for the heart if, you, pardoning him, made it so that we could arrive in Peking just like old times . . .

SIHANOUK: When I was amidst the world's uproar, how I struggled! I lived all, won all, lost all, I saw correctly, I saw falsely, I saw too soon, I didn't see the dagger in my back, I was mistaken, I wasn't mistaken, I often lied, I many times spoke the truth, too many times.
And now at fifty-six, I'm three thousand years old. I have nothing left to lose. I'm sitting on the cusp of time. It's been centuries since Sihanouk emerged from the river. Here, there is no more error, no more rage. Before me lies the immense tranquil field of legend. I could stretch out, rest. Still living, I've grown as wise and as old as the dead. I no longer have the strength, the courage to make errors, to run the race, to do what's necessary to take part in the games of the earth. I'll never more speak word.

THE PRINCESS: It won't last long. This silence. What will you do up there, in your exalted wisdom?

SIHANOUK: I'll write the history of my country. First episode: *Para-*

dise Lost.[48] Next, how Lon Nol worked for Pol Pot. Next, how Pol Pot worked for Vietnam. And me?

I'm without a future and I'm not dead. I'm the victim of a miracle. I'm going off now to the other side of the world, where Asia and its demons won't pursue me.

THE PRINCESS: They'll pursue you there because you are needed. History isn't over.

SIHANOUK: If they need me, they'll find me again. One always finds what one needs. *[to Penn Nouth]*

You owe me an explanation, we'll talk about it again up there.

[They exit. The Vietnamese attack increases.]

PART 2, ACT 5, FINAL SCENE 5

[Cambodia. The dead enter: King Suramarit, Queen Kossomak, Mom Savay, and Khieu Samnol. Then Madame Lamné and Yukanthor enter with a bike.]

SURAMARIT: It's the hour of Great Exile. The sweet land of Cambodia is no longer the country of Khmers. We have come to say good-bye, good-bye and good luck. You must leave before dawn.

KHIEU SAMNOL: When you're going through the forest, watch out for mines, my son, watch where you set foot.

MADAME LAMNÉ: To be separated from each other again, to lose you once more! I know we have to leave, but what sorrow overcomes my heart! Our dear departed, when we're no longer here, what will become of all of you?

MOM SAVAY: We know that you'll think of us because we are your loving past.

KHIEU SAMNOL: Oh! To listen to the rain without you! To see the seasons turn! We'll miss you! We'll miss you. Remember me wherever you go, wherever you go it's all the same to me, as long as you let me know.

MADAME LAMNÉ: Wherever I go to live, my beloved Samnol, you'll

---

[48] English in the original. TR

220

rise again in my heart each morning like the sun and each evening like the moon.

[Enter Ong Meang, carrying Dith Boun Suo on his back.]

ONG MEANG: Pardon me, Majesty. He has just arrived. He's still quite upset.

QUEEN KOSSOMAK: Dith Boun Suo! Dear, dear, Dith Boun Suo! So my poor friend, you weren't able to wait a little longer! My son will be sad!

DITH BOUN SUO: Your Majesty, I tried, I tried, but yesterday morning my heart cracked. Crack!

MOM SAVAY: But where were you during the terrible years?

DITH BOUN SUO: In the canton of Kaak Srok. For two years, I ate nothing but rice soup and leaves from trees. That's why I suffered from anemia and extreme emaciation. And I suffered a lot because, excuse me, Majesty, I was made the shit collector, fertilizer number 1.
But I was able to rescue Your Grace's parasol. I hid it and finally brought it, safe and sound, all the way here.

QUEEN KOSSOMAK: Now the dead, the millions of dead will tend Cambodia. You're leaving. And we'll wait for you. We'll wait till the Cambodian children return, the children who'll live and pronounce our names in our country's air.

SURAMARIT: So, in this regard, Yukanthor, wherever you may live, in a second country, in a third country, in Europe, or in far America . . .

KHIEU SAMNOL: In America! Dear me! No, me, I . . .

MADAME LAMNÉ: But let me hear His Majesty.

SURAMARIT: As I was saying, whatever foreign country you end up living in, don't forget our language, our sweet Khmer language. Speak it everyday. Don't let it die out.

QUEEN KOSSOMAK: Because our language is the water of the Mekong, it's our source, our liberty, our sublime land, our survival, our memory, and our pride. As long as our source flows in the world, our people, living and dead—not one of us can be forgotten.

MOM SAVAY: And the second source is the dance. Our royal dance.[49] You must save our dance.

YUKANTHOR: Oh! Buddha, the royal dance? How's it done?

ONG MEANG: There's a grandniece of mine, Sihamino. Madame Savay, you know her, she was your student. She lives in Vancouver, Canada.

KHIEU SAMNOL: Canada, the poor thing!

[Enter Hou Youn, then the other dead in succession.]

SURAMARIT: And when at last one day a slight opening is made in this exile's high wall, then our descendants will rush through toward eternal Cambodia, where we'll be waiting for them.

YUKANTHOR: One day, Your Majesty, when's that?

SURAMARIT: I don't know what day, my son. One day in the future.

KHIEU SAMNOL: In any case, a day is a day. What counts is that this day will arrive one day.

SURAMARIT: On your way now. Across the forests up to the Cardamom Mountains, we'll watch over you. But after that, past the Cardamoms over to the plains of Thailand, you must ask for Buddha's protection.

MADAME LAMNÉ: Yes, but day by day, after walking and walking, we'll get to the other side of the mountains, to the Thais' country, and then what will happen to us? I'm scared!

YUKANTHOR: Oh! Then there'll be such a celebration! Because everyone will have a heart full of goodness when the world learns of our terrible misfortune.

MADAME LAMNÉ: You think so?

YUKANTHOR: That's how it happens, naturally, when an innocent

---

[49] Pol Pot's regime murdered approximately 90 percent of those who knew the royal dance, which has now been reconstructed, abroad, through the instruction of a handful of surviving old teachers. TR

country has too long endured an evil destiny. In such a case, the big countries of the West who are very rich and happy, such as Canada, Switzerland, France, the U.S.A., and Australia, as soon as they know, they will come immediately to find us and make amends for so much grief.

KHIEU SAMNOL: Is that so, My Uncle?

SURAMARIT: I don't know. Come on, come on. The living and the dead must part company, now.

MADAME LAMNÉ: Having known you living, Samnol, that was the greatest joy of my life.
I'm ready. Farewell and good-bye. Farewell and good-bye.

YUKANTHOR: I'll return to honor you, with my whole family.

[They bow to each other. Ong Meang holds out something for Madame Lamné.]

MADAME LAMNÉ: What is it?

ONG MEANG: A bit of our earth.

SURAMARIT: We are ripe for the final putting asunder.

[Madame Lamné and Yukanthor exit.]

KHIEU SAMNOL: Madame Lamné! Marie-Madeleine! My dear! Does she hear me? I wanted to tell you: maybe you could get to Paris? To Paris, France! Do you hear me?

MADAME LAMNÉ: [from far off] What are you saying?

KHIEU SAMNOL: To Paris!
Doesn't she hear me anymore? [to the Queen and Mom Savay] I always wanted to go to Paris, where I've never been, it's so beautiful! And I also have a cousin in Paris, he lives in Besançon. Can you still see them, Mom Savay, with your good eyes?

MOM SAVAY: Our friends are now approaching the end of our country.

KHIEU SAMNOL: Oh! My god, Buddha, stand by! They are quite near the border!

MOM SAVAY: Ah! I no longer see them!

KHIEU SAMNOL: You no longer see them?

MOM SAVAY: They've arrived, Madame Khieu Samnol. In Thailand. In Kao-I-Dang.

KHIEU SAMNOL: In Thailand! How anxious I am! Who will watch over you now, poor Cambodian exiles, without your dead thinking of you all the time the way we have?!
Ah! How alone we are here now, all of us!

QUEEN KOSSOMAK: Our voices are low, but we are so numerous, we the people of the dead Cambodians, so numerous that perhaps if we howled altogether, then perhaps the weakened howl of our people will be heard by someone down there among the great noise of the living.
Today in captive Cambodia, millions of our fellows, standing around their immense tomb, are crying, crying, crying. They cry: Cambodia! Only that: Cambodia! Hush. Listen, hush . . .

End of Act 5, scene 5.

VARIANT, PART 2, ACT 5, FINAL SCENE 5

KHIEU SAMNOL: You no longer see them?!

MOM SAVAY: They've arrived, Madame Khieu Samnol. In Thailand. At Kao-I-Dang.

KHIEU SAMNOL: In Thailand! How anxious I am! Who will watch over you now, poor Cambodian exiles, without your dead thinking of you all the time the way we have?
Ah! How alone we are now here, all of us!

THE FATHER: And now, to work! We must hope.

KHIEU SAMNOL: Hope! But from here to hope is as far as from Phnom Penh to the moon! Tell me a bit how we can hope, when there is only night around us, as if we had buried the sun.

QUEEN KOSSOMAK: How? Let's hope by hoping every day, day after day.

KHIEU SAMNOL: Life is short, death long—what makes me laugh is that perhaps my dear Marie-Madeleine, that perhaps she'll have one of those telephones that were always flying around in her dreams.

MOM SAVAY: I'm thinking of the poor Cambodians, leaning on the sills of foreign windows, and thinking of us.

KHIEU SAMNOL: To be Khmer is very difficult, it's even more difficult in these times, but just the same, for me, that's what I choose.

—End—

VARIANT, PART 2, ACT 5, SCENE 1

[Night. Camp Veal Vong. Enter Khieu Samnol, then Madame Lamné.]

KHIEU SAMNOL: What's that I hear? What's this music? Do you hear it? No? I do. What's happening to me?
O, My Buddha! Is it your bells I'm hearing?! Already!
Madame Lamné! Madame Lamné! Marie-Madeleine!

MADAME LAMNÉ: Ah! What is it? What's the matter?

KHIEU SAMNOL: It's nothing. It's nothing. It's me. You know, my sister, I'm sorry, but I must leave you in a little while.

MADAME LAMNÉ: You, leave me? I don't believe it. It's not true!

KHIEU SAMNOL: I'm sorry, but it's true. I've had the warning. You know, for some days now my health has been going. I have complete spinal collapse and heart failure and my body is overrun with disease. Still, I don't want to die. So, I'll try to live on and on. There's nothing to be done about it, my dear. Three days from now, when I wake up, I'll be on the other side. . . . Each time I come back here now, dragging myself along, it gets more and more difficult, as if the river were widening. Then afterward I begin to understand that soon I won't be able to stay close to you much longer, starting now. I'm sorry that the end comes for me in this infernal camp where I never would have wanted to see you suffer so, because it grieves me so mortally.

MADAME LAMNÉ: Oh! No, no! My dearest! No! I beg you! Say it isn't so! Say you're wrong, say you're getting better, I'll take care of you the way you have taken care of me.

KHIEU SAMNOL: But what am I going to do, my little Lamné? I'm sorry but I could never stand this Christian name of Marie-Madeleine, you know? Oh! My god, Mary and Jesus, you who are my sister's holy divinities, what am I going to do with my poor dear when I die?
And I, who was afraid, when I saw her so sick and gray, that she was going to abandon me! And it's poor Samnol who is leaving poor Lamné. Ah! But what an awful and horrible destiny! Because you know, I'd have preferred to see you die if I had known that it was going to come to me so quickly, don't you know?

MADAME LAMNÉ: Ah! My adorable one! I don't want you to leave. I'm against death and for life, but if you must go, I'll go with you. All this is because of those cursed dollars. If we hadn't succeeded in making them work, I'd be extinct for three weeks already, as planned, and today both of us would be dead. But this injustice is too much, my god.

KHIEU SAMNOL: Tell me, my sweet, what time is it? Because I would certainly like to say good-bye to Yukanthor, the poor dear.

MADAME LAMNÉ: It's two o'clock in the morning. He won't be late. Usually he arrives at the camp by three.

KHIEU SAMNOL: But perhaps he would prefer that I be already gone, do you think? Because he already sleeps so little, the poor thing.

MADAME LAMNÉ: All the same, it's better to go at night my love, if you can, because at least we're together and they cannot separate us.

KHIEU SAMNOL: When I'm on the other side, my dearest, as long as you're here, a miserable prisoner, I'll think of you all the time, I swear.

MADAME LAMNÉ: Oh! I too, I too, my treasure, my thoughts will never leave you, never, until my death, I beg Jesus, Mary, the Lord, and all the Buddhas to send me on as fast as possible. Amen. [Enter Yukanthor.]

226

KHIEU SAMNOL: Amen. But nonetheless, I'd like to stay a bit in Cambodia if possible because I'm also thinking about my poor country. All those living who can, must still wait, must remain alive the longest time possible, because if we all die, only the Pol Pots would be left on our dear land. And also, I'd like it if you looked after this fellow here a bit . . .

YUKANTHOR: Oh, Grandmother, what is it?

MADAME LAMNÉ: She's dying, my son, she's dying.

KHIEU SAMNOL: So you, you obey Madame Lamné now, alright? Because, at your age, you know nothing except how to dig and dig, because of these monsters. Do you hear?

MADAME LAMNÉ: What? What?

YUKANTHOR: There's no one there, Grandmother.

KHIEU SAMNOL: Music. I hear it. I have to hurry, Madame Lamné, make him read, write, count. Be strict, okay?

MADAME LAMNÉ: And a little French, too?

KHIEU SAMNOL: Yes, what was I saying? Ah! Yes. Say, Madame Lamné, nevertheless, weren't the dollars beautiful?

MADAME LAMNÉ: Oh! Yes, my treasure, they were beautiful!

KHIEU SAMNOL: We were winning! We were winning. Ah! There's Her Majesty, the Queen.

MADAME LAMNÉ: *[to Yukanthor]* Do you see her?

YUKANTHOR: No, no.

MADAME LAMNÉ: You're mistaken, my dear sister.

KHIEU SAMNOL: But no, I do see her! Because I already have the eyes of the other side. Ah! There's Mom Savay! Now then, my beloved, I must say farewell and good-bye to you, and with regret I'm going to go away, while wiping away my tears.

YUKANTHOR: Beloved Grandmother, I disobeyed you sometimes.

KHIEU SAMNOL: Pardon this death. And also, my dear sister, I want to tell you: this week, I was unable to wash myself, you'll be willing to pardon me?

227

MADAME LAMNÉ: Me neither, my dove. So you see.

Oh! Don't go! Don't go, my dear, don't leave me all alone in this desert exile where nothing grows but despair.

KHIEU SAMNOL: It hurts! It hurts! It's hard to die. Help me! Alas! I see the eminent people who are waiting for me on the other side! But say, I see a man also!

MADAME LAMNÉ: She also sees a man? And who is it?

KHIEU SAMNOL: Ah! My sister, but it's Mr. Hou Youn, don't you remember?

MADAME LAMNÉ: Mr. Hou Youn!!! Well is it him, yes?! And not Madame Lamné? This can't be so.

KHIEU SAMNOL: O, o, o! Look out because I see the kamaphibal, the mustachioed spy is also coming along the footpath. Oh! My dear, it's best for me to leave you right now. . . . Let me be, let me be, now. . . . Take my hand and say nothing . . . hush . . . I adore you. Amen. Silence . . . *[Silence]*

MADAME LAMNÉ: Ah! Lord! She's dying! Yukanthor! She's dying!

YUKANTHOR: The kamaphibal . . . ! I hear him. I see him too, and he's quite alive, he is. Let's be quiet, Madame Lamné.

MADAME LAMNÉ: Samnol! Take me away! Help! I don't want to stay in Pol Pot's infernal misery! She's gone, my bird! She has returned to her nest!

YUKANTHOR: Hush! Grandmother! Hush!

MADAME LAMNÉ: Oh! How peaceful you're going to be now in your new dwelling! And I, left alone, without repose, I walk without forgetfulness under a night without stars. Life kills us, death separates us. I'm thinking of those I love.

[Enter the kamaphibal.]

THE KAMAPHIBAL: What's wrong now? Who's disturbing the village at this hour, hey? Ah! It's you again, comrade witch! Every time it's you . . .

MADAME LAMNÉ: Oh, venerable comrade! It's my sister! It's my sister who has just died! Ah! Let me cry for five minutes, I beg you, let me cry for my sister!

THE KAMAPHIBAL: Cry! Cry! That's all you know how to do! Go on, let her be, comrade. We'll throw her in a ditch tomorrow. Go on, rest now. She'll make grade two fertilizer. We don't give a damn for these old rotten bones, in the end!

MADAME LAMNÉ: Don't touch my sister! Help! Help!

YUKANTHOR: Comrade! That's my grandmother! *[Enter Hou Youn.]*

THE KAMAPHIBAL: *[to Yukanthor]* Come closer. You want me to make your grandmother shut up?

YUKANTHOR: I beg of you!

HOU YOUN: Don't touch the grandmother, comrade.

THE KAMAPHIBAL: What?! Huh? Who's there?

HOU YOUN: *[seizing the Kamaphibal from behind]* It's Hou Youn! The General Hou Youn! Go on, Yukanthor! Hurry! I've got him. Go on! Go on! Kill him! Kill him!

YUKANTHOR: Ah! Ah! Eat that, comrade! Die, die!

MADAME LAMNÉ: Kill him! Kill him!

HOU YOUN: Eat that, Pol Pot! Die Ieng Sary! Die Khieu Samphan! Excuse . . .

MADAME LAMNÉ: Not at all.

YUKANTHOR: Is he dead? Did I kill him?

HOU YOUN: You've killed him.

YUKANTHOR: Me? I've killed a Khmer Rouge? I've really killed one of them?! Oh Merciful Buddha! And to think that once I prayed to kill an American! Oh! I've killed a Khmer Rouge, Grand-mother!

MADAME LAMNÉ: But my god, what are we going to do with him?

HOU YOUN: I'll take him away, Madame Lamné. Don't you worry. I leave you with the deceased. And if you pray, take pity on Hou Youn, too, in your invocations.

229

YUKANTHOR: Mr. Hou Youn, I thank you, it's been an honor and a joy.

HOU YOUN: It's I who thanks you, my son, for your gift. You know, we who are dead, we have desires, but no power. *[He leaves, carrying the Khmer Rouge.]*

MADAME LAMNÉ: *[to the tune of "My Dear Doll"]*
"My dear little dolly, doesn't want to sleep all alone.
Sleep dolly, sleep. Sleep or I'll die. When day comes I'll wash
   you
And I'll dress you in your clothes,
Such beautiful clothes . . ."
I crouch all alone in the depths of my deserted heart.
An icy wind blows through the country.
Even the dead have fled far away from this bitter season.
I beg my bird to come back, but I don't know if she hears me.
Vietnam, Cambodia. How I feel for you.
Life is going out, night gains on infinity,
As high as its wings carry it, hope can not perceive the promise
   of day.

Artemisia
By Anna Banti
Translated by Shirley D'Ardia Caracciolo

Bitter Healing
German Women Writers from 1700 to 1830
An Anthology
Edited by Jeannine Blackwell and Susanne Zantop

The Maravillas District
By Rosa Chacel
Translated by d. a. démers

The Book of Promethea
By Hélène Cixous
Translated by Betsy Wing

Maria Zef
By Paola Drigo
Translated by Blossom Steinberg Kirschenbaum

Woman to Woman
By Marguerite Duras and Xavière Gauthier
Translated by Katherine A. Jensen

Hitchhiking
Twelve German Tales
By Gabriele Eckart
Translated by Wayne Kvam

231

The Tongue Snatchers
By Claudine Herrmann
Translated by Nancy Kline

Mother Death
By Jeanne Hyvrard
Translated by Laurie Edson

The House of Childhood
By Marie Luise Kaschnitz
Translated by Anni Whissen

The Panther Woman
Five Tales from the Cassette Recorder
By Sarah Kirsch
Translated by Marion Faber

Daughters of Eve
Women Writing from the German Democratic Republic
Translated by Nancy Lukens and Dorothy Rosenberg

On Our Own Behalf
Women's Tales from Catalonia
Edited by Kathleen McNerney

Absent Love
A Chronicle
By Rosa Montero
Translated by Cristina de la Torre and Diana Glad

The Delta Function
By Rosa Montero
Translated by Kari A. Easton and Yolanda Molina Gavilan

Music from a Blue Well
By Torborg Nedreaas
Translated by Bibbi Lee

232

Nothing Grows by Moonlight
By Torborg Nedreaas
Translated by Bibbi Lee

Why Is There Salt in the Sea?
By Brigitte Schwaiger
Translated by Sieglinde Lug

The Same Sea as Every Summer
By Esther Tusquets
Translated by Margaret E. W. Jones